CLIFFSCOMPLETE

Shakespeare's
Twelfth Night

Edited by Sidney Lamb

Associate Professor of English

Sir George Williams University, Montreal

Complete Text + Commentary + Glossary

Commentary by Chris Stroffolino and David Rosenthal

WILEY

Wiley Publishing, Inc.

CLIFFSCOMPLETE

Shakespeare's

Twelfth Night

About the Author

Chris Stroffolino received his Ph.D. in Shakespearean studies from SUNY Albany and has published five books of poetry, one book of literary criticism, and is currently finishing his book on Shakespeare called *Making Fun of Tragedy*. He lives in New York City and plays keyboard with the rock band, Volumen.

David Rosenthal received his MFA in Dramatic Writing at the Tisch School of the Arts at New York University. His plays have been performed in New York, Los Angeles, San Diego, and Philadelphia.

Publisher's Acknowledgments

Editorial

Project Editor: Michael Kelly

Acquisitions Editor: Gregory W. Tubach

Editorial Director: Kristin Cocks

Illustrator: DD Dowden

Composition

Indexer: Sherry Massey

Proofreader: Vickie Broyles

Wiley Indianapolis Composition Services

CliffsComplete Shakespeare's Twelfth Night

Published by:
Wiley Publishing, Inc.
111 River Street
Hoboken, NJ 07030
www.wiley.com

Copyright © 2000 Wiley Publishing, Inc., New York, New York
Library of Congress Control Number: 00-101110
ISBN: 0-7645-8577-0

10 9 8 7 6 5 4 3
1O/RV/QZ/QU/IN
Published by Wiley Publishing, Inc., New York, NY
Published simultaneously in Canada

CLIFFSCOMPLETE

Shakespeare's

Twelfth Night

CONTENTS AT A GLANCE

CLIFFSCOMPLETE

Shakespeare's

Twelfth Night

TABLE OF CONTENTS

Shakespeare's

TWELFTH NIGHT

INTRODUCTION TO WILLIAM SHAKESPEARE

William Shakespeare, or the "Bard" as people fondly call him, permeates almost all aspects of our society. He can be found in our classrooms, on our televisions, in our theatres, and in our cinemas. Speaking to us through his plays, Shakespeare comments on his life and culture, as well as our own. Actors still regularly perform his plays on the modern stage and screen. The 1990s, for example, saw the release of cinematic versions of *Romeo and Juliet, Hamlet, Othello, A Midsummer Night's Dream,* and many more of his works.

In addition to the popularity of Shakespeare's plays as he wrote them, other writers have modernized his works to attract new audiences. For example, *West Side Story* places *Romeo and Juliet* in New York City, and *A Thousand Acres* sets *King Lear* in Iowa corn country. Beyond adaptations and productions, his life and works have captured our cultural imagination. The twentieth century witnessed the production of a play about two minor characters from Shakespeare's *Hamlet* in *Rosencrantz and Guildenstern are Dead* and a fictional movie about Shakespeare's early life and poetic inspiration in *Shakespeare in Love.*

Despite his monumental presence in our culture, Shakespeare remains enigmatic. He does not tell us which plays he wrote alone, on which plays he collaborated with other playwrights, or which versions of his plays to read and perform. Furthermore, with only a handful of documents available about his life, he does not tell us much about Shakespeare the person, forcing critics and scholars to look to historical references to uncover the true-life great dramatist.

Anti-Stratfordians — modern scholars who question the authorship of Shakespeare's plays — have used this lack of information to argue that William Shakespeare either never existed or, if he did exist, did not write any of the plays we attribute to him. They believe that another historical figure, such as Francis Bacon or Queen Elizabeth I, used the name as a cover. Whether or not a man named William Shakespeare ever actually existed is ultimately secondary to the recognition that the group of plays bound together by that name does exist and continues to educate, enlighten, and entertain us.

An engraved portrait of Shakespeare by an unknown artist, ca. 1607. Culver Pictures, Inc./SuperStock

Family life

Though scholars are unsure of the exact date of Shakespeare's birth, records indicate that his parents — Mary and John Shakespeare — baptized him on April 26, 1564, in the small provincial town of Stratford-upon-Avon — so named because it sat on the banks of the Avon river. Because common practice was to baptize infants a few days after they were born, scholars generally recognize April 23, 1564, as Shakespeare's birthday. Coincidentally, April 23 is the day of St. George, the patron saint of England, as well as the day upon which Shakespeare would die 52 years later. William was the third of Mary and John's eight children and the first of four sons. The house in which scholars believe Shakespeare to have been born stands on Henley Street, and despite many modifications over the years, you can still visit it today.

Shakespeare's father

Prior to Shakespeare's birth, John Shakespeare lived in Snitterfield, where he married Mary Arden, the daughter of his landlord. After moving to Stratford in 1552, he worked as a glover, a moneylender, and a dealer in agricultural products such as wool and grain. He also pursued public office and achieved a variety of posts including bailiff, Stratford's highest elected position — equivalent to a small town's mayor. At the height of his career, sometime near 1576, he petitioned the Herald's Office for a coat of arms and thus the right to be a gentleman. But the rise from the middle class to the gentry did not come right away, and the costly petition expired without being granted.

About this time, John Shakespeare mysteriously fell into financial difficulty. He became involved in serious litigation, was assessed heavy fines, and even lost his seat on the town council. Some scholars suggest that this decline could have resulted from religious discrimination because the Shakespeare family may have supported Catholicism, the practice of which was illegal in England. However, other scholars point out that not all religious dissenters (both Catholics and radical Puritans) lost their posts due to their religion. Whatever the cause of his decline, John did regain some prosperity toward the end of his life. In 1596, the Herald's Office granted the Shakespeare family a coat of arms at the petition of William, by now a successful playwright in London. And John, prior to his death in 1601, regained his seat on Stratford's town council.

Childhood and education

Our understanding of William Shakespeare's childhood in Stratford is primarily speculative because children do not often appear in the legal records from which many scholars attempt to reconstruct Shakespeare's life. Based on his father's local prominence, scholars speculate that Shakespeare most likely attended King's New School, a school that usually employed Oxford graduates and was generally well respected. Shakespeare would have started *petty school* — the rough equivalent to modern preschool — at the age of four or five. He would have learned to read on a *hornbook*, which was a sheet of parchment or paper on which the alphabet and the Lord's Prayer were written. This sheet was framed in wood and covered with a transparent piece of horn for durability. After two years in petty school, he would have transferred to grammar school, where his school day would have probably lasted from 6 or 7 o'clock in the morning (depending on the time of year) until 5 o'clock in the evening, with only a handful of holidays.

While in grammar school, Shakespeare would primarily have studied Latin, reciting and reading the works of classical Roman authors such as Plautus, Ovid, Seneca, and Horace. Traces of these authors' works can be seen in his dramatic texts. Toward his last years in grammar school, Shakespeare would have acquired some basic skills in Greek as well. Thus the remark made by Ben Jonson, Shakespeare's well-educated friend and contemporary playwright, that Shakespeare knew "small Latin and less Greek" is accurate. Jonson is not saying that when

Shakespeare's birthplace.
SuperStock

Shakespeare left grammar school he was only semi-literate; he merely indicates that Shakespeare did not attend University, where he would have gained more Latin and Greek instruction.

Wife and children

When Shakespeare became an adult, the historical records documenting his existence began to increase. In November 1582, at the age of 18, he married 26-year-old Anne Hathaway from the nearby village of Shottery. The disparity in their ages, coupled with the fact that they baptized their first daughter, Susanna, only six months later in May 1583, has caused a great deal of modern speculation about the nature of their relationship. However, sixteenth-century conceptions of marriage differed slightly from our modern notions. Though all marriages needed to be performed before a member of the clergy, many of Shakespeare's contemporaries believed that a couple could establish a relationship through a premarital contract by exchanging vows in front of witnesses. This contract removed the social stigma of pregnancy before marriage. (Shakespeare's plays contain instances of marriage prompted by pregnancy, and *Measure for Measure* includes this kind of premarital contract.) Two years later, in February 1585, Shakespeare baptized his twins Hamnet and Judith. Hamnet would die at the age of 11 when Shakespeare was primarily living away from his family in London.

For seven years after the twins' baptism, the records remain silent on Shakespeare. At some point, he traveled to London and became involved with the theatre, but he could have been anywhere between 21 and 28 years old when he did. Though some have suggested that he may have served as an assistant to a schoolmaster at a provincial school, it seems likely that he went to London to become an actor, gradually becoming a playwright and gaining attention.

The plays: On stage and in print

The next mention of Shakespeare comes in 1592 by a University wit named Robert Greene when Shakespeare apparently was already a rising actor and playwright for the London stage. Greene, no longer a successful playwright, tried to warn other University wits about Shakespeare. He wrote:

> *For there is an upstart crow, beautified with our feathers, that with his "Tiger's heart wrapped in a player's hide" supposes he is as well able to bombast out a blank verse as the best of you, and, being an absolute Johannes Factotum, is in his own conceit the only Shake-scene in a country.*

This statement comes at a point in time when men without a university education, like Shakespeare, were starting to compete as dramatists with the University wits. As many critics have pointed out, Greene's statement recalls a line from *3 Henry VI*, which reads, "O tiger's heart wrapped in a woman's hide!" (I.4.137). Greene's remark does not indicate that Shakespeare was generally disliked. On the contrary, another University wit, Thomas Nashe, wrote of the great theatrical success of *Henry VI*, and Henry Chettle, Greene's publisher, later printed a flattering apology to Shakespeare. What Greene's statement does show us is that Shakespeare's reputation for poetry had reached enough of a prominence to provoke the envy of a failing competitor.

In the following year, 1593, the government closed London's theatres due to an outbreak of the bubonic plague. Publication history suggests that during this closure, Shakespeare may have written his two narrative poems, *Venus and Adonis*, published in 1593, and *The Rape of Lucrece*, published in 1594. These are the only two works that Shakespeare seems to have helped into print; each carries a dedication by Shakespeare to Henry Wriothesley, Earl of Southampton.

A ground plan of London after the fire of 1666, drawn by Marcus Willemsz Doornik.
Guildhall Library, London/AKG, Berlin/SuperStock

Stage success

When the theatres reopened in 1594, Shakespeare joined the Lord Chamberlain's Men, an acting company. Though uncertain about the history of his early dramatic works, scholars believe that by this point he had written *The Two Gentlemen of Verona, The Taming of the Shrew,* the *Henry VI* trilogy, and *Titus Andronicus*. During his early years in the theatre, he primarily wrote history plays, with his romantic comedies emerging in the 1590s. Even at this early stage in his career, Shakespeare was a success. In 1597, he was able to purchase New Place, one of the two largest houses in Stratford, and secure a coat of arms for his family.

In 1597, the lease expired on the Lord Chamberlain's playhouse, called The Theatre. Because the owner of The Theatre refused to renew the lease, the acting company was forced to perform at various playhouses until the 1599 opening of the now famous Globe Theatre, which was literally built with lumber from The Theatre. (The Globe, later destroyed by fire, has recently been reconstructed in London and can be visited today.)

Recent scholars suggest that Shakespeare's great tragedy, *Julius Caesar*, may have been the first of Shakespeare's plays performed in the original playhouse. When this open-air theatre on the Thames River opened, financial papers list Shakespeare's name as one of the principal investors. Already an actor and a playwright, Shakespeare was now becoming a "Company Man." This new status allowed him to share in the profits of the theatre rather than merely getting paid for his plays, some of which publishers were beginning to release in quarto format.

Publications

A *quarto* was a small, inexpensive book typically used for leisure books such as plays; the term itself indicates that the printer folded the paper four times. The modern day equivalent of a quarto would be a paperback. In contrast, the first collected works of Shakespeare were in folio format, which means that the printer folded each sheet only once. Scholars call the collected edition of Shakespeare's works the *First Folio*. A folio was a larger and more prestigious book than a quarto, and printers generally reserved the format for works such as the Bible.

No evidence exists that Shakespeare participated in the publication of any of his plays. Members of Shakespeare's acting company printed the First Folio seven years after Shakespeare's death. Generally, playwrights wrote their works to be performed on stage, and publishing them was a novel innovation at the time. Shakespeare probably would not have thought of them as books in the way we do. In fact, as a principal investor in the acting company (which purchased the play as well as the exclusive right to perform it), he may not have even thought of them as his own. He would probably have thought of his plays as belonging to the company.

For this reason, scholars have generally characterized most quartos printed before the Folio as "bad" by arguing that printers pirated the plays and published them illegally. How would a printer have received a pirated copy of a play? The theories range from someone stealing a copy to an actor (or actors) selling the play by relating it from memory to a printer. Many times, major differences exist between a quarto version of the play and a folio version, causing uncertainty about which is Shakespeare's true creation. *Hamlet*, for example, is almost twice as long in the Folio as in quarto versions. Recently, scholars have come to realize the value of the different versions. The *Norton Shakespeare*, for example, includes all three versions of *King Lear* — the quarto, the folio, and the *conflated* version (the combination of the quarto and folio).

Prolific productions

The first decade of the 1600s witnessed the publication of additional quartos as well as the production of most of Shakespeare's great tragedies, with *Julius Caesar* appearing in 1599 and *Hamlet* in 1600–1601. After the death of Queen Elizabeth in 1603, the Lord Chamberlain's Men became the King's Men under James I, Elizabeth's successor. Around the time of this transition in the English monarchy, the famous tragedy *Othello* (1603–1604) was most likely written and performed, followed closely by *King Lear* (1605–1606), *Antony and Cleopatra* (1606), and *Macbeth* (1606) in the next two years.

Shakespeare's name also appears as a major investor in the 1609 acquisition of an indoor theatre known as the Blackfriars. This last period of Shakespeare's career, which includes plays that considered the acting conditions both at the Blackfriars and the open-air Globe Theatre, consists primarily of romances or tragicomedies such as *The Winter's Tale* and *The Tempest*. On June 29, 1613, during a performance of *All is True*, or *Henry VIII*, the thatching on top of the Globe caught fire and the playhouse burned to the ground. After this incident, the King's Men moved solely into the indoor Blackfriars Theatre.

Final days

During the last years of his career, Shakespeare collaborated on a couple of plays with contemporary dramatist John Fletcher, even possibly coming out of retirement — which scholars believe began sometime in 1613 — to work on *The Two Noble Kinsmen* (1613–1614). Three years later, Shakespeare died on April 23, 1616. Though the exact cause of death remains unknown, a vicar from Stratford in the mid-seventeenth-century wrote in his diary that Shakespeare, perhaps celebrating the marriage of his daughter, Judith, contracted a fever during a night of revelry with fellow literary figures Ben Jonson and Michael Drayton. Regardless, Shakespeare may have felt his death was imminent in March of that year because he altered his will. Interestingly, his will mentions no book or theatrical manuscripts, perhaps indicating the lack of value that he put on printed versions of his dramatic works and their status as company property.

Seven years after Shakespeare's death, John Heminges and Henry Condell, fellow members of the King's Men, published his collected works. In their preface, they claim that they are publishing the true versions of Shakespeare's plays partially as a response to the previous quarto printings of 18 of his plays, most of these with multiple printings. This Folio contains 36 plays to which scholars generally add *Pericles* and *The Two Noble Kinsmen*. This volume of Shakespeare's plays began the process of constructing Shakespeare not only as England's national poet but also as a monumental figure whose plays would continue to captivate imaginations at the end of the millenium with no signs of stopping. Ben Jonson's prophetic line about Shakespeare in the First Folio — "He was not of an age, but for all time!" — certainly holds true.

Chronology of Shakespeare's plays

1590–1591	The Two Gentlemen of Verona
	The Taming of the Shrew
1591	2 Henry VI
	3 Henry VI
1592	1 Henry VI
	Titus Andronicus
1592–1593	Richard III
	Venus and Adonis
1593–1594	The Rape of Lucrece
1594	The Comedy of Errors
1594–1595	Love's Labour's Lost
1595	Richard II
	Romeo and Juliet
	A Midsummer Night's Dream
1595–1596	Love's Labour's Won
	(This manuscript was lost.)
1596	King John
1596–1597	The Merchant of Venice
	1 Henry IV
1597–1598	The Merry Wives of Windsor
	2 Henry IV
1598	Much Ado About Nothing
1598–1599	Henry V
1599	Julius Caesar
1599–1600	As You Like It
1600–1601	Hamlet

1601	Twelfth Night, or What You Will
1602	Troilus and Cressida
1593–1603	Sonnets
1603	Measure for Measure
1603–1604	A Lover's Complaint
	Othello
1604–1605	All's Well That Ends Well
1605	Timon of Athens
1605–1606	King Lear
1606	Macbeth
	Antony and Cleopatra
1607	Pericles
1608	Coriolanus
1609	The Winter's Tale
1610	Cymbeline
1611	The Tempest
1612–1613	Cardenio (with John Fletcher; this manuscript was lost.)
1613	All is True (Henry VIII)
1613–1614	The Two Noble Kinsmen (with John Fletcher)

This chronology is derived from Stanley Wells's and Gary Taylor's *William Shakespeare: A Textual Companion*, which is listed in the "Works consulted" section below.

A note on Shakespeare's language

Readers encountering Shakespeare for the first time usually find Early Modern English difficult to understand. Yet, rather than serving as a barrier to Shakespeare, the richness of this language should form part of our appreciation of the Bard.

One of the first things readers usually notice about the language is the use of pronouns. Like the King James Version of the Bible, Shakespeare's pronouns are slightly different from our own and can cause confusion. Words like "thou" (you), "thee" and "ye" (objective cases of you), and "thy" and "thine" (your/yours) appear throughout Shakespeare's plays. You may need a little time to get used to these changes. You can find the definitions for other words that commonly cause confusion in the notes column on the right side of each page in this edition.

Iambic pentameter

Though Shakespeare sometimes wrote in prose, he wrote most of his plays in poetry, specifically blank verse. Blank verse consists of lines in unrhymed *iambic pentameter. Iambic* refers to the stress patterns of the line. An *iamb* is an element of sound that consists of two beats — the first unstressed (da) and the second stressed (DA). A good example of an iambic line is Hamlet's famous line "To be or not to be," in which you do not stress "to," "or," and "to," but you do stress "be," "not," and "be." *Pentameter* refers to the *meter* or number of stressed syllables in a line. *Penta*-meter has five stressed syllables. Thus, Romeo's line "But soft, what light through yonder window breaks?" (II.2.2) is a good example of an iambic pentameter line.

Wordplay

Shakespeare's language is also verbally rich as he, along with many dramatists of his period, had a fondness for wordplay. This wordplay often takes the forms of double meanings, called *puns*, where a word can mean more than one thing in a given context. Shakespeare often employs these puns as a way of illustrating the distance between what is on the surface — *apparent* meanings — and what meanings lie underneath. Though recognizing these puns may be difficult at first, the notes in the far right column point many of them out to you.

If you are encountering Shakespeare's plays for the first time, the following reading tips may help ease you into the plays. Shakespeare's lines were meant to be spoken; therefore, reading them aloud or speaking them should help with comprehension. Also, though most of the lines are poetic, do not forget to read complete sentences — move from period to period as well as from line to line. Although Shakespeare's language can be difficult at first, the rewards of immersing yourself in the richness and fluidity of the lines are immeasurable.

Works consulted

For more information on Shakespeare's life and works, see the following:

Bevington, David, ed. *The Complete Works of Shakespeare.* New York: Longman, 1997.

Evans, G. Blakemore, ed. *The Riverside Shakespeare.* Boston: Houghton Mifflin Co., 1997.

Greenblatt, Stephen, ed. *The Norton Shakespeare.* New York: W.W. Norton and Co., 1997.

Kastan, David Scott, ed. *A Companion to Shakespeare.* Oxford: Blackwell, 1999.

McDonald, Russ. *The Bedford Companion to Shakespeare: An Introduction with Documents.* Boston: Bedford-St. Martin's Press, 1996.

Wells, Stanley and Gary Taylor. *William Shakespeare: A Textual Companion.* New York: W.W. Norton and Co., 1997.

INTRODUCTION TO EARLY MODERN ENGLAND

William Shakespeare (1564–1616) lived during a period in England's history that people have generally referred to as the English Renaissance. The term *renaissance*, meaning rebirth, was applied to this period of English history as a way of celebrating what was perceived as the rapid development of art, literature, science, and politics: in many ways, the rebirth of classical Rome.

Recently, scholars have challenged the name "English Renaissance" on two grounds. First, some scholars argue that the term should not be used because women did not share in the advancements of English culture during this time period; their legal status was still below that of men. Second, other scholars have challenged the basic notion that this period saw a sudden explosion of culture. A rebirth of civilization suggests that the previous period of time was not civilized. This second group of scholars sees a much more gradual transition between the Middle Ages and Shakespeare's time.

Some people use the terms *Elizabethan* and *Jacobean* when referring to periods of the sixteenth and seventeenth centuries. These terms correspond to the reigns of Elizabeth I (1558–1603) and James I (1603–1625). The problem with these terms is that they do not cover large spans of time; for example, Shakespeare's life and career span both monarchies.

Scholars are now beginning to replace Renaissance with the term Early Modern when referring to this time period, but people still use both terms interchangeably. The term *Early Modern* recognizes that this period established many of the foundations of our modern culture. Though critics still disagree about the exact dates of the period, in general, the dates range from 1450 to 1750. Thus, Shakespeare's life clearly falls within the Early Modern period.

Shakespeare's plays live on in our culture, but we must remember that Shakespeare's culture differed greatly from our own. Though his understanding of human nature and relationships seems to apply to our modern lives, we must try to understand the world he lived in so we can better understand his plays. This introduction helps you do just that. It examines the intellectual, religious, political, and social contexts of Shakespeare's work before turning to the importance of the theatre and the printing press.

Intellectual context

In general, people in Early Modern England looked at the universe, the human body, and science very differently from the way we do. But while we do not share their same beliefs, we must not think of people during Shakespeare's time as lacking in intelligence or education. Discoveries made during the Early Modern period concerning the universe and the human body provide the basis of modern science.

Cosmology

One subject we view very differently than Early Modern thinkers is cosmology. Shakespeare's contemporaries believed in the astronomy of Ptolemy, an intellectual from Alexandria in the second century A.D. Ptolemy thought that the earth stood at the center of the universe, surrounded by nine concentric rings. The celestial bodies circled the earth in the following order: the moon, Mercury, Venus, the sun, Mars, Jupiter, Saturn, and the stars. The entire system was controlled by the *primum mobile*, or Prime Mover, which initiated and maintained the movement of the celestial bodies. No one had yet discovered the last three planets in our solar system, Uranus, Neptune, and Pluto.

In 1543, Nicolaus Copernicus published his theory of a sun-based solar system, in which the sun stood at the center and the planets revolved around it. Though this theory appeared prior to Shakespeare's birth, people didn't really start to change their minds until 1610, when Galileo used his telescope to confirm Copernicus's theory. David Bevington asserts in the general introduction to his edition of Shakespeare's works that during most of Shakespeare's writing career, the cosmology of the universe was in question, and this sense of uncertainty influences some of his plays.

Universal hierarchy

Closely related to Ptolemy's hierarchical view of the universe is a hierarchical conception of the Earth (sometimes referred to as the Chain of Being). During the Early Modern period, many people believed that all of creation was organized hierarchically. God existed at the top, followed by the angels, men, women, animals, plants, and rocks. (Because all women were thought to exist below all men on the chain, we can easily imagine the confusion that Elizabeth I caused when she became queen of England.

She was literally "out of order," an expression that still exists in our society.) Though the concept of this hierarchy is a useful one when beginning to study Shakespeare, keep in mind that distinctions in this hierarchical view were not always clear and that we should not reduce all Early Modern thinking to a simple chain.

Elements and humors

The belief in a hierarchical scheme of existence created a comforting sense of order and balance that carried over into science as well. Shakespeare's contemporaries generally accepted that four different elements composed everything in the universe: earth, air, water, and fire. People associated these four elements with four qualities of being. These qualities — hot, cold, moist, and dry — appeared in different combinations in the elements. For example, air was hot and moist; water was cold and moist; earth was cold and dry; and fire was hot and dry.

In addition, people believed that the human body contained all four elements in the form of *humors* — blood, phlegm, yellow bile, and black bile — each of which corresponded to an element. Blood corresponded to air (hot and moist), phlegm to water (cold and moist), yellow bile to fire (hot and dry), and black bile to earth (cold and dry). When someone was sick, physicians generally believed that the patient's humors were not in the proper balance. For example, if someone were diagnosed with an abundance of blood, the physician would bleed the patient (using leeches or cutting the skin) in order to restore the balance.

Shakespeare's contemporaries also believed that the humors determined personality and temperament. If a person's dominant humor was blood, he was considered light-hearted. If dominated by yellow bile (or choler), that person was irritable. The dominance of phlegm led a person to be dull and kind. And if black bile prevailed, he was melancholy or sad. Thus, people of Early Modern England often used the humors to explain behavior and emotional outbursts. Throughout Shakespeare's plays, he uses the concept of the humors to define and explain various characters.

Yet *Twelfth Night, or What You Will,* never adheres to a simple notion of the humors. In fact, it has been argued that, in *Twelfth Night,* Shakespeare is satirizing the playwright Ben Jonson's "comedy of humors." In Jonson's plays, the characters — their actions and behaviors — are defined by their humors alone. As in popular psychology today, humors reduced the complexities of human behavior to a few overly simplified concepts, which were to be applied to almost any situation. Shakespeare scorns this reductive view; he presents life. He captures and reveals human behavior in more complex terms, allowing his characters to embody contradictions. A person may behave rationally in certain situations and choleric in others within a play by Shakespeare. With Jonson, this dynamic is never the case; his characters are created to exemplify one specific humor. Many critics believe that the practical joke played upon the choleric Malvolio in *Twelfth Night* mirrors Shakespeare's own sanguine joke upon the choleric Ben Jonson. In effect, *Twelfth Night* is Shakespeare mocking Jonson as a playwright for being overtly moralizing (and self-satisfied, in the manner of Malvolio), as well as reductive in his rendering of the human condition.

Religious context

Shakespeare lived in an England full of religious uncertainty and dispute. From the Protestant Reformation to the translation of the Bible into English, the Early Modern era is punctuated with events that have greatly influenced modern religious beliefs.

The Reformation

Until the Protestant Reformation, the only Christian church was the Catholic, or "universal," church. Beginning in Europe in the early sixteenth century, religious thinkers such as Martin Luther and John Calvin, who claimed that the Roman Catholic

Church had become corrupt and was no longer following the word of God, began what has become known as the Protestant Reformation. The Protestants ("protestors") believed in salvation by faith rather than works. They also believed in the primacy of the Bible and advocated giving all people access to reading the Bible.

Many English people initially resisted Protestant ideas. However, the Reformation in England began in 1527 during the reign of Henry VIII, prior to Shakespeare's birth. In that year, Henry VIII decided to divorce his wife, Catherine of Aragon, for her failure to produce a male heir. (Only one of their children, Mary, survived past infancy.) Rome denied Henry's petitions for a divorce, forcing him to divorce Catherine without the Church's approval, which he did in 1533.

A portrait of King Henry VIII, artist unknown, ca. 1542.
National Portrait Gallery, London/SuperStock

The Act of Supremacy

The following year, the Pope excommunicated Henry VIII while Parliament confirmed his divorce and the legitimacy of his new marriage through the *Act of Succession*. Later in 1534, Parliament passed the *Act of Supremacy*, naming Henry the "Supreme Head of the Church in England." Henry continued to persecute both radical Protestant reformers and Catholics who remained loyal to Rome.

Henry VIII's death in 1547 brought Edward VI, his 10-year-old son by Jane Seymour (the king's third wife), to the throne. This succession gave Protestant reformers the chance to solidify their break with the Catholic Church. During Edward's reign, Archbishop Thomas Cranmer established the foundation for the Anglican Church through his 42 articles of religion. He also wrote the first *Book of Common Prayer*, adopted in 1549, which was the official text for worship services in England.

Bloody Mary

Catholics continued to be persecuted until 1553, when the sickly Edward VI died and was succeeded by Mary, his half-sister and the Catholic daughter of Catherine of Aragon. The reign of Mary witnessed the reversal of religion in England through the restoration of Catholic authority and obedience to Rome. Protestants were executed in large numbers, which earned the monarch the nickname *Bloody Mary*. Many Protestants fled to Europe to escape persecution.

Elizabeth, the daughter of Henry VIII and Anne Boleyn, outwardly complied with the mandated Catholicism during her half-sister Mary's reign, but she restored Protestantism when she took the throne in 1558 after Mary's death. Thus, in the space of a single decade, England's throne passed from Protestant to Catholic to Protestant, with each change carrying serious and deadly consequences.

Though Elizabeth reigned in relative peace from 1558 to her death in 1603, religion was still a serious concern for her subjects. During Shakespeare's life, a great deal of religious dissent existed in England.

Many Catholics, who remained loyal to Rome and their church, were persecuted for their beliefs. At the other end of the spectrum, the Puritans were persecuted for their belief that the Reformation was not complete. (The English pejoratively applied the term *Puritan* to religious groups that wanted to continue purifying the English church by such measures as removing the *episcopacy,* or the structure of bishops.)

The Great Bible

One thing agreed upon by both the Anglicans and Puritans was the importance of a Bible written in English. Translated by William Tyndale in 1525, the first authorized Bible in English, published in 1539, was known as the Great Bible. This Bible was later revised during Elizabeth's reign into what was known as the Bishop's Bible. As Stephen Greenblatt points out in his introduction to the *Norton Shakespeare,* Shakespeare would probably have been familiar with both the Bishop's Bible, heard aloud in Mass, and the Geneva Bible, which was written by English exiles in Geneva. The last authorized Bible produced during Shakespeare's lifetime came within the last decade of his life when James I's commissioned edition, known as the King James Bible, appeared in 1611.

Political context

Politics and religion were closely related in Shakespeare's England. Both of the monarchs under whom Shakespeare lived had to deal with religious and political dissenters.

Elizabeth I

Despite being a Protestant, Elizabeth I tried to take a middle road on the religious question. She allowed Catholics to practice their religion in private as long as they outwardly appeared Anglican and remained loyal to the throne.

Elizabeth's monarchy was one of absolute supremacy. Believing in the divine right of kings, she styled herself as being appointed by God to rule England. To oppose the Queen's will was the equivalent of opposing God's will. Known as *passive obedience,* this doctrine did not allow any opposition even to a tyrannical monarch because God had appointed the king or queen for reasons unknown to His subjects on earth. However, as Bevington notes, Elizabeth's power was not as absolute as her rhetoric suggested. Parliament, already well established in England, reserved some power, such as the authority to levy taxes, for itself.

Elizabeth I lived in a society that restricted women from possessing any political or personal autonomy and power. As queen, Elizabeth violated and called into question many of the prejudices and practices against women. In a way, her society forced her to "overcome" her sex in order to rule effectively. However, her position did nothing to increase the status of women in England.

A portrait of Elizabeth I by George Gower, ca. 1588.
National Portrait Gallery, London/SuperStock

One of the rhetorical strategies that Elizabeth adopted in order to rule effectively was to separate her position as monarch of England from her natural body — to separate her *body politic* from her *body natural*. In addition, throughout her reign, Elizabeth brilliantly negotiated between domestic and foreign factions — some of whom were anxious about a female monarch and wanted her to marry — appeasing both sides without ever committing to one.

She remained unmarried throughout her 45-year reign, partially by styling herself as the Virgin Queen whose purity represented England herself. Her refusal to marry and her habit of hinting and promising marriage with suitors both foreign and domestic helped Elizabeth maintain internal and external peace. Not marrying allowed her to retain her independence, but it left the succession of the English throne in question. In 1603, on her deathbed, she named James VI, King of Scotland and son of her cousin Mary, as her successor.

James I

When he assumed the English crown, James VI of Scotland became James I of England. (Some historians refer to him as James VI and I.) Like Elizabeth, James was a strong believer in the divine right of kings and their absolute authority.

Upon his arrival in London to claim the English throne, James made his plans to unite Scotland and England clear. However, a long-standing history of enmity existed between the two countries. Partially as a result of this history and the influx of Scottish courtiers into English society, anti-Scottish prejudice abounded in England. When James asked Parliament for the title of "King of Great Britain," he was denied.

As scholars such as Bevington have pointed out, James was less successful than Elizabeth was in negotiating between the different religious and political factions in England. Although he was a Protestant, he began to have problems with the Puritan sect of the House of Commons, which ultimately led to a rift between the court (which also started to have Catholic sympathies) and the Parliament. This rift between the monarchy and Parliament eventually escalated into a civil war that would erupt during the reign of James's son, Charles I.

In spite of its difficulties with Parliament, James's court was a site of wealth, luxury, and extravagance. James I commissioned elaborate feasts, masques, and pageants, and in doing so he more than doubled the royal debt. Stephen Greenblatt suggests that Shakespeare's *The Tempest* may reflect this extravagance through Prospero's magnificent banquet and accompanying masque. Reigning from 1603 to 1625, James I remained the King of England throughout the last years of Shakespeare's life.

Social context

Shakespeare's England divided itself roughly into two social classes: the aristocrats (or nobility) and everyone else. The primary distinctions between these two classes were ancestry, wealth, and power. Simply put, the aristocrats were the only ones who possessed all three.

Aristocrats were born with their wealth, but the growth of trade and the development of skilled professions began to provide wealth for those not born with it. Although the notion of a middle class did not begin to develop until after Shakespeare's death, the possibility of some social mobility did exist in Early Modern England. Shakespeare himself used the wealth gained from the theatre to move into the lower ranks of the aristocracy by securing a coat of arms for his family.

Shakespeare was not unique in this movement, but not all people received the opportunity to increase their social status. Members of the aristocracy feared this social movement and, as a result, promoted harsh laws of apprenticeship and fashion, restricting certain styles of dress and material. These laws dictated that only the aristocracy could wear certain articles of clothing, colors, and materials. Though enforcement was a difficult task, the Early Modern aristocracy considered dressing above one's station a moral and ethical violation.

The status of women

The legal status of women did not allow them much public or private autonomy. English society functioned on a system of patriarchy and hierarchy (see "The Chain of Being" earlier in this introduction), which means that men controlled society beginning with the individual family. In fact, the family metaphorically corresponded to the state. For example, the husband was the king of his family. His authority to control his family was absolute and based on divine right, similar to that of the country's king. People also saw the family itself differently than today, considering apprentices and servants part of the whole family.

The practice of *primogeniture* — a system of inheritance that passed all of a family's wealth through the first male child — accompanied this system of patriarchy Thus women did not generally inherit their family's wealth and titles. In the absence of a male heir, some women, such as Queen Elizabeth, did. But after women married, they lost almost all of their already limited legal rights, such as the right to inherit, to own property, and to sign contracts. In all likelihood, Elizabeth I would have lost much of her power and authority if she married.

Furthermore, women did not generally receive an education and could not enter certain professions, including acting. Instead, society relegated women to the domestic sphere of the home.

In *Twelfth Night,* however, we see such gender stereotypes challenged in many ways. The strongest character in the play, Viola, is sympathetically portrayed as adopting a male disguise in order to transcend the typical gender restrictions of her time. It is perhaps more than a mere coincidence that this play, like the other comedies in which women dress as men to achieve power over, or at least parity with, men, was written while England was ruled by a Queen. When Elizabeth died, and James became king, Shakespeare largely eschewed such plays that celebrated a largely untamed feminine spirit.

There are other ways in which traditional gender roles are inverted in *Twelfth Night.* Olivia, who like Queen Elizabeth, is head of her household, is in a position of authority throughout the play, trying to maintain peace between the choleric Malvolio and the sanguineous Toby. We see her controlling her household, while Orsino, by contrast, is somewhat less authoritative: He would rather lounge about his house passively and recite poetry than go hunting, either for deer or for Olivia.

Daily life

Daily life in Early Modern England began before sun-up — exactly how early depended on one's station in life. A servant's responsibilities usually included preparing the house for the day. Families usually possessed limited living space, and even among wealthy families multiple family members tended to share a small number of rooms, suggesting that privacy may not have been important or practical.

Working through the morning, Elizabethans usually had lunch about noon. This midday meal was the primary meal of the day, much like dinner is for modern families. The workday usually ended around sundown or 5 p.m., depending on the season. Before an early bedtime, Elizabethans usually ate a light repast and then settled in for a couple of hours of reading (if the family members were literate and could bear the high cost of books) or socializing.

Mortality rates

Mortality rates in Early Modern England were high compared to our standards, especially among infants. Infection and disease ran rampant because physicians did not realize the need for antiseptics and sterile equipment. As a result, communicable diseases often spread very rapidly in cities, particularly London.

In addition, the bubonic plague frequently ravaged England, with two major outbreaks — from 1592–1594 and in 1603 — occurring during Shakespeare's lifetime. People did not understand the plague and generally perceived it as God's punishment. (We now know that the plague was spread by fleas and could not be spread directly from human to human.) Without a cure or an understanding of what transmitted the disease, physicians could do nothing to stop the thousands of deaths that resulted from each outbreak. These outbreaks had a direct effect on Shakespeare's career, because the government often closed the theatres in an effort to impede the spread of the disease.

London life

In the sixteenth century, London, though small compared to modern cities, was the largest city of Europe, with a population of about 200,000 inhabitants in the city and surrounding suburbs. London was a crowded city without a sewer system, which facilitated epidemics such as the plague. In addition, crime rates were high in the city due to inefficient law enforcement and the lack of street lighting.

Despite these drawbacks, London was the cultural, political, and social heart of England. As the home of the monarch and most of England's trade, London was a bustling metropolis. Not surprisingly, a young Shakespeare moved to London to begin his professional career.

The theatre

Most theatres were not actually located within the city of London. Rather, theatre owners built them on the South bank of the Thames River (in Southwark) across from the city in order to avoid the strict regulations that applied within the city's walls. These restrictions stemmed from a mistrust of public performances as locations of plague and riotous behavior. Furthermore, because theatre performances took place during the day, they took laborers away from their jobs. Opposition to the theatres also came from Puritans who believed that they fostered immorality. Therefore, theatres moved out of the city, to areas near other sites of restricted activities, such as dog fighting, bear- and bull-baiting, and prostitution.

Despite the move, the theatre was not free from censorship or regulation. In fact, a branch of the government known as the Office of the Revels attempted to ensure that plays did not present politically or socially sensitive material. Prior to each performance, the Master of the Revels would read a complete text of each play, cutting out offending sections or, in some cases, not approving the play for public performance.

Performance spaces

Theatres in Early Modern England were quite different from our modern facilities. They were usually open-air, relying heavily on natural light and good weather. The rectangular stage extended out into an area that people called the *pit* — a circular, uncovered area about 70 feet in diameter. Audience members had two choices when purchasing admission to a theatre. Admission to the pit, where the lower classes (or *groundlings*) stood for the performances,

The recently reconstructed Globe Theatre.
Chris Parker/PAL

was the cheaper option. People of wealth could purchase a seat in one of the three covered tiers of seats that ringed the pit. At full capacity, a public theatre in Early Modern England could hold between 2,000 and 3,000 people.

The stage, which projected into the pit and was raised about five feet above it, had a covered portion called the *heavens*. The heavens enclosed theatrical equipment for lowering and raising actors to and from the stage. A trapdoor in the middle of the stage provided theatrical graves for characters such as Ophelia and also allowed ghosts, such as Banquo in *Macbeth*, to rise from the earth. A wall separated the back of the stage from the actors' dressing room, known as the *tiring house*. At each end of the wall stood a door for major entrances and exits. Above the wall and doors stood a gallery directly above the stage, reserved for the wealthiest spectators. Actors occasionally used this area when a performance called for a difference in height — for example, to represent Juliet's balcony or the walls of a besieged city. A good example of this type of theatre was the original Globe Theatre in London in which Shakespeare's company, The Lord Chamberlain's Men (later the King's Men), staged its plays. However, indoor theatres, such as the Blackfriars, differed slightly because the pit was filled with chairs that faced a rectangular stage. Because only the wealthy could afford the cost of admission, the public generally considered these theatres private.

Some question exists as to whether Shakespeare wrote *Twelfth Night* to be performed in a more popular theatre or in a private theatre. Certainly,

Shakespeare in Love *shows how the interior of the Globe would have appeared.*
The Everett Collection

Shakespeare was able to include enough in the play to please an aristocratic audience as well as a less educated one.

Actors and staging

Performances in Shakespeare's England do not appear to have employed scenery. However, theatre companies developed their costumes with great care and expense. In fact, a playing company's costumes were its most valuable items. These extravagant costumes were the object of much controversy because some aristocrats feared that the actors could use them to disguise their social status on the streets of London.

Costumes also disguised a player's gender. All actors on the stage during Shakespeare's lifetime were men. Young boys whose voices had not reached maturity played female parts. This practice no doubt influenced Shakespeare's and his contemporary playwrights' thematic explorations of cross-dressing.

Though historians have managed to reconstruct the appearance of the early modern theatre, such as the recent construction of the Globe in London, much of the information regarding how plays were performed during this era has been lost. Scholars of Early Modern theatre have turned to the scant external and internal stage directions in manuscripts in an effort to find these answers. While a hindrance for modern critics and scholars, the lack of detail about Early Modern performances has allowed modern directors and actors a great deal of flexibility and room to be creative.

Ultimately, there is no one "correct" way for *Twelfth Night* to be performed. It is possible that Shakespeare went out of his way to purposely "erase" statements of how his plays were performed in order to allow more room for interpretation. In directing *Twelfth Night* and other Shakespeare plays, as in writing about them, we are in some ways co-authoring it, just as each harpsichordist who interprets a Bach concerto, although reading the music note for note, achieves a unique effect. The bare stage puts a greater emphasis not only on the actors' costume, but also on their ability to use words. Accustomed as we are, in the early twenty-first century, to special effects, in the theatre as well as in movies (which have, in many ways, more in common with the Shakespearean theatre than contemporary theatre does), we may initially downplay the importance of words in Shakespeare. For Shakespeare, language was not only the means by which characters communicate to each other but also served a function that today is largely served by so-called special effects.

The printing press

If not for the printing press, many Early Modern plays may not have survived until today. In Shakespeare's time, printers produced all books by *sheet* — a single large piece of paper that the printer would fold in order to produce the desired book size. For example, a folio required folding the sheet once, a quarto four times, an octavo eight, and so on. Sheets would be printed one side at a time; thus, printers had to simultaneously print multiple nonconsecutive pages.

In order to estimate what section of the text would be on each page, the printer would *cast off* copy. After the printer made these estimates, *compositors* would set the type upside down, letter by letter. This process of setting type produced textual errors, some of which a proofreader would catch. When a proofreader found an error, the compositors would fix the piece or pieces of type. Printers called corrections made after printing began *stop-press* corrections because they literally had to stop the press to fix the error. Because of the high cost of paper, printers would still sell the sheets printed before they made the correction.

Printers placed frames of text in the bed of the printing press and used them to imprint the paper. They then folded and grouped the sheets of paper into gatherings, after which the pages were ready for sale. The buyer had the option of getting the new play bound.

The printing process was crucial to the preservation of Shakespeare's works, but the printing of drama in Early Modern England was not a standardized practice. Many of the first editions of Shakespeare's plays appear in quarto format and, until recently, scholars regarded them as "corrupt." In fact, scholars still debate how close a relationship exists between what appeared on the stage in the sixteenth and seventeenth centuries and what appears on the printed page. The inconsistent and scant appearance of stage directions, for example, makes it difficult to determine how close this relationship was.

We know that the practice of the theatre allowed the alteration of plays by a variety of hands other than the author's, further complicating any efforts to extract what a playwright wrote and what was changed by either the players, the printers, or the government censors. Theatre was a collaborative environment. Rather than lament our inability to determine authorship and what exactly Shakespeare wrote, we should work to understand this collaborative nature and learn from it.

Unlike many other plays that appeared in a bootlegged quarto form while he was still alive, *Twelfth Night* did not appear in print until 1623 in the First Folio of Shakespeare's plays compiled by his friends, Heminges and Condell. (Shakespeare discouraged publication of his plays while he was alive because publication would allow rival acting troupes to perform the plays and thus threaten his economic livelihood.) While this fact means that much of the textual debate that surrounds other Shakespeare plays (such as *Hamlet,* whose quarto and folio versions are significantly different) is avoided when considering the text of *Twelfth Night,* it in no way ensures that the text we have today is what Shakespeare wrote. It is quite possible, for example, that the actor who played Feste, Robert Armin, had at least some hand in writing his own lines. Some have suggested that Armin, a professional fool and author, as well as an actor who played one, actually improvised his jokes so that each night a theatre audience would see a somewhat different play.

Shakespeare wrote his plays for the stage, and the existing published texts reflect the collaborative nature of the theater as well as the unavoidable changes made during the printing process. A play's first written version would have been the author's *foul papers,* which invariably consisted of blotted lines and revised text. From there, a scribe would recopy the play and produce a *fair copy.* The theatre manager would then copy out and annotate this copy into a playbook (what people today call a *promptbook*).

At this point, scrolls of individual parts were copied out for actors to memorize. (Due to the high cost of paper, theatre companies could not afford to provide their actors with a complete copy of the play.) The government required the company to send the playbook to the Master of the Revels, the government official who would make any necessary changes or mark any passages considered unacceptable for performance.

Printers could have used any one of these copies to print a play. We cannot determine whether a printer used the author's version, the modified theatrical version, the censored version, or a combination when printing a given play. Refer back to the "Publications" section of the Introduction to William Shakespeare for further discussion of the impact printing practices has on our understanding of Shakespeare's works.

Works cited

For more information regarding Early Modern England, consult the following works:

Bevington, David. "General Introduction." *The Complete Works of William Shakespeare.* Updated Fourth edition. New York: Longman, 1997.

Greenblatt, Stephen. "Shakespeare's World." *Norton Shakespeare.* New York: W.W. Norton and Co., 1997.

Kastan, David Scott, ed. *A Companion to Shakespeare.* Oxford: Blackwell, 1999.

McDonald**,** Russ**.** *The Bedford Companion to Shakespeare: An Introduction with Documents.* Boston: Bedford-St. Martin's Press, 1996.

INTRODUCTION TO TWELFTH NIGHT

Before considering *Twelfth Night, or What You Will,* in its own right, it's important to consider the play in relation to its dramatic genre. Up until quite recently, most Shakespearean critics and scholars have steadfastly adhered to a false, one-sided hierarchy, which claims that tragedy is a more serious, ambitious, and important dramatic genre than comedy.

Comedies and tragedies — the critical context

It has become a critical commonplace to claim that Shakespeare's masterpieces are primarily his tragedies (specifically, *Hamlet, King Lear, Othello,* and *Macbeth*). His comedies, however charming, have generated significantly less ink and are often relegated to second-class status as lighter plays or, in extreme cases, mere apprentice works written more to entertain the vulgar sensibilities of the groundlings in the cheap seats than to educate and challenge a more sophisticated audience's sensibilities.

This viewpoint, while it has produced some excellent readings and interpretations of the tragedies, nonetheless gives us a lopsided view of Shakespeare's achievements. Luckily, in the past 30 years, a gradual, yet pronounced, re-evaluation of this hierarchy capaciously allows us access to the breadth of Shakespeare's plays without having to subordinate the comedies to the tragedies. Such a re-evaluation has come from several quarters, the most significant of which are the following:

* Feminist critics have convincingly shown that the traditional preference for tragedies over comedies, in most cases, implies a gender bias. These critics argue that the tragedies deal far more with the problematics of a male subjectivity left largely unchecked by women, while the comedies divide their concerns more equally between men and women.

* Other critics have shown that the traditional privileging of tragedy over comedy is usually accompanied by a spurious notion that higher poetic diction is synonymous with superior moral insight. Thus, because the comedies abound with quick witty dialogue while the tragedies are more full of long speeches and soliloquies, the comedies are often deemed less poetic. Yet if we broaden our idea of poetry to allow for wit and dialogue, we may find that the comedies are at least as poetic as the tragedies, especially when considering *Twelfth Night,* which has both long speeches with high poetic diction and quick witty banter.

In fact, the witty banter and emphasis on dialogue in Shakespearean comedy is very much a comment on these tragic conventions. In *Twelfth Night,* Shakespeare employs comic conventions to keep tragedy in check: The unfettered subjectivity, isolation, and alienation of the tragic hero, destructive to himself as well as to the society of which he is a part, is satirized and often successfully countered by the serious foolery in this play. *Twelfth Night* has no tragic heroes, though the characters of both Orsino and Malvolio contain elements of the tragic hero. The fact that Shakepeare's comedies rarely offer a privileged access to the characters' personal torment may seem, to some sensibilities, a more superficial approach. But life requires constant compromises and accommodations with society in general, as well as with other individuals, and the comedies, with their plurality of perspectives and seemingly gratuitous banter (which require an acute attentiveness to language and the slipperiness of the present), have much to teach us.

The conclusion of *Twelfth Night* adheres to Shakespearean comic convention: the promise of multiple weddings. From the 1996 film, *Twelfth Night,* with Helena Bonham Carter, Toby Stephens, Imogen Stubbs, and Stephen Mackintosh. The Everett Collection

When we speak of *Shakespearean comedy,* we do not use the term in the same way that it is used today. Generally speaking, comedy is opposed to tragedy insofar as the latter plays end in death while the former end in marriage. The difference between comedy and tragedy is largely a function of how the plays end; one sleight of the authorial pen, and *Romeo and Juliet* becomes a comedy and *Twelfth Night* a tragedy.

Shakespeare, throughout his career, manipulated and complicated this convention. *Love's Labour's Lost,* an early comedy, teases us, as well as its leading male characters, by violating the comic convention and deferring the expected marriage until a year after the play ends. Nor does the mere fact that a play ends in marriage necessarily mean that it has a "happy ending." In *Measure for Measure* and *All's Well That Ends Well,* two plays generally classified as comedies, the marriages that end the plays are practically viewed as a form of punishment for the majority of the characters.

Even in the more "festive" comedies, such as *Much Ado About Nothing,* many questions have been raised about the plausibility and soundness of the marriage of certain characters. One could argue that some of the tragedies, which end in death, may actually have happier endings than some of Shakespeare's most celebrated comedies. For example, Antony and Cleopatra seem more united in death than they ever did in life. Thus, when we consider Shakespeare's comedies, we are looking at something far more complex than a fairy-tale story with a happy ending. What we see in the endings of Shakespeare's plays is more likely a tentative, new beginning, than a happy ending.

Twelfth Night, one of Shakespeare's comic masterpieces (and by most accounts, the last comedy he wrote before turning to the period of the great tragedies), presents a case in point. The play adheres to comic conventions. Three couples are paired off by the end of the play, and a brother and sister are reunited — yet the *world* that the play presents is, in the final analysis, more the point of the play than whether or not the ending is happy.

Generally speaking, Shakespearean comedy is also distinguished from tragedy by several other factors.

* In tragedy, character is more important, while in comedy, plot is more important.
* In tragedy, feeling is more important, while in comedy, thought reigns.
* No character is central to a comedy in the way that a tragic hero is. While tragedies often take their name from their central characters, none of the comedies do.
* Men dominate the world of tragedies, while in the comedies, women are more dominant than, or at least equal with, the men in a way they are not in tragedy (with the possible exception of *Antony and Cleopatra*).
* Long speeches, so central to the tragedies (and to the history plays), are less prevalent, and even satirized, in the comedies, in which witty banter is more prevalent.
* In comedies, the individual must learn to accommodate his or her needs and feelings to the demands of society, while in tragedy, the *pathos* of the individual is indulged in.

While all of these distinguishing factors may be seen in *Twelfth Night,* we must remember that each play (whatever its generic classification) handles these themes differently. *Twelfth Night,* for example, evokes much more sympathy and empathy in the way characters are portrayed than an earlier comedy such as *A Midsummer Night's Dream,* in which we look at the amorous follies of the central human characters through the eyes of the mischievous sprite Puck, who, in laughing at them — "what fools these mortals be!" — makes it harder to sympathize with them. In *Twelfth Night,* we are still invited to laugh, but more typically the laughter is *with* the characters rather than at them; even when we laugh at Malvolio, our laughter cannot help but turn uncomfortably on ourselves. We are not afforded any omniscient, Puck-like perspective from which to gaze on the follies brought on by love in *Twelfth Night*. In this, *Twelfth Night* is a somewhat more "realistic" play than many of Shakespeare's earlier comedies, and it also has more tragic elements, insofar as tragedy is more concerned with feeling than comedy typically is. This is not to say that *Twelfth Night* is an especially dark play, but that it contains a harmonious balance between comic and tragic elements.

The comic character, Malvolio, from a 1994 Royal Shakespeare Company production of Twelfth Night.
Clive Barda/PAL

Cesario, and s/he is most "willing apt" to let him. Even though all these threats come to nought, they serve as a reminder of how *eros* (love), in Shakespeare, can so quickly slide over into *thanatos* (death). In fact, many of the characters speak of love in terms of death. Although speaking of love as a kind of death was a (Petrarchan) convention in Shakespeare's day, and in many instances had become meaningless and cliched by overuse, Shakespeare is able to breathe new life into this metaphor by embodying it dramatically on stage.

In *Twelfth Night*, love is seen as similar to death, because both pose a threat, or at the very least, a challenge to the singular self that is afraid of change, the self that, in the words of Sir Toby Belch, acts as if it "will never die." To be able to love another requires that one must accept change, to accept that one cannot entirely control one's fate, or even one's will. The very language that one uses to communicate with another may end up meaning more, or at least differently, than what one intended.

The characters in the play that cling to a singular sense of self that does not allow for change are often the ones for whom change happens most violently. Malvolio is the most notable example of this, but Orsino, too, although he claims to be open to love, is, beneath all his high rhetoric, deeply afraid of any mutual love relationship. In some ways, it's much easier for him to pine for Olivia and send middlemen to woo her, precisely because it flatters his ego to feel he loves more than she loves him back. By

Death and love in *Twelfth Night*

Although no actual deaths occur in *Twelfth Night*, death haunts this play throughout. At the beginning of the play, Olivia is mourning a dead brother. Sebastian and Viola, fraternal twins, have just survived a shipwreck, and each spends the majority of the play thinking the other dead. Yet in both of these cases, the severing by death of a fraternal bond, seems to force these characters to ready themselves for a more mature adult love.

Later in the play, when the plot entanglements heat up, we learn of other near-brushes with death. Antonio, captured by Orsino's men, is threatened with death. Pranks orchestrated by Sir Toby and Sir Andrew lead them perilously close to being killed by Sebastian. Most significantly, Orsino threatens to kill contrast, Viola embraces forces that are beyond her control (time, for example) and gives of herself more freely to others. Perhaps because, being shipwrecked on a strange land and having lost her brother (though not her money!), she now realizes that she has nothing to lose, and this frees her to play a wide range of roles and "sing both high and low."

Love and the self

Perhaps the comedies are more important to a young person for whom love is a more pressing issue than death is. As the poet Richard Wilbur wrote, love "calls us to things of this world." Certainly *Twelfth Night's* overriding concern is love and the havoc that sexual desire may wreak upon the self. When one is in love, of course, one may have to sacrifice one's sense of identity and try to see oneself with another's eyes, rather than steadfastly cling to one's self-image by ignoring or deprecating what others may say. What may be a virtue in other realms of experience becomes a debilitating stubbornness when it comes to erotic love.

When Olivia concludes at the end of Act I, Scene 5

> *I do I know not what, and fear to find*
> *Mine eye too great a flatterer for my mind.*
> *Fate, show thy force; ourselves we do not owe.*
> *What is decreed must be — and this be so!*

Shakespeare, in the person of Olivia here, gets to the heart of the relationship between self and love. When we fall in love, we almost necessarily lose our self-composure, cease to be able to see our actions with our own eyes (or realize, perhaps for the first time, that we could never see our actions in the first place). Yet even though Olivia fears that her attraction to Viola will come to nought, she is willing to risk it, because love, or at least intense attraction, allows her to leave her "mind" behind and give herself up to fate. This quote embodies Shakespeare's

Olivia (right) woos Viola, disguised as Duke Orsino's male servant, Cesario. From the 1996 film, Twelfth Night, with Imogen Stubbs and Helena Bonham Carter. *The Everett Collection*

lesson about the most noble, if not necessarily rewarding, attitude to take toward the risk that love entails: for Olivia, it is better to have loved and lost than never to have loved at all.

Of course, such a stoic attitude is easier said than done, and many of the follies of this play result from the characters' inability to truly live up to their own wisdom. Their lapses and mini-tragedies occur when they try to control a situation that, by definition, must remain beyond their control. Yet when Olivia exclaims, "ourselves we do not owe" ("owe" meaning primarily what we mean by "own" today), she states a truth that makes her both more noble and more profound than not only Malvolio (whom she characterizes as "sick of self love") but also Sir Toby Belch and Orsino (who do not come to this realization except, perhaps, in the play's final recognition scene).

For if we do not owe ourselves, then somebody else does, and *every* relationship with others actually creates our self, our sense of identity, much more than any pre-existing sense of essence does. This is not to say that we must therefore give up our "will" and become entirely passive in letting fate, or time, have its way with us.

The heroine of this play, Viola, although extremely passive when it comes to expressing (and acting *directly* on) her own desire for Orsino, is nonetheless extremely active in moving the plot of the play along. But will in Shakespeare's time was a more complex word than it is in its common usage today. Will is not only what we intend, or the act by which we attempt to control things, but also that which cannot be controlled (roughly equivalent to "lust"). As long as a word may have two meanings, and these meanings are in what common sense would term "radical contradiction" to each other, we must realize not only how unstable (or as Feste would say, how "unreliable") words are but also come to find that even the self is an "always already" social entity. For if we cannot control even our own (allegedly internal) will, then we really have nothing to lose by giving ourselves up to love, or to another's whim. We do not have control over who loves us, and we do not have control over whom we love.

Identity will always be fragmentary and incomplete until one is able to love, regardless of whether one is loved in return. Yet if that love is frustrated (and in Shakespearean comedy, it almost always is at first, as frustration is precisely what moves the plot), it may sometimes turn into hate. While neither Viola nor Olivia is guilty of doing so, Orsino is, whose "love" for Olivia is so often blended with hate. Even Malvolio, in his pathetic attempt to please Olivia, shares more of the wisdom that Olivia expresses in the above quote than Orsino does.

We see both the Duke's twisted attitude and Shakespeare's "foolish" attempt at correcting it as late in the play as Act V:

Duke *I know thee well. How dost thou, my good fellow?*

Clown *Truly, sir, the better for my foes and the worse for my friends.*

Duke *Just the contrary, the better for thy friends.*

Clown *No, sir, the worse.*

Duke *How can that be?*

Clown *Marry, sir, they praise me and make an ass of me; now my foes tell me plainly I am an ass: so that by my foes, sir, I profit in the knowledge of myself, and by my friends I am abused: so that, conclusions to be as kisses, if your four negatives make your two affirmatives, why then, the worse for my friends and the better for my foes.*

Duke *Why, this is excellent.*

The fool, here as elsewhere, is like a zen-master, using absurdity to point out the absurdity of common sense. The fool's wisdom here is so clearly what this play has to teach not only Orsino but also ourselves. Even though Orsino, in contrast to Malvolio, can act graciously to the fool and intellectually appreciate (as well as economically reward) the fool's speech, the speech's meaning has obviously fallen on deaf ears up to this point in the play. Orsino's desire to be flattered and his fear of the risk involved in truly giving himself to another are clearly the biggest problems that he refuses to confront. He simply cannot see how he may profit by his enemies, by those who thwart his desires.

When Viola, with characteristic self-effacement, tries to convince him that Olivia simply *cannot* (as opposed to *will* not) love him, Orsino limply responds, "I cannot so be answered." He doesn't think that he has to be *changed* in order to fall in love, perhaps because, being the Duke, he thinks he can buy love, or keep sending middlemen who allow him to avoid the intimacy that even a *direct* rejection would grant.

Identity and disguise

One of the central motifs of this play is identity and mistaken identity. Identity (like so many words in this play) has a double sense. On the one hand, identity differentiates one thing from another by noting the individuality of each. On the other hand, identity also implies likeness or resemblance. When we say two things are identical, we usually mean they are exactly the same, like identical twins. And this tension between likeness and difference generates much of the action in the comic and romantic plots. Both plots depend on Viola and Sebastian being identical in appearance, yet two different people.

Shakespeare's genius for playing with words and his ability to reveal the tenuous connection between words and the things they represent is both astounding and unsettling. His ability to reveal the unstable nature of identity itself, however, is profoundly disturbing. All the characters in this play are either taken in by another character's disguise or perpetrate a deception regarding their own identity. The subtitle, *or What You Will,* may be this play's guiding principle: *What you will* in this play is the basis for who you are. In Illyria, characters (like actors) take on fictive roles, and the line between being someone and playing someone is as tenuous as the line between reality and illusion.

Orsino plays the role of an unrequited lover and performs his suffering in scene after scene. Olivia plays the role of a woman grieving; her somber clothes and veil are her costume. Only when Viola enacts the role of Cesario, a young gentleman, does Olivia exchange her mourning costume for that of an active participant in love's pageant. Malvolio, Olivia's steward, performs the role of Olivia's lover for his own shadow (for himself). But in short order, Maria scripts his performance with a counterfeit love letter, supplying him with a larger audience (Toby, Andrew, and Fabian) and a guide to costuming (cross-gartered yellow stockings). Maria promises to make Malvolio a "common recreation," and he becomes just that, a piece of sublime theater. Poor Sir Andrew lacks the intelligence and imagination to successfully play the role he would will, a respected gentleman; so Sir Toby must direct Sir Andrew's performance every step of the way, like a "mannikin" in a puppet show. Yet all of these characters are unconscious of the fact that they are playing roles at all.

While the other characters delude themselves into believing that they are who they play at being, only Feste and Viola consciously disguise themselves as others, Feste as Sir Topas and Viola as Cesario. This knowledge sets them apart; they know just how changeable identity really is. Viola is aware that life in Illyria is like a play in which characters choose roles and enact their identities, but she is also aware of the wickedness of disguise (hers has deceived Olivia) and its limitations (it prevents her from being loved by Orsino). Feste, the Fool, is no less aware of the deceptive nature of appearance when it comes to identity. His role as Fool provides the other characters with a mirror in which they see themselves without illusion, an inverted fun house mirror, correcting instead of creating distortions.

Similarly, Shakespeare has created a play that acts as a mirror, showing his audience that identity itself is a convenient lie, its underlying instability the greatest truth. Shakespeare undermines the notion of identity as a stable, immutable form at every level. The similarity between the names of Olivia, Malvolio, and Viola — spoken aloud, their resemblance is palpable — is no accident; their difference is almost indistinguishable. They not only sound alike, they are anagrams of each other. As critic Stevie Davies has noted, Olivia is a juggled Viola plus the letter I, and Malvolio contains Olivia.

Viola, as Cesario, is just one example of identity confusion prevalent in Twelfth Night. *From a 1994 Royal Shakespeare Company production of* Twelfth Night. *Michael Ward/PAL.*

Another level of identity confusion in *Twelfth Night* is gender identity. Viola embodies this confusion when she assumes the identity of a boy, Cesario. Of course, in Shakespeare's time all female roles were played by boys, so in this case a boy actor plays a woman character (Viola) who dissembles herself as a boy (Cesario). In a patriarchal culture, sexual difference is held to be an immutable law; traditional gender role behavior was based on a natural biological fact rather than social convention. The indeterminacy of Viola/Cesario's sexual identity would show that maleness and femaleness were just aspects of a role, qualities that are learned, not immutable physical traits. When Cesario and Sir Andrew face each other in a duel, it is revealed that both are dissembling the role of being a man. The biological fact of Sir Andrew's maleness is superfluous.

Music in *Twelfth Night*

The craze for music in Elizabethan England reached its zenith at the close of the sixteenth century. Many popular folk songs and ballads were collected and published in songbooks around the time that *Twelfth Night* was written. Some of these songs found their way into this play in the catches and fragments of songs that Toby, Andrew, and Feste sing. The music serves to create a festive carnival atmosphere in *Twelfth Night,* while the lyrics act as an additional level of commentary on the many themes within the play.

The importance of music to this play cannot be doubted; the play begins with Orsino's discourse on music, accompanied by musicians, and ends with Feste singing a song directly to the audience. Viola, the play's heroine, is named after a renaissance instrument called the Viol, and she obtains her position in Orsino's house because she "can sing and speak to him in many sorts of music."

Shakespeare's comedies begin in a world out of balance with itself and progress toward an end in which harmony is re-established. This play, especially, begins with a world that has lost all sense of proportion — it is out of tune with itself. *Twelfth Night* modulates between lyricism and riotous disorder. Orsino's delicate lyricism is never far from the caterwauling of Sir Toby, Andrew, and Feste's catches. The characters' desires, their individual wills, are like different parts in a song, which must unite by marrying their individual voices into one ordered and harmonious whole.

Language in *Twelfth Night*

The importance and power of the English language had grown enormously by the sixteenth century. As a result, there was extraordinary interest in language, theories about language, and the uses of rhetoric. One of the main concerns at the time was whether or not words could be trusted to tell the truth. Was rhetoric (the art of persuasion) to be used to tell the truth, or was it rather a technique by which a false argument could be made to appear true?

In this play, Feste calls our attention to the dissembling nature of words. He shows how easily the meaning of a sentence can be turned inside out. Problems arise whenever one word has two or more distinct meanings. In fact, much of the humor in this play is based on the double sense of words and the confusion it engenders.

Shakespeare creates his characters, in part, through his choice of language. Each character has a distinctive style of diction, based on their vocabulary and syntax. Orsino's vocabulary is erudite, yet pompous; his syntax is highly ornate, yet languorous. Malvolio's vocabulary is equally as pompous, but his syntax is highly condensed and efficient. Sir Toby has the slurred speech of a drunk; he mispronounces old words and creates new words in the process.

In addition to defining character traits, Shakespeare also uses language to define a character's mood. The diction of a character can reflect the character's level of sincerity or the immediacy of a need to communicate. For example, when Orsino muses about the nature of love, he uses extended metaphors and high poetic language; when he speaks to his officers, he gives straightforward commands. When characters have an immediate need to communicate something, or when they are speaking from the heart, they tend to speak in simple plain language. When they want to dissemble a fact, their language becomes obscure or full of puns. When they want to dissemble a feeling, they tend to decorate their speech with high poetic language and the stock clichés of a Petrarchan lover.

The Feast of Epiphany and Roman Saturnalia

If one accepts Dr. Leslie Hotson's date, *Twelfth Night* was first performed January 6, 1601, on Twelfth Night, or the Feast of the Epiphany — the last night of the Christmas revels. This period was one of great celebration, as the Christian ritual of Epiphany combined with the older Roman Saturnalia, a festival where presents were exchanged, and all people were freed from their customary restraints. Shakespeare's play, as the critic C.L. Barber has noted, partakes of this carnival atmosphere, creating a world of indulgence and excess, music and temporary inversions of the traditional social hierarchy.

Although it is titled *Twelfth Night,* the action within the play does not take place during Twelfth Night, and the play has no references to the time of year or the holiday season. For this reason, the subtitle of the play, *or What You Will,* is perhaps the better title. While Harold Bloom interprets this subtitle as "Have At You!" — a threat or challenge to the audience, in the spirit of *As You Like It* or *Much Ado About Nothing* — the more obvious reading is that of a promise that the audience shall have what it desires. A third and more subtle reading suggests that, within the world of the play, "what you will" is what you are, that is, reality is what you make of it.

Date of composition

Lord Hunsdon, the Lord Chamberlain to Queen Elizabeth I and patron of Skakespeare's company of the King's Men, was charged by the Queen with the commissioning of a play to be given at an important royal occasion in 1601. Lord Hunsdon required a play that "shalbe best furnished with rich apparell, have great variety and change of Musicke and sauncs, and of a subject that may be most pleasing to her Majestie." From other evidence not connected with the royal occasion, we infer that *Twelfth Night* was written between 1599 and 1600, for performance on January 6, 1601.

Dr. Leslie Hotson believes that the play was written, rehearsed, and presented within a fortnight, which is not unusual with Shakespeare's plays. The play seems to have been written at a leisurely pace so that it might be produced on the stage with a minimum of alteration. Despite Leslie Hotson's interesting attempt to show that the play was commissioned for performance before the Queen and court at Whitehall on January 6, 1601, most other scholars accept an entry of February 2, 1602, in the diary of John Manningham, a barrister of the Middle Temple. The diary entry points to the play's first production in the Middle Temple hall on the Twelfth Night of that year: "At our feast we had a play called Twelve Night, or What You Will, much like the Comedy of Errors or Menechmi in Plautus, but most like an neere to that in Italian called Inganni."

The romantic plot is derived from a popular Italian comedy, *Gl'Ingannati (The Deceived),* first performed in Siena in 1531 by an amateur society, which, amazed at its own ambition, called itself *Gli Intronati,* or The Thunderstruck. After passing through eight Italian editions, this work was translated into French and then into a Latin edition entitled *Laelia.* Shakespeare's main source, however, is Barnabe Riche's "Of Apolonius and Silla," the second story in his *Farewell to Militarie Profession* (1581). Riche's story is derived ultimately from *Gl'Ingannati,* by way of prose versions in Bandello's *Novelle* (1554) and Francois de Belleforest's *Histoires Tragiques* (1571). According to Leslie Hotson's theory, the character of Malvolio is based on Sir William Knollys, Elizabeth's puritanical comptroller of the household and a familiar object of ridicule in court circles.

CHARACTERS IN THE PLAY

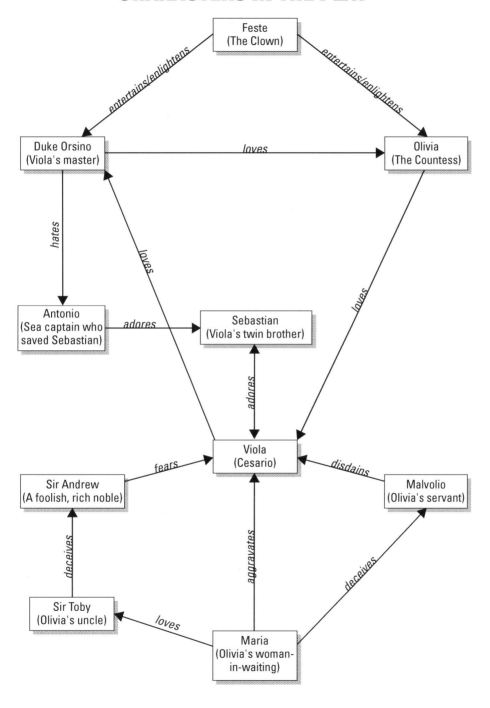

TWELFTH NIGHT
ACT I

Duke *O, when mine eyes did see Olivia first,*
Methought she purged the air of pestilence!
That instant was I turn'd into a hart;
And my desires, like fell and cruel hounds,
E'er since pursue me.

. . . .

Olivia *Your lord does know my mind. I cannot love him;*
Yet I suppose him virtuous, know him noble...
A gracious person: but yet I cannot love him;
He might have took his answer long ago.

Act I, Scene 1

At his court, the lovesick Duke listens to music while waiting for news of Olivia. His messenger arrives, and Orsino learns that Olivia's brother has died, and she will see no man for seven years' time.

ACT I, SCENE 1
A room in the Duke's palace.

[Enter DUKE, CURIO, and other Lords; Musicians attending.]

Duke If music be the food of love, play on;
　Give me excess of it, that, surfeiting,
　The appetite may sicken, and so die.
　That strain again! it had a dying fall.
　O, it came o'er my ear like the sweet south　　　　　5
　That breathes upon a bank of violets,
　Stealing and giving odour! Enough; no more.
　'Tis not so sweet now as it was before.
　O spirit of love! how quick and fresh art thou!
　That, nothwithstanding thy capacity　　　　　　10
　Receiveth as the sea, nought enters there,
　Of what validity and pitch soe'er,
　But falls into abatement and low price,
　Even in a minute: so full of shapes is fancy,
　That it alone is high fantastical.　　　　　　　15

Curio Will you go hunt, my lord?

Duke　　　　　　　　　　What, Curio?

Curio The hart.

Duke Why, so I do, the noblest that I have.
　O, when mine eyes did see Olivia first,　　　　　20
　Methought she purged the air of pestilence!
　That instant was I turn'd into a hart;
　And my desires, like fell and cruel hounds,
　E'er since pursue me.
　[Enter VALENTINE.]
　How now! what news from her?

Valentine So please my lord, I might not be admitted;　　25
　But from her handmaid do return this answer:

NOTES

2.　　*surfeiting:* having more than enough.

5.　　*south:* wind (this makes much more sense than the word sound which has mistakenly crept into many other editions). Pope's emendation.

12.　　*pitch:* height.

13.　　*abatement:* falling of powers.

14.　　*fancy:* both love and imagination.

18.　　*hart:* male deer or stag. Notice the deliberate rhetorical effects employed in Orsino's opening speech. The alliteration of the sibilant-sounds in lines 2 and 3 is noteworthy; the assonance (play on vowel-sounds) in lines 1–15 is also remarkable. The effect is heavy and sensual.

19.　　*noblest:* The word hart (or perhaps heart) is understood to follow, to make clear the transition from hunting deer to Olivia.

21.　　*pestilence:* infection (she purified the air).

23.　　*desires, like... hounds:* an implied and slightly oblique reference to the myth of Acteon, who was turned into a hart by the goddess Diana, and who could not escape from being torn to pieces by his own hounds. This was his punishment for having accidentally viewed Diana and her nymphs while they were bathing.

The element itself, till seven years' heat,
Shall not behold her face at ample view;
But, like a cloistress, she will veiled walk
And water once a day her chamber round   30
With eye-offending brine: all this to season
A brother's dead love, which she would keep fresh
And lasting in her sad remembrance.

Duke O, she that hath a heart of that fine frame
To pay, this debt of love but to a brother,   35
How will she love, when the rich golden shaft
Hath kill'd the flock of all affections else
That live in her; when liver, brain, and heart,
These sovereign thrones, are all supplied, and fill'd
Her sweet perfections with one self king!   40
Away before me to sweet beds of flowers;
Love-thoughts lie rich when canopied with bowers.
[Exeunt.]

27.   *element:* sky.

29.   *cloistress:* nun.

31.   *brine:* salt tears.
       season: preserve or keep fresh.

34.   *frame:* quality or texture.

36.   *shaft:* love arrow (of Cupid).

38.   *liver, brain, and heart:* The liver vied with the heart as the seat of the bodily passions in the Elizabethan physiology; the brain was the seat of reason, which was to control the exercise of both the affections and the passions.

40.   *one self king:* himself (as husband or lover).

COMMENTARY

At the Duke's palace, sweet melancholy music introduces the tone of the scene as well as the mood of the Duke, Orsino, who is sometimes portrayed reclining on a divan surrounded by his musicians and courtiers. His character is based on the archetype of the Petrarchan courtly lover; he is an aesthete, inclined towards moodiness and brooding rather than masterful self-assertion — hence his reclining posture. The musicians set a lyrical tone for the scene and subtly add to our understanding of the Duke's character. Surrounded by musicians rather than soldiers, the Duke is introduced by delicate courtly music in contradistinction to the caterwauling of the revelers in scenes to come.

Orsino's first speech serves a choral function, introducing the play's main themes: love, fancy, and the excess of appetite. Shakespeare also uses the manner of the Duke's speech — the affectedly rich, round open vowel sounds, the lilting cadence — to express his character, hinting at his extravagance and insincerity. His appreciation of music in the first few lines smacks of high romanticism and hyperbole; if his appreciation were sincere, would he so quickly sicken of it? These few lines call attention to the Duke's self-absorption, as well as foreshadow his lack of constancy. There are elements of profundity in the speech, also, as Orsino is an adept thinker when it comes to the mechanics of desire.

From Orsino's speech, we see that he is far more in love with the idea of love, high language, and his own self-importance, than he is with the Countess Olivia (whose refusal of his love has prompted this outpouring of erotic philosophy).

After his initial rapture, Orsino's pleasure in the musicians quickly fades (line 7), and he sends them away. This dismissal acts as a material echo of his discourse on the surfeiting, or excess, of appetite. Shakespeare often presents an idea and follows it up with its dramatic proof. His dismissal is also a clue to Orsino's character; his mercurial mood swing should be well noted — if he loves music and sickens of it so quickly, what does that say about his proclaimed love for Olivia, or anyone for that matter?

Orsino sullenly imagines that Olivia considers his love as reduced in value as he himself now finds the musicians. Curio recognizes his mood, and attempts to distract him by mentioning hunting. Orsino says he would rather hunt after Olivia's heart, and extending the metaphor to include wordplay, Orsino becomes the hart, punished by his own desires in the form of cruel hounds.

Valentine, Orsino's messenger, returns from attempting to deliver a message to Olivia, who has refused to see him. He reports that Olivia will mourn the death of her brother for seven years and live cloistered like a nun. Is this Olivia's way of saying she feels love for no man alive? We can assume, at least in part, this is the tenor of her message to Orsino. Similar to Orsino, Olivia seems to have a penchant for excessive shows of emotion.

Undeterred by this news, Orsino imagines that a woman capable of such devotion to a brother will, once she has fallen in love with Orsino, give him the finest kind of love.

From this scene we gather Orsino is a wealthy gentleman pining away for the love of Olivia. His speeches are beautiful, but such persuasive rhetoric may belie the sincerity of his feelings. His understanding that satisfaction is the death of desire suggests he has experienced enough love conquests in his day to be jaded and consequently somewhat cynical. But now he has found his match in Olivia. But is she worthy of him simply *because* she has refused him? Orsino must be aware that desire dies the moment it is satisfied; he expresses this knowledge in clear and concise terms in his discourse about music. The love between a husband and wife is based on mutuality and caring; it lacks, however, the "high fantastical" powers of desire that Orsino seeks. What better way to enjoy the fever of desire without end, then by choosing Olivia, the one woman he cannot have.

Act I, Scene 2

On the coast of Illyria, Viola, who has been saved from a shipwreck in which she believes her brother drowned, learns of Olivia and Orsino from a sea captain. Viola desires to serve Olivia, but as it is not possible, she decides to serve Orsino instead. The captain promises to present her to the Duke disguised as a boy.

ACT I, SCENE 2
The sea-coast.

[Enter VIOLA, a Captain, and Sailors.]

Viola What country, friends, is this?

Captain This is Illyria, lady.

Viola And what should I do in Illyria?
My brother he is in Elysium.
Perchance he is not drown'd. What think you, sailors? 5

Captain It is perchance that you yourself were saved.

Viola Oh, my poor brother! and so perchance may he be.

Captain True, madam; and, to comfort you with chance,
Assure yourself, after our ship did split,
When you and those poor number saved with you 10
Hung on our driving boat, I saw your brother,
Most provident in peril, bind himself,
Courage and hope both teaching him the practice,
To a strong mast that lived upon the sea;
Where, like Arion on the dolphin's back, 15
I saw him hold acquaintance with the waves
So long as I could see.

Viola For saying so, there's gold.
Mine own escape unfoldeth to my hope,
Where to thy speech serves for authority, 20
The like of him. Know'st thou this country?

Captain Ay, madam, well; for I was bred and born
Not three hours' travel from this very place.

Viola Who governs here?

Captain A noble Duke, in nature as in name. 25

Viola What is his name?

Captain Orsino.

NOTES

2. *Illyria:* a mythical land somewhere in the Mediterranean.

4. *Elysium:* paradise. In Greek Mythology, where the blessed go after death.

5. *Perchance:* perhaps.

6. *perchance:* by chance.

15. *Arion on the dolphin's back:* Arion was the poet-musician of the Greek island of Lesbos; about to be put to death by pirates, he asked for a last chance to play his lyre, then leaped overboard and was carried ashore by a dolphin that had been enchanted by the music.

19. *Mine...the like of him:* My escape makes me believe my brother might have escaped, and your speech encourages that hope.

Viola Orsino! I have heard my father name him.
   He was a bachelor then.

Captain And so is now, or was so very late;   30
   For but a month ago I went from hence,
   And then 'twas fresh in murmur, — as, you know,
   What great ones do the less will prattle of, —
   That he did seek the love of fair Olivia.

Viola What's she?   35

Captain A virtuous maid, the daughter of a count
   That died some twelvenmonths since; then leaving her
   In the protection of his son, her brother,
   Who shortly also died: for whose dear love,
   They say, she hath abjured the company   40
   And sight of men.

Viola   O that I served that lady,
   And might not be deliver'd to the world,
   Till I had made mine own occasion mellow,
   What my estate is!

Captain   That were hard to compass,
   Because she will admit no kind of suit,   45
   No, not the duke's.

Viola There is a fair behaviour in thee, captain;
   And though that nature with a beauteous wall
   Doth oft close in pollution, yet of thee
   I will believe thou hast a mind that suits   50
   With this thy fair and outward character.
   I prithee, and I'll pay thee bounteously,
   Conceal me what I am, and be my aid
   For such disguise as haply shall become
   The form of my intent. I'll serve this Duke;   55
   Thou shalt present me as an eunuch to him.
   It may be worth thy pains; for I can sing
   And speak to him in many sorts of music,
   That will allow me very worth his service.
   What else may hap to time I will commit;   60
   Only shape thou thy silence to my wit.

Captain Be you his eunuch, and your mute I'll be.
   When my tongue blabs, then let mine eyes not see.

Viola I thank thee; lead me on. [*Exeunt.*]

---

32.   *murmur:* rumor, gossip.

33.   *the less:* those of lower rank.

40.   *abjured:* solemnly sworn to give up, sacrifice.

42.   *be delivered...mellow:* until the time was ripe for revealing my state.

44.   *to compass:* to bring about.

45.   *suit:* wooing, formal petition.

49.   *close in pollution:* Nature often encloses things nasty or evil in a beautiful exterior.

54.   *disguise:* Viola is a young lady of good birth; she would have difficulty obtaining a suitable position at Orsino's court owing to the fact that the Duke was a bachelor.

56.   *eunuch:* boy with a high voice (counter-tenor, male alto, or even castrato).

59.   *very worth:* worthy of.

60.   *hap:* happen.

62.   *mute:* silent person.

COMMENTARY

On the sea-coast of Illyria, an imaginary country ruled by Duke Orsino, we meet a young woman (Viola), a Captain, and several sailors who have washed ashore after a shipwreck. On stage, this scene is often played before the curtain to speed up the production. Originally, the play was performed on a bare stage — no traverses (areas formed by using a partition or curtain), balconies or inner rooms — enabling the scenes to change constantly from place to place without breaking up the flow of action.

Believing they are the only survivors, Viola grieves for her brother, who was also aboard the ship and, she imagines, has drowned with the rest of the crew. She sobs, "My brother he is in Elysium," that is, my brother is in heaven. Although we have yet to meet Olivia, we know that she has also recently lost a brother.

The Captain suggests that Viola's brother may still be alive, as he saw her brother bind himself to a mast and use it as a raft to float on top of the waves. Viola, conveniently surviving the wreckage with purse intact, rewards the Captain's optimism with gold. Even in her grief, she reveals an uncommon generosity of spirit. Though she has just been set on a foreign shore with no other possessions than her clothes and the small sum of gold in her purse, Viola rewards the Captain without a second thought.

Although Viola is new to Illyria, the Captain knows the country well and tells her that Duke Orsino rules these lands. Viola has heard of the Duke from her father and wonders whether he is still a bachelor. The Captain provides some information, suggesting that Orsino is still a bachelor, though he has heard gossip that Orsino is in love with the Countess Olivia. We also learn that Olivia's father died shortly before she lost her brother, leaving Olivia the sole mistress of the household. According to the Captain, in her grief, she has sworn to see no men.

Often in Shakespeare's plays we find two characters with different temperaments put into similar predicaments: the one acting as a foil to the other, allowing the audience to decide what an appropriate action in such a circumstance might be. Laertes and Fortinbras, for example, were foils to Hamlet; their active and swift revenge of a father's death makes us aware of Hamlet's indecision. Here, Viola's heartfelt but temperate response to her brother's supposed death should give us pause before accepting Olivia's overzealous grieving as a natural response to a brother's death.

Viola decides that she wants to serve Olivia. As they are both grieving the loss of a brother, her service would provide her with an opportunity to share her grief with someone who would really understand. Her desire to "serve," however, is not so simple; Viola possesses gold and was raised as a gentlewoman, not a servant. Perhaps she believes serving someone else may prove an effective means to avoid morbid self-pity. Rather than cloister herself like Olivia, putting her own grief at the center of her existence, she chooses to abnegate her self in service of another. The Captain, however, informs her that Olivia will admit no kind of suit (that is, she will not grant any public audiences, to wooers or anyone else) during her mourning period. Viola quickly adopts a new strategy. She will serve the Duke disguised as a boy. This cross-gender strategy is required, because as a woman, Viola would have been denied entry to the Duke's house. Here, Viola exhibits her immense improvisational talents, surprising the Captain with her determination, resourcefulness, and ingenuity.

Viola enlists the Captain's help in concealing her identity. But first, with subtle irony, she questions whether she can trust his outward appearance of goodness, immediately following up her rhetorical question about the truth of appearances by creating a deceptive appearance for herself. The slippery nature of identity in this play is first hinted at here; Shakespeare subtly calls our attention to this fact by warning us not to trust appearances.

Viola, as the heroine of this play, embodies all that is most virtuous in Shakespeare: She can sing and speak "in many sorts of music" and adapt herself to the demands of any situation. Compare her relationship to music to that of Orsino. Viola uses music to give pleasure, while Orsino is a consumer of music, someone who gluts himself and then quickly sickens of it. His taste in music is significantly more narrow than hers. Orsino fixates on one or two songs; Viola is open and receptive to new music and things at all times. Although Orsino may believe that music is the food of love, we might do better to think of music as a surrogate for love. From this standpoint, the manner in which a character experiences music hints at the way they experience love.

The Captain agrees to help Viola disguise herself as a eunuch and promises not to tell her secret; then he leads her on to Orsino's court.

Act I, Scene 3

At Olivia's manor house, we meet Sir Toby Belch, Olivia's uncle; Sir Andrew Aguecheek, a foolish knight whom Toby has convinced to woo Olivia; and Maria, Olivia's gentle woman. Maria proves Sir Andrew to be a fool.

ACT I, SCENE 3
A room in Olivia's house.

[Enter SIR TOBY BELCH and MARIA.]

Sir Toby What a plague means my niece, to take the death of her brother thus? I am sure care's an enemy to life.

Maria By my troth, Sir Toby, you must come in earlier o' nights. Your cousin, my lady, takes great exceptions to your ill hours.   5

Sir Toby Why, let her except, before excepted.

Maria Ay, but you must confine yourself within the modest limits of order.

Sir Toby Confine! I'll confine myself no finer than I am. These clothes are good enough to drink   10
in; and so be these boots too. An they be not, let them hang themselves in their own straps.

Maria That quaffing and drinking will undo you. I heard my lady talk of it yesterday; and of a foolish knight that you brought in one night here to be her   15
wooer.

Sir Toby Who, Sir Andrew Aguecheek?

Maria Ay, he.

Sir Toby He's as tall a man as any's in Illyria.

Maria What's that to the purpose?

Sir Toby Why, he has three thousand ducats a year.   20

Maria Ay, but he'll have but a year in all these ducats; he's a very fool and a prodigal.

Sir Toby Fie, that you'll say so! He plays o' the viol-de-gamboys, and speaks three or four languages word for word without book, and hath all the   25
good gifts of nature.

NOTES

4.   *cousin:* general term to indicate close kinship.

6.   *except before excepted:* Toby's adaptation of a legal phrase meaning, excepting those things which are to be excepted.

9.   *Confine myself:* dress myself.

20.   *ducats:* Spanish coin.

22.   *prodigal:* wastrel.

24.   *viol -de-gamboys:* (Italian gamba, leg) a stringed instrument like a violincello, held between the knees and scraped with a bow.

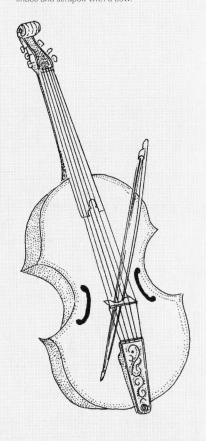

Maria He hath indeed, almost natural: for besides
that he's a fool, he's a great quarreller; and but that
lie hath the gift of a coward to allay the gust he hath
in quarrelling, 'tis thought among the prudent he
would quickly have the gift of a grave.   30

Sir Toby By this hand, they are scoundrels and
substractors that say so of him. Who are they?

Maria They that add, moreover, he's drunk nightly
in your company.

Sir Toby With drinking healths to my niece. I'll   35
drink to her as long as there is a passage in my throat
and drink in Illyria. He's a coward and a coystrill
that will not drink to my niece till his brains turn o'
the toe like a parish-top. What, wench! Castiliano
vulgo! for here comes sir Andrew Agueface.   40

[Enter SIR ANDREW AGUECHEEK.]

Sir Andrew Sir Toby Belch! how now, Sir Toby
Belch!

Sir Toby Sweet Sir Andrew!

Sir Andrew Bless you, fair shrew.

Maria And you too, sir.

Sir Toby Accost, Sir Andrew, accost.   45

Sir Andrew What's that?

Sir Toby My niece's chamber-maid.

Sir Andrew Good Mistress Accost, I desire better
acquaintance.

Maria My name is Mary, sir.

Sir Andrew Good Mistress Mary Accost, —   50

Sir Toby You mistake, knight: accost is, front her,
board her, woo her, assail her.

Sir Andrew By my troth, I would not undertake her
in this company. Is that the meaning of accost?

Maria Fare you well gentlemen.   55

26.   *natural:* a born idiot.

28.   *gust:* appetite or gusto (taste for).

32.   *substractors:* Sir Toby cannot say subtractors after
all the drink he has taken. He means detractors,
those who take away a man's reputation by gossip-
ing about him behind his back.

37.   *coystrill:* knave or base fellow.

39.   *Castiliano vulgo:* either put on the grave manner of
the Castilian aristocrat, for here comes the "knight
of the sorrowful countenance" Sir Andrew Agueface, or think of the common *castilians* (coins).
Andrew supplied Toby with money.

45.   *accost:* speak to first. A nautical term, when one
ship comes alongside of another.

48.   *Accost:* He mistakenly believes Accost is her name.

53.   *troth:* in truth.

Sir Toby An thou let part so, Sir Andrew, would thou mightst never draw sword again.

Sir Andrew An you part so, mistress, I would I might never draw sword again. Fair lady, do you think you have fools in hand? 60

Maria Sir, I have not you by the hand.

Sir Andrew Marry, but you shall have; and here's my hand.

Maria Now, sir, thought is free. I pray you, bring your hand to the butter-bar and let it drink.

Sir Andrew Wherefore, sweetheart? what's your 65 metaphor?

Maria It's dry, sir.

Sir Andrew Why, I think so; I am not such an ass but I can keep my hand dry. But what's your jest?

Maria A dry jest, sir.

Sir Andrew Are you full of them? 70

Maria Ay, sir; I have them at my fingers' ends: marry, now I let go your hand I am barren.
[Exit MARIA.]

Sir Toby O knight, thou lackest a cup of canary. When did I see thee so put down?

Sir Andrew Never in your life, I think, unless you 75 see canary put me down. Methinks sometimes I have no more wit than a Christian or an ordinary man has; but I am a great eater of beef, and I believe that does harm to my wit.

Sir Toby No question.

Sir Andrew An I thought that, I'd forswear it. I'll 80 ride home to-morrow, Sir Toby.

Sir Toby Pourquoi, my dear knight?

Sir Andrew What is "pourquoi"? do or not do? I would I had bestowed that time in the tongues that I have in fencing, dancing, and bear-baiting. O, had 85 I but followed the arts!

64. *butter-bar:* a room or pantry in which the wines and liquors are kept.

73. *canary:* light sweet wine from the Canary Islands.

80. *forswear it:* swear to give it up.

82. *Pourquoi:* Fr. for why.

Sir Toby Then hadst thou had an excellent head of
hair.

Sir Andrew Why, would that have mended my hair?

Sir Toby Past question, for thou seest it will not
curl by nature.

Sir Andrew But it becomes me well enough, does't
not?   90

Sir Toby Excellent; it hangs like flax on a distaff.

Sir Andrew Faith, I'll home to-morrow, Sir Toby.
Your niece will not be seen; or if she be, it's four to
one she'll none of me. The count himself here hard   95
by woos her.

Sir Toby She'll none o' the count. She'll not match
above her degree, neither in estate, years, nor wit.
I have heard her swear't. Tut, there's life in't, man.

Sir Andrew I'll stay a month longer. I am a fellow o'   100
the strangest mind i' the world; I delight in masques
and revels sometimes altogether.

Sir Toby Art thou good at these kickshawses,
knight?

Sir Andrew As any man in Illyria, whatsoever he be,
under the degree of my betters; and yet I will not   105
compare with an old man.

Sir Toby What is thy excellence in a galliard,
knight?

Sir Andrew Faith, I can cut a caper.

Sir Toby And I can cut the mutton to't.

Sir Andrew And I think I have the back-trick   110
simply as strong as any man in Illyria.

Sir Toby Wherefore are these things hid? where
fore have these gifts a curtain before 'em? are they
like to take dust, like Mistress Mall's picture? why
dost thou not go to church in a galliard and come home   115
in a coranto? My very walk should be a jig. What
dost thou mean? Is it a world to hide virtues in? I

86.   *hair:* Sir Andrew was probably bald under the large
wig he affected.

92.   *distaff:* staff used for spinning thread from wool or
flax.

101.   *masques:* dramatic entertainments set to music.

103.   *kickshawses:* fancy dishes (revels, here).

106.   *galliard:* quick and lively dance in triple time.

108.   *cut a caper:* leap about. (A caper is also an ingredient used in sauce to spice mutton.)

110.   *back-trick:* a difficult acrobatic leap.

114.   *Mistress Mall's picture:* perhaps a reference to Mistress Mary, or Mall, Fitton, one of Queen Elizabeth's
maids-of-honor who had fallen from royal favor.

116.   *coranto:* dance with a running step.

jig: lively dance often in triple time.

did think, by the excellent constitution of thy leg, it was formed under a star of a galliard.

120

Sir Andrew Ay, 'tis strong, and it does indifferent well in a flame-coloured stock. Shall we set about some revels?

Sir Toby What shall we do else? were we not born under Taurus?

125

Sir Andrew Taurus! That's sides and heart.

Sir Toby No, sir; it is legs and thighs. Let me see thee caper. Ha! higher; ha, ha! excellent!
[Exeunt.]

120. *formed under a star...:* reference to the belief that the stars determine our destiny (astrological).

122. *stock:* stocking.

125. *Taurus:* the Bull; second of the twelve signs of the zodiac. Andrew confuses Taurus with Leo, as Toby points out.

COMMENTARY

We meet a third group of people at Olivia's house. Although Olivia is in mourning, the rest of her household, with one notable exception (Malvolio), is in a more festive mood, drinking, singing, and carousing. Olivia quietly disapproves, and the duty of restoring order falls to her puritanical steward, Malvolio, whom we meet later in this act.

Olivia's uncle, Sir Toby Belch, is the life of this party. He's a gentleman by title, an armed retainer of the house by occupation, and an exuberant, rude drunk in action. Discussing his niece with Maria, Toby's opinion is that "care is an enemy to life," and Olivia's mourning has put the damper on their festivities for too long.

Maria, Olivia's mischievous but goodhearted woman-in-waiting, warns Toby that Olivia will no longer tolerate his late night drinking sessions and that Olivia has threatened to send him away if he doesn't control himself. Chances are that Maria has her own reasons for keeping Toby around. He is a gentleman, and if Maria were to marry him, she would move a step up the social ladder. Yet there are indications that Maria, too, would prefer a less drunk Sir Toby. She may find his drinking amusing at times, but as a prospective wife, how could she not find his excessive drinking a concern for the future? For as she warns him, quaffing and drinking will undo him.

Another complaint of Olivia's is directed to Toby's annoying companion Andrew Aguecheek. Sir Andrew is a ridiculous, cowardly knight with a shallow wit and deep pockets. He has an income of 3,000 ducats a year. Similar to Slender, a foppish moron in *The Merry Wives of Windsor,* and anticipating the gull Roderigo in *Othello,* Sir Andrew is an ineffectual suitor of Olivia who trusts his courtship to a middleman (Toby) who abuses that trust. For Toby, Andrew's one redeeming feature is his money; for the audience, however, it is the part he plays in this unique comic duo. Sir Andrew is tall and thin, and he is often portrayed wearing a yellow wig of straw-like hair — as Sir Toby notes, it will not curl and hangs like flax on a distaff.

Sir Andrew is a perfect foil for Sir Toby's larger girth and quicker wit. Although one might compare Sir Toby to Falstaff, from *Henry IV,* the similarities are superficial. Sir Toby lacks Falstaff's depth and comprehensive intelligence. Sir Toby also has a potential for cruelty that Falstaff does not possess. Even though Toby's wit may seem quick compared to Sir Andrew, it seems slow and clownish when compared to Feste's, the fool in this work.

The over-the-top greetings between Toby and Andrew set the tone of their comedic scenes throughout the story — an exaggerated, silly, drunken, near slapstick humor. They shout like old drunken pals who haven't seen each other in years, though in reality it has likely only been a matter of hours or days. Andrew's affection for Toby, though playful, is genuine. We can assume, however, that Toby does not reciprocate the genuineness; Toby's banter with Andrew has an underlying tone of mockery and condescension.

In this scene, Shakespeare introduces his use of the double meanings of words and phrases to humorous effect, which he will continue throughout the play. At times, the characters are unaware of the word play, as when Andrew misinterprets the meaning of "accost" (48), adding to the humor of the wordplay.

At other times, however, characters consciously use wordplay to their advantage. Maria plays with words in order to put down Andrew (64–71). Taking his hand, she tells him to let it drink. A confused Andrew asks what her meaning is. She responds, "It's dry, sir," leading Andrew to assume she refers to his hand's dryness — a fair conclusion. But Maria has already shifted to the ironic; it is her own jest to which "dry" refers. Andrew — one step behind — asks whether she is full of dry jests, but too late; Maria has shifted once again, from the abstract idea of a joke to Andrew himself, a "joke" standing at her fingers' ends. And finally, as she lets go of him, she shifts once more; she is barren, that is, she is dry of humor, having no more jokes to make at his expense.

This exchange highlights how Andrew is usually portrayed as a boastful idiot, though he does have moments of incipient self-recognition. His need to be liked, however, prevents him from being too honest with himself or others. If he were only a little bit smarter, he might be capable of the kind of self-awareness that leads to growth. But his attention, or brainpower, falls just short of critical mass. His bewilderment by the French word, "pourquoi," prompts him to regret not spending the time to learn languages or follow the arts. Of course, he has boasted of these skills (or attempted to pass himself off as one in the know) prior to this scene and does not learn from his embarrassment, as he is once again flummoxed by Viola's French in Act III.

Maria stays one step ahead of Sir Andrew with her dry jests. From a 1994 Royal Shakespeare Company production of *Twelfth Night*.
Clive Barda /PAL

On the pretense of helping Andrew court his niece Olivia, Toby has kept Andrew at the house, using his money to keep the festivities going. Andrew, however, has lost faith, seeing his courtship with Olivia as a bust. He knows he doesn't have a chance against the handsome — and wealthier — Duke Orsino. Toby assures him that Olivia isn't interested in the Duke, and Andrew promises to stay a month longer.

If his appetite for food and drink leads Toby to endure the tedious company of Andrew to maintain his supplies, Andrew is driven by his need to be well liked and respected. In this play, characters glut themselves on their appetites and are made fools of by their own desires.

Toby takes great pleasure in tricking Andrew into playing the idiot — or at least exhibiting his silliness and stupidity. Toby encourages Andrew to brag and then consistently puts his bragging to the test. Their talk of dance steps is an egregious example of this dynamic. At Toby's encouragement, Andrew prances around like a fool. Their exit is often staged with Andrew (the self-proclaimed master of the back-trick) cutting a ridiculous figure as he attempts to cut a caper and lands on the seat of his pants.

Act I, Scene 4

At Orsino's court, Viola serves the Duke disguised as Cesario. Orsino entrusts Viola as his messenger to woo Olivia. Viola, in an aside to the audience, confides that she is in love with Orsino.

ACT I, SCENE 4
The Duke's palace.

[Enter VALENTINE, and VIOLA in man's attire.]

Valentine If the duke continue these favours towards you Cesario, you are like to be much advanced. He hath known you but three days, and already you are no stranger.

Viola You either fear his humour or my negligence, that you call in question the continuance of his love. Is he inconstant, sir, in his favours?   5

Valentine No, believe me.

Viola I thank you. Here comes the count.

[Enter DUKE, CURIO, and Attendants.]

Duke Who saw Cesario, ho?

Viola On your attendance, my lord; here.   10

Duke Stand you a while aloof. Cesario,
Thou know'st no less but all. I have unclasp'd
To thee the book even of my secret soul;
Therefore, good youth, address thy gait unto her;
Be not denied access, stand at her doors,   15
And tell them, there thy fixed foot shall grow
Till thou have audience.

Viola   Sure, my noble lord,
If she be so abandon'd to her sorrow
As it is spoke, she never will admit me.

Duke Be clamorous and leap all civil bounds   20
Rather than make unprofited return.

Viola Say I do speak with her, my lord, what then?

Duke Oh, then unfold the passion of my love,
Surprise her with discourse of my dear faith

NOTES

1. *these favours:* confiding in Cesario and sending him on confidential missions to Olivia.

2. *advanced:* promoted in the ducal service.

4. *humour:* mood, temperament, whim.

6. *inconstant:* inconsistent or unreliable.

11. *aloof:* waiting at some distance (out of earshot).

14. *gait:* footsteps (walking).

21. *unprofited return:* do not return without accomplishing anything positive.

23. *unfold the passion of my love:* Foreign as the custom is to us in the twentieth century, wooing by proxy was often practised in Britain and Europe. The danger was that the proxy (the messenger) would reap personal advantage from the encounter.

It shall become thee well to act my woes;   25
She will attend it better in thy youth
Than in a nuncio's of more grave aspect.

Viola I think not so, my lord.

Duke   Dear lad, believe it;
For they shall yet belie thy happy years,
That say thou art a man. Diana's lip   30
Is not more smooth and rubious; thy small pipe
Is as the maiden's organ, shrill and sound;
And all is semblative a woman's part
I know thy constellation is right apt
For this affair. Some four or five attend him,   35
All, if you will; for I myself am best
When least in company. Prosper well in this,
And thou shalt live as freely as thy lord,
To call his fortunes thine.

Viola   I'll do my best
To woo your lady; *[Aside.]* yet, a barful strife!   40
Whoe'er I woo, myself would be his wife.
[Exeunt.]

27.   *nuncio's of more grave aspect:* messenger's older and more serious appearance.

30.   *Diana's lip:* goddess' lip.

33.   *semblative:* resembling.

34.   *constellation:* zodiacal pattern; stars that govern your success.

40.   *barful strife:* obstacle that causes turmoil.

COMMENTARY

At Orsino's palace, we meet Viola again. She has successfully carried out her plan, having already served in Orsino's house for three days, disguised as Cesario, a boy. We learn from Valentine, the Duke's messenger, that Orsino has taken an immediate liking to Cesario, and if all goes well, he will soon promote Cesario. The Duke's constancy is questioned by Viola and defended by Valentine. This theme comes into play throughout *Twelfth Night.* In a later scene, Feste mocks Orsino for his inconstancy. Orsino himself says that he is constant in his affection for Olivia and inconstant in everything else. (Yet, his action at the play's conclusion calls even this much into question.) Viola's curiosity about Orsino's constancy may be our first hint that she is attracted to him.

Orsino enters, dismisses his attendants, and takes Cesario aside. He means to send Cesario to Olivia to plead his love for her. He implores Cesario to do whatever it takes to see Olivia in person: "Be clamorous and leap all civil bounds / Rather than make unprofited return" (20–21). In other words, be rude if you have to, but don't return without speaking to her. Cesario accepts the task, but wonders why he should be successful after so many failures by others.

Orsino tells Cesario to unfold the passions of his love, adding that he will be well rewarded for acting his woes, that is, presenting his love sickness to Olivia in a moving manner. The idea of performing his woes comes naturally to Orsino; he does perform them himself. His passionate longing and suffering for love has a self dramatizing quality. The Duke, being a rich noble, has few responsibilities and plenty of leisure time, so why not perform "courtly love" for his own amusement? His penchant for sending messengers rather than going himself hints at Orsino's strange combination of self-knowledge and self-delusion. Orsino probably has concluded that Olivia would reject him outright, ending his courtship once and for all.

Orsino insists Cesario's youth will win Olivia's attention. Clearly, the youth has caught Orsino's eye. He praises Cesario's rubious lip and feminine voice and all his parts that would seem beautiful on a woman. Orsino's immediate affection for Cesario is at least partially dependent on Cesario's feminine qualities. To Orsino (and the audience as well) the indeterminacy of Cesario's gender is seductive; it creates a tension that is difficult to resolve or ignore. Viola seems to enjoy all this attention and praise from the Duke; notice there is something teasingly intimate and almost flirty in Orsino's tone.

In Shakespeare's theater, all the actors were male, and Viola was played by a boy. For an audience today, the difficulty lies in believing that Cesario, played by a woman, can pass for a man. Shakespeare's audience, however, would have found it harder to imagine Viola as a woman, and harder still to keep a clear sense of Cesario's gender identity when Viola (a boy playing a woman) disguises herself as Cesario (a boy playing a woman playing a boy). Much of the comedy in this play depends on the elusiveness of identity (gender or otherwise).

Viola promises to woo Olivia. But having fallen in love with Orsino herself, she has no love of the task. She would pursue him herself, but how can she, disguised as a boy? The love complications have just begun.

Act I, Scene 5

Malvolio and Feste engage in a verbal skirmish, and Olivia sides with Feste. Viola arrives at Olivia's manor, disguised as Cesario, and asks to speak to Olivia alone. While Viola presents Orsino's wooing message, Olivia falls in love with Viola. After Viola leaves, Olivia sends Malvolio after her to "return" Viola's ring.

ACT I, SCENE 5
Olivia's house.

[Enter MARIA and Clown.]

Maria Nay, either tell me where thou hast been, or
I will not open my lips so wide as a bristle may enter in way of thy excuse. My lady will hang thee for
thy absence.

Clown Let her hang me; he that is well hanged in
this world needs to fear no colours.   5

Maria Make that good.

Clown He shall see none to fear.

Maria A good lenten answer. I can tell thee where
that saying was born, of "I fear no colours."

Clown Where, good Mistress Mary?   10

Maria In the wars; and that may you be bold to
say in your foolery.

Clown Well, God give them wisdom that have it;
and those that are fools, let them use their talents.

Maria Yet you will be hanged for being so long   15
absent; or, to be turned away, is not that as good as
a hanging to you?

Clown Many a good hanging prevents a bad marriage; and, for turning away, let summer bear it out.

Maria You are resolute, then?   20

Clown Not so, neither; but I am resolved on two
points.

Maria That if one break, the other will hold; or, if
both break, your gaskins fall.

NOTES

SD.   *Clown:* Feste (the jester).

5.   *fear no colours:* fear no enemy (colors are regimental insignia or flags).

6.   *Make that good:* prove that.

8.   *lenten:* short and spare (one fasts during the penitential season of Lent).

19.   *for turning away...:* that can be endured now that summer is coming in.

20.   *resolute:* resolved, determined.

22.   *points:* tagged lace for attaching hose to the doublet and fastening various parts where buttons came to be used.

24.   *gaskins:* breeches.

Clown Apt, in good faith, very apt. Well, go thy   25
way; if Sir Toby would leave drinking, thou wert as
witty a piece of Eve's flesh as any in Illyria.

Maria Peace, you rogue, no more o'that. Here comes
my lady. Make your excuse wisely, you were best.
[Exit.]

Clown Wit, an't be thy will, put me into good fooling! Those wits, that think they have thee, do very   30
oft prove fools; and I, that am sure I lack thee, may
pass for a wise man. For what says Quinapalus?
"Better a witty fool than a foolish wit."
[Enter LADY OLIVIA with MALVOLIO.]
God bless thee, lady!

Olivia Take the fool away.

Clown Do you not hear, fellows? Take away the lady.   35

Olivia Go to, you're a dry fool; I'll no more of you.
Besides, you grow dishonest.

Clown Two faults, madonna, that drink and good
counsel will amend: for give the dry fool drink,
then is the fool not dry; bid the dishonest man mend   40
himself; if he mend, he is no longer dishonest; if he
cannot, let the botcher mend him. Anything that's
mended is but patched: virtue that transgresses is but
patched with sin; and sin that amends is but patched
with virtue. If that this simple syllogism will serve,   45
so; if it will not, what remedy? The lady bade take
away the fool; therefore, I say again, take her away.

Olivia Sir, I bade them take away you.

Clown Misprision in the highest degree! Lady, cucul-   50
lus non facit monachum. That's as much to say as I
wear not motley in my brain. Good madonna, give
me leave to prove you a fool.

Olivia Can you do it?

Clown Dexteriously, good madonna.   55

Olivia Make your proof.

Clown I must catechize you for it, madonna. Good
my mouse of virtue, answer me.

32.   *Quinapalus:* a fictitious, learnedsounding name.

36.   *dry fool:* dull. Olivia is in mourning and she has no patience for foolery.

45.   *syllogism:* Feste, the jester, employs a kind of logical reasoning called the syllogism, consisting of the major and minor premises followed by a conclusion. His argument is a parody of the syllogistic method.

50–51.   *Misprision:* misunderstanding.

cuculius non facit monachum: the cowl does not make the monk.

55.   *Dexteriously:* neatly and skillfully.

57.   *catechize:* question formally.

58.   *mouse:* term of affection.

Olivia Well, sir, for want of other idleness, I'll bide
your proof.   60

Clown Good madonna, why mournest thou?

Olivia Good fool, for my brother's death.

Clown I think his soul is in hell, modonna.

Olivia I know his soul is in heaven, fool.

Clown The more fool, madonna, to mourn for   65
your brother's soul being in heaven. Take away the fool,
gentlemen.

Olivia What think you of this fool, Malvolio? doth
he not mend?

Malvolio Yes, and shall do till the pangs of death   70
shake him. Infirmity, that decays the wise, doth ever
make the better fool.

Clown God send you sir, a speedy infirmity, for the
better increasing your folly! Sir Toby will be sworn
that I am no fox; but he will not pass his word for   75
two pence that you are no fool.

Olivia How say you to that, Malvolio?

Malvolio I marvel your ladyship takes delight in
such a barren rascal. I saw him put down the other
day with an ordinary fool that has no more brain
than a stone. Look you now, he's out of his guard   80
already. Unless you laugh and minister occasion to
him, he is gagged. I protest, I take these wise men,
that crow so at these set kind of fools, no better
than the fools' zanies.

Olivia O, you are sick of self-love, Malvolio, and   85
taste with a distempered appetite. To be generous,
guiltless, and of free disposition, is to take those
things for bird-bolts that you deem cannon-bullets.
There is no slander in an allowed fool, though he do
nothing but rail; nor no railing in a known discreet   90
man, though he do nothing but reprove.

Clown Now Mercury endue thee with leasing, for
thou speakest well of fools!

[Re-enter MARIA.]

71.   *Infirmity:* Malvolio thinks the Clown is weak and sick.

78.   *barren rascal:* empty of jests.
     put down: defeated (in a battle of wits) by.

84.   *fools' zanies:* clowns' assistants.

86.   *distempered:* disordered, diseased.

87.   *free disposition:* generous outlook and manner.

88.   *bird-bolts:* blunt-headed arrows for shooting birds.

90.   *rail:* scold, revile, upbraid.

92.   *Mercury:* god of lies.
     leasing: the power of telling lies.

Maria Madam, there is at the gate a young gentleman much desires to speak with you.   95

Olivia From the Count Orsino, is it?

Maria I know not, madam; 'tis a fair young man,
and well attended.

Olivia Who of my people hold him in delay?

Maria Sir Toby, madam, your kinsman.   100

Olivia Fetch him off, I pray you; he speaks nothing
but madman; fie on him! *[Exit Maria.]* Go you,
Malvolio. If it be a suit from the count, I am sick,
or not at home — what you will, to dismiss it. *[Exit
Malvolio.]* Now you see, sir, how your fooling   105
grows old, and people dislike it.

Clown Thou hast spoke for us, madonna, as if thy
eldest son should be a fool, whose skull Jove cram
with brains! for, — here he comes, — one of thy kin
has a most weak pia mater.   110

    [Enter SIR TOBY.]

Olivia By mine honour, half drunk. What is he at
the gate, cousin?

Sir Toby A gentleman.

Olivia A gentleman! what gentleman?

Sir Toby 'Tis a gentleman here — a plague o'these
pickle-herring! How now, sot!   115

Clown Good Sir Toby!

Olivia Cousin, cousin, how have you come so early
by this lethargy?

Sir Toby Lechery? I defy lechery. There's one at   120
the gate.

Olivia Ay, marry, what is he?

Sir Toby Let him be the devil, an he will, I care not.
Give me faith, say I. Well, it's all one.
[Exit.]

Olivia What's a drunken man like, fool?

107. *madonna:* my lady.

107–108. *as... fool:* a reference to the proverb "wise men
have fools to their children."

110. *pia mater:* brain.

115. *pickle-herring:* these have caused that indiges-
tion for which Sir Toby's family name (Belch) is
descriptive.

120. *lechery:* Sir Toby's tongue cannot get around the
awkward th-sound in lethargy.

Clown Like a drowned man, a fool, and a madman: one draught above heat makes a fool; the second mads him; and a third drowns him. 125

Olivia Go thou and seek the crowner, and let him sit o' my coz; for he's in the third degree of drink, he's drowned. Go, look after him. 130

Clown He is but mad yet, madonna; and the fool shall look to the madman.
[Exit.]

[Re-enter MALVOLIO.]

Malvolio Madam, yond young fellow swears he will speak with you. I told him you were sick; he takes on him to understand so much, and therefore comes to speak with you. I told him you were asleep; he 135 seems to have a foreknowledge of that too, and therefore comes to speak with you. What is to be said to him, lady? he's fortified against any denial.

Olivia Tell him he shall not speak with me.

Malvolio Has been told so; and he says, he'll 140 stand at your door like a sheriff's post, and be the supporter to a bench, but he'll speak with you.

Olivia What kind o'man is he?

Malvolio Why, of mankind. 145

Olivia What manner of man?

Malvolio Of very ill manner; he'll speak with you, will you or no.

Olivia Of what personage and years is he?

Malvolio Not yet old enough for a man, nor young 150 enough for a boy; as a squash is before 'tis a peascod, or a codling when 'tis almost an apple. 'Tis with him in standing water, between boy and man. He is very well favoured and he speaks very shrewishly; one would think his mother's milk were scarce out of 155 him.

Olivia Let him approach. Call in my gentlewoman.

Malvolio Gentlewoman, my lady calls.

---

128. *crowner:* coroner (one who conducts inquests).

129. *sit:* technical term applied to the holding of an inquest.

141. *sheriff's post:* a sheriff's noticeboard or messenger bearing notices of wanted men, rewards, proclamations etc.

142. *bench:* magistrates' bench in court, or wooden seat.

151. *squash... peascod:* unripe peascod before it becomes mature (leguminous vegetable).

152. *codling... apple:* half-grown apple before it reaches full size.

153. *standing water:* at the turn of the tide; half way between.

154. *shrewishly:* scoldingly, in a bad-tempered manner, sharply.

[Exit.]
[Re-enter MARIA.]

Olivia Give me my veil. Come throw it o'er my face. We'll once more hear Orsino's embassy.

[Enter VIOLA and Attendants.]

Viola The honourable lady of the house, which is she?   160

Olivia Speak to me; I shall answer for her. Your will?

Viola Most radiant, exquisite and unmatchable beauty, — I pray you, tell me if this be the lady of the house, for I never saw her. I would be loath to cast away my speech, for besides that it is excel-   165 lently well penned, I have taken great pains to con it. Good beauties, let me sustain no scorn; I am very comptible, even to the least sinister usage.

Olivia Whence came you sir?

Viola I can say little more than I have studied, and   170 that question's out of my part. Good gentle one, give me modest assurance if you be the lady of the house, that I may proceed in my speech.

Olivia Are you a comedian?

Viola No my profound heart; and yet by the   175 very fangs of malice I swear, I am not that I play. Are you the lady of the house?

Olivia If I do not usurp myself, I am.

Viola Most certain, if you are she, you do usurp yourself; for what is yours to bestow is not yours   180 to reserve. But this is from my commission. I will on with my speech in your praise, and then show you the heart of my message.

Olivia Come to what is important in't; I forgive you the praise.

Viola Alas, I took great pains to study it, and 'tis   185 poetical.

Olivia It is the more like to be feigned; I pray you, keep it in. I heard you were saucy at my gates, and allowed your approach rather to wonder at you

164.   *loath:* reluctant.

166.   *con:* construe or learn by heart.

168.   *comptible:* sensitive.
          sinister usage: unfavorable treatment.

178.   *usurp:* wrongfully hold possession of herself.

than to hear you. If you be not mad, be gone; if you
have reason, be brief. 'Tis not that time of moon   190
with me to make one in so skipping a dialogue.

Maria Will you hoist sail, sir? here lies your way.

Viola No, good swabber; I am to hull here a little
longer. Some mollification for your giant, sweet
lady. Tell me your mind, I am a messenger.   195

Olivia Sure, you have some hideous matter to deliver, when the courtesy of it is so fearful. Speak
your office.

Viola It alone concerns your car. I bring no overture
of war, no taxation of homage. I hold the olive in
my hand; my words are as full of peace as matter.   200

Olivia Yet you began rudely. What are you? What
would you?

Viola The rudeness that hath appeared in me have I
learned from my entertainment. What I am, and
what I would, are as secret as maidenhead; to your   205
ears, divinity; to any other's, profanation.

Olivia Give us the place alone; we will hear this
divinity. [*Exeunt MARIA and Attendants.*]
Now, sir, what is your text?

Viola Most sweet lady, —

Olivia A comfortable doctrine, and much may be   210
said of it. Where lies your text?

Viola In Orsino's bosom.

Olivia In his bosom! In what chapter of his bosom?

Viola To answer by the method, in the first of his
heart.

Olivia Oh, I have read it; it is heresy. Have you no   215
more to say?

Viola Good madam, let me see your face.

Olivia Have you any commission from your lord to
negotiate with my face? You are now out of your
text; but we will draw the curtain and show you the   220

192.   *hoist sail:* note the nautical metaphor.

193.   *swabber:* deck-washer.

       hull: moor. Note how neatly Cesario retorts, turning
       Maria's metaphor back to her.

194.   *giant:* ironic hyperbole. Maria was small.

201.   *what would you:* What do you want?

204.   *my entertainment:* the manner in which I was
       received by your servants.

205.   *maidenhead:* virginity.

206.   *profanation:* violation.

208.   *text:* sustains the image of divinity (suggests the
       Bible).

210.   *comfortable doctrine:* sustains the idea of preach-
       ing from the text such divinity.

213.   *chapter:* continues the scriptural metaphors; ironi-
       cally cited.

218.   *commission:* order.

219.   *out of your text:* beyond the limits of your job.

picture. Look you, sir, such a one I was this present.
Is't not well done? *[Unveiling.]*

Viola Excellently done, if God did all.

Olivia 'Tis in grain sir; 'twill endure wind and
weather.

Viola 'Tis beauty truly blent, whose red and white   225
Nature's own sweet and cunning hand laid on.
Lady, you are the cruell'st she alive,
If you will lead these graces to the grave
And leave the world no copy.

Olivia Oh, sir, I will not be so hard-hearted; I will   230
give out divers schedules of my beauty. It shall be
inventoried, and every particle and utensil labelled
to my will: as, item, two lips, indifferent red; item,
two grey eyes, with lids to them; item, one neck, one
chin, and so forth. Were you sent hither to praise   235
me?

Viola I see you what you are, you are too proud;
But, if you were the devil, you are fair.
My lord and master loves you. O, such love
Could be but recompensed, though you were crown'd
The nonpareil of beauty!   240

Olivia   How does he love me?

Viola With adorations, fertile tears,
With groans that thunder love, with sighs of fire.

Olivia Your lord does know my mind. I cannot love him;
Yet I suppose him virtuous, know him noble,
Of great estate, of fresh and stainless youth;   245
In voices well divulged, free, learn'd and valiant;
And in dimension and the shape of nature
A gracious person: but yet I cannot love him;
He might have took his answer long ago.

Viola If I did love you in my master's flame,   250
With such a suffering, such a deadly life,
In your denial I would find no sense;
I would not understand it.

Olivia   Why, what would you?

224. *in grain:* natural (part of the wood, not painted on).

231. *divers schedules:* various lists.

232. *inventoried:* itemized in a list, counted item by item.

239. *but recompensed:* no more than returned on equal terms.

240. *nonpareil:* without equal or parallel.

Viola Make me a willow cabin at your gate,
And call upon my soul within the house;   255
Write loyal cantons of contemned love
And sing them loud even in the dead of night;
Halloo your name to the reverberate hills,
And make the babbling gossip of the air
Cry out "Olivia!" Oh, you should not rest   260
Between the elements of air and earth,
But you should pity me!

Olivia   You might do much.
What is your parentage?

Viola Above my fortunes, yet my state is well;
I am a gentleman.   265

Olivia   Get you to your lord;
I cannot love him. Let him send no more;
Unless, perchance, you come to me again,
To tell me how he takes it. Fare you well.
I thank you for your pains; spend this for me.

Viola I am no fee'd post, lady; keep your purse.   270
My master, not myself, lacks recompense.
Love make his heart of flint that you shall love;
And let your fervour, like my master's, be
Placed in contempt! Farewell, fair cruelty.
[Exit.]

Olivia "What is your parentage?"   275
"Above my fortunes, yet my state is well;
I am a gentleman." I'll be sworn thou art.
Thy tongue, thy face, thy limbs, actions, and spirit,
Do give thee five-fold blazon. Not too fast: soft, soft !
Unless the master were the man. How now!   280
Even so quickly may one catch the plague?
Methinks I feel this youth's perfections
With an invisible and subtle stealth
To creep in at mine eyes. Well, let it be.
What ho, Malvolio!   285

[Re-enter MALVOLIO.]

Malvolio   Here, madam, at your service.

---

254.   *willow cabin:* small hut with willow (the sign of unrequited love) before it.

256.   *cantons:* love songs (cantos).

        contemned love: love that is given but not returned.

254–262. *babbling gossip:* reference to Echo, a nymph from Greek Mythology. The impression of hallooing, reverberating, and babbling gossip is very brilliantly and masterfully created in this passage by the use of vowel sounds, assonance, and alliterative onomatopoeia.

270.   *no fee'd post:* no paid messenger.

271.   *recompense:* reward.

279.   *blazon:* proclamation (like a coat-of-arms, or possibly, a triumphant blast on the trumpet).

280.   *master:* Orsino.

        the man: the messenger; that is, unless Cesario were the master delivering his own message.

Olivia Run after that same peevish messenger,
The county's man. He left this ring behind him,
Would I or not. Tell him I'll none of it.
Desire him not to flatter with his lord,
Nor hold him tip with hopes; I am not for him.   290
If that the youth will come this way to-morrow,
I'll give him reasons for't. Hie thee, Malvolio.

Malvolio Madam, I will.
[Exit.]

Olivia I do I know not what, and fear to find
Mine eye too great a flatterer for my mind   295
Fate, show thy force; ourselves we do not owe.
What is decreed must be, and be this so.
[Exit.]

286. *peevish:* to the servants Cesario had been cross and fretful. Olivia keeps up this pretense to avoid letting Malvolio suspect that she, the countess, has fallen in love with Cesario.

292. *Hie thee:* hurry up.

296. *owe:* own.

COMMENTARY

At Olivia's house, Maria and Feste (the Clown) match wits. They have served together in Olivia's household for years and are on good terms. Their rapid-fire one-liners attest to their familiarity with one another. In fact, Maria is likely recycling Feste's old jokes and using them on him.

Although the text refers to Feste as a clown, portraying him in a traditional clown costume is not necessary. Feste is one of Shakespeare's wittiest and wisest fools. He possesses the melancholy wisdom of a man who has accepted his own failings, and is free from ambition and illusions — although he still tries to "fool" money out of the people he meets. This self-acceptance leaves him free to poke fun at the desires of others, as when he teases Maria about wanting to marry Sir Toby (25–27). Feste can be seen as the guiding spirit of the play; the fool confers self knowledge on his patrons and/or victims by acting as a mirror in which he shows them their own folly — much like Hamlet's explanation of the purpose of playing.

Maria questions Feste about his unexplained absences from Olivia's household and warns him he may be turned away. Feste reminds her that it's summertime, and he can risk being homeless. We sense Feste may be weary of his role in the house.

Maria exits, and Olivia appears, looking very grave, dressed in black and wearing a mourning veil. Her steward Malvolio, also in black, is a stiff, no-nonsense person. Besides his grave demeanor, Malvolio's most noticeable character trait is his supercilious, haughty attitude toward other characters, with the exception of Olivia. The two together are a fool's worst nightmare. Feste puts his hands together in a mock prayer to Wit (the fool invokes the spirit of good humor, or Wit, as if it were a god), to make him funny.

To maintain the somber mood of her grief, Olivia imperiously commands, "Take the fool away." Feste counters that it is Olivia who is the fool. She replies that he is a dry fool and dishonest. His answer is a slightly longwinded and irrational way of saying what he can fix, he will, and what can't be fixed, one must accept, which could serve as his life's philosophy. Accordingly, Olivia is a fool to persist in grieving over her brother's death, for if it can't be fixed, it must be accepted. Feste's pun about giving the "dry" fool drink echoes Maria's "dry" jokes on Sir Andrew in Scene 3.

Feste asks Olivia for permission to prove she is a fool. She grants it, and he poses her questions that prove she is foolish to cry for her dead brother as his soul is in heaven, a better place than earth. This thought pleases her, as it takes her out of herself. This is exactly the purpose of a fool, to give people perspective on their folly via humor.

We see that Feste's humor warms Olivia's tone; she is less imperious. For Feste's part, Olivia challenges him to be at his best, and his humor improves from the tedious early monologue to very witty dialogue. The nature of comedy depends upon both the wit of the comedian and the receptivity of the audience.

Olivia asks whether the fool mends, that is, gives pleasure. Malvolio shows nothing but scorn for Feste and denies any positive effects that fooling might provide. Why? Malvolio is the perfect companion for Olivia while she mourns; he is serious and somber. But once Olivia's grieving ends, she becomes less like him and, consequently, won't spend as much time with Malvolio. So, if the fool mends her, Malvolio is no longer needed as his lady's constant companion, which he will not accept without a fight as he is secretly in love with her.

Like the Puritans who condemned the theater in the late sixteenth and early seventeenth century in England, Malvolio undervalues the role of feelings in life and over-emphasizes social utility and reason. Malvolio scorns people who laugh at fools and encourage their jests, as if it were time and labor wasted, rather than a mutually beneficial merriment. Although there are numerous jests leveled at the Puritans in this play, Shakespeare's animus was directed at people who were not capable of enjoying the pleasure of a good time, rather than any direct animosity toward the Puritan religion.

Despite Feste's absences and questionable honesty, Olivia is fond of her old fool. Olivia tells Malvolio that he is sick of self-love and cannot appreciate a good joke. And that he's too serious and makes mountains out of molehills. It takes one to know one; and Olivia is not so different from her steward, at least with regard to being sick of self-love (overly self-absorbed and self-important). Yet, her ability to diagnose Malvolio may signify that she herself has the potential for self-knowledge — the only cure for this particular disease. The sickness of self-love hits epidemic proportions in this play; Malvolio is just the only sufferer who does not belong to the nobility. His self-love, combined with his instinct for social climbing, makes it more obtrusive and repugnant to the sensibilities of the other characters.

Maria reports there's someone at the gate to see Olivia. Olivia rightly assumes that the guest must be a messenger from Orsino and tells Malvolio to send him away. Sir Toby has been delaying him in the interim.

Sir Toby staggers onto stage, excessively drunk and belching, blaming his intoxication and belching on the pickled herring he has been eating. Toby reports that Cesario — the visitor — is a gentleman and staggers off.

Olivia plays another round of question and answer with her fool. Feste's answers reveal a subtle intellect that differentiates his wit from the low comedy of Toby and Andrew. Feste is a thoughtful fool, whereas Toby is a clownish gentleman. Olivia orders Feste to attend to Toby, who is in the third degree of drink — he's drowned (note the reference to the coroner).

Feste exits, and Malvolio re-enters, saying that the young fellow at the gate demands to speak with Olivia and won't accept no for an answer. He reports that the visitor will stand at her door like a court officer that must deliver his subpoena or summons personally. Shakespeare dramatizes Viola's persistence and Olivia's stubbornness by giving us a series of introductions — Maria, Toby, and Malvolio — before Olivia grants Viola the admission.

Malvolio's description of Viola piques Olivia's interest. Notice that he does not define Viola by what she is, but what she is not; she is not yet a man, but not young enough for a boy. Again, the enigmatic quality of Cesario's identity interests Olivia, as well as the fact that Cesario is said to be a gentleman and handsome.

Olivia and Maria prepare to meet the messenger; Maria covers Olivia's face with a veil. The veil serves a double purpose here. First, the veil signifies that Olivia is in mourning, and as such, it is not an appropriate time to court her. Second, the veil allows Olivia to shroud her identity in mystery. Because the enigmatic quality of Cesario has piqued Olivia's interest, she invests herself with a touch of the unknown, too. Cesario enters and launches into his prepared speech, but unsure of whom to address, he breaks off his speech and asks which one is the lady of the house. Olivia says she will answer for the lady of the house. Not satisfied with this equivocal answer, Cesario refuses to resume his speech; he doesn't want to waste it on the wrong person.

Olivia asks whether Cesario is a comedian, that is, an actor, as he is so unwilling to speak anything except the speech he has memorized. No, Cesario says, playfully adding, "I am not that I play." The levels of identity at play here are complex. First, we have Viola, the woman. Second, we have Cesario, the young man she counterfeits. And finally, we have the role of an actor speaking for Orsino by proxy with a prepared speech. For her part, though Olivia is the lady of the house, she has left her identity ambiguous until she claims, "If I do not usurp myself, I am."

Cesario returns to his memorized speech in praise of Olivia, saying that he will show the heart of the message. Note the play on "heart" in this line (183). The word is used both as the heart, or central core, of the message, and as a love message, revealing the heart of Orsino.

Olivia, sure that she has heard it all before, asks Cesario to be brief. She wants the messenger to get to the matter and skip the praise part, which is likely to be false. Just the thought of listening to more of Orsino's nonsense has made her irritable and impatient. She wonders why she has even let this rude messenger take up this much of her time. But despite her comments to the contrary, she may also be more interested in hearing the messenger himself speak.

Maria, sensing her mood, comes forward and tells Cesario to "hoist sail," a nautical term for hit the road. Cesario refuses, asking Olivia to mollify, or calm down, her giant. Originally, Shakespeare's smallest boy actor played the part of Maria. Calling Maria a giant is both a self-conscious (meta-theatric) nod to the smallness of the boy actor playing Maria and a comic put-down of Maria herself. Shakespeare is masterful in his handling of dramatic irony. The irony of Viola's comments as Cesario, which allude to her feminine identity, call our attention to the duplicitous nature of identity in this play. In a similar manner, Shakespeare goes one step further by reminding the audience that there are actors playing roles — a boy playing Maria — and falsifying identity in the same manner as Viola does as Cesario.

A veiled Olivia hears Orsino's messenger, Cesario.

Olivia tells him to speak, but Cesario refuses until they are alone. Olivia's irrepressible curiosity makes her cry out, "What are you? What would you?" Orsino's desire is transparent, making it a bore, but Cesario's mysteriousness has unsettled Olivia. She agrees to Cesario's demand and dismisses Maria.

Now alone, Cesario begins to recite Orsino's prepared speech. Olivia cannot contain her contempt for Orsino's tedious love messages. She sarcastically undermines Cesario's delivery of the speech. Why? She is interested in the messenger, not the message.

Cesario asks to see Olivia's face. She removes her veil as though revealing a work of art. But Cesario does not give her the admiration she has come to expect from men — no wonder, as Cesario is not a man. Cesario mockingly wonders whether her beauty is painted on with makeup. It is natural, replies Olivia. Cesario tells her it would be a shame to leave the world no copy of such beauty, that is, without bearing a child, offering another reason to accept Orsino's love. (Shakespeare deals with this theme in the first 17 of his sonnets.) Olivia maintains her sarcastic tone, saying she will leave her beauty, like goods in a store, to be inventoried.

Cesario tells Olivia that she is too proud. Some current productions play this as the moment when Olivia unknowingly falls in love with Cesario, suggesting that Olivia, who disdains the fawning nature of Orsino's love, is excited by the scorn and indifference to her beauty that Cesario shows her.

Cesario tells her that Orsino loves her, and asks whether this means nothing to her? How can she be so hard-hearted? Olivia says that she cannot love Orsino, though she is aware of his many good points. Cesario says that if he loved her with such passion as Orsino does, he would find no sense in her answer.

Olivia asks what Cesario would do if he loved Olivia, and he responds passionately describing a highly romantic ideal courtship. This is the point that most traditional productions define as the moment when Olivia falls in love with Cesario. Yet, Cesario's quick wit, such as when she deviates from Orsino's set speech, is just as likely to have attracted Olivia. Orsino's speeches may sound highly romantic, but they are riddled with worn out clichés of courtly love, and their hollowness resounds. Cesario's words, however, are alive; they may sting at times, but perhaps that sting is precisely what Olivia needs — something to snap her out of her neurasthenic mourning.

Olivia's question about his parentage signals her interest in Cesario romantically. And her assurance that he is a gentleman clinches the deal. Olivia tells Cesario to return to Orsino and tell him she cannot love him, and he must send no more. But if Cesario would like to come again, she would be glad to see him.

She offers him money, but Cesario refuses the gift, saying his master, not himself, lacks reward. Once again we find Viola's natural inclination toward self-sacrifice and other-directed thinking; showing no interest in her own reward, she thinks only of Orsino. After Cesario has left, Olivia recounts to herself this conversation, and savors his replies.

She calls Malvolio and tells him to run after Cesario and return a ring that he left behind. We know of course that this is a trick, which she will explain away if the boy comes again. She tells Malvolio to hurry off and do it.

Olivia is falling in love. She reasons that love is like fate, and that because it is out of our control, she will accept whatever happens. Even though we know that Olivia is misguided in her choice of love object, her statement reveals an insight into the nature of love that makes her a more sympathetic and attractive character than Orsino at this point in the play. Love demands the surrender of the self to the beloved, and Olivia voluntarily gives over her authority and her self-control, sending a servant — Cesario — her ring.

As Act I ends, the situation is complicated. The Countess loves a girl (Viola) masquerading as a boy (Cesario), while the Duke Orsino loves the Countess, who rejects him, and is in turn loved by the girl Viola, who is a mere youth — and a boy at that — to the Duke. The double dramatic irony is delicious.

Notes

Notes

Notes

TWELFTH NIGHT
ACT II

Viola *I am the man. If it be so, as 'tis,*
Poor lady, she were better love a dream.
Disguise, I see, thou art a wickedness,
Wherein the pregnant enemy does much.

. . . .

Malvolio *In my stars I am above thee; but be not afraid of*
greatness: some are born great, some achieve greatness, and
some have greatness thrust upon 'em.

Act II, Scene 1

Sebastian, Viola's twin brother, has also survived the shipwreck; he was saved by Antonio. Sebastian is on his way to Orsino's court, and despite the risk of danger to himself, Antonio decides to follow Sebastian on his journey.

ACT II, SCENE 1
The sea-coast.

[Enter ANTONIO and SEBASTIAN.]

Antonio Will you stay no longer? nor will you not
   that I go with you?

Sebastian By your patience, no. My stars shine
   darkly over me. The malignancy of my fate might
   perhaps distemper yours; therefore I shall crave of   5
   you your leave that I may bear my evils alone. It were
   a bad recompense for your love, to lay any of them
   on you.

Antonio Let me know of you whither you are bound.

Sebastian No, sooth, sir. My determinate voyage is
   mere extravagancy. But I perceive in you so excel-   10
   lent a touch of modesty, that you will not extort
   from me what I am willing to keep in; therefore it
   charges me in manners the rather to express myself.
   You must know of me then, Antonio, my name is
   Sebastian, which I called Roderigo. My father was   15
   that Sebastian of Messaline, whom I know you have
   heard of. He left behind him myself and a sister,
   both born in an hour. If the heavens had been
   pleased, would we had so ended I but you, sir, altered
   that; for some hour before you took me from the   20
   breach of the sea was my sister drowned.

Antonio Alas the day!

Sebastian A lady, sir, though it was said she much
   resembled me, was yet of many accounted beautiful;
   but, though I could not with such estimable wonder
   overfar believe that, yet thus far I will boldly pub-   25
   lish her; she bore a mind that envy could not but
   call fair. She is drowned already, sir, with salt water,

NOTES

1.   *nor... not:* A double negative was permissible in Elizabethan English for the sake of emphasis.

4.   *malignancy of my fate:* the evil course of my destiny.

5.   *distemper yours:* spread like an illness and upset yours.

10.   *mere extravagancy:* only for recreation.

16.   *Messaline:* probably based on the Latin Massiliensis, Fr. Marseilles.

23.   Note the contrast between Sebastian's commonsensical, calm, balanced, measured sentences, and Viola's poetic flights of passion.

though I seem to drown her remembrance again
with more.

Antonio Pardon me, sir, your bad entertainment.

Sebastian O good Antonio, forgive me your trouble.   30

Antonio If you will not murder me for my love, let
me be your servant.

Sebastian If you will not undo what you have done,
that is, kill him whom you have recovered, desire it
not. Fare ye well at once: my bosom is full of kind-   35
ness, and I am yet so near the manners of my mother,
that upon the least occasion more mine eyes will tell
tales of me. I am bound to the Count Orsino's
court. Farewell.
[Exit.]

Antonio The gentleness of all the gods go with thee!   40
I have many enemies in Orsino's court,
Else would I very shortly see thee there.
But, come what may, I do adore thee so,
That danger shall seem sport, and I will go.
[Exit.]

29.   *your bad entertainment:* pardon me your poor
reception as my guest.

COMMENTARY

On another part of the sea-coast of Illyria, we meet
two more survivors of the shipwreck that we
learned about in Act I, Scene 2. Sebastian is a young
man and Viola's twin brother (in some productions they
are played by the same person). Antonio is the sea
captain of the ship that rescued Sebastian. The relationship of these two minor characters is somewhat
ambiguous; although they appear to be friends, a subtle homoerotic subtext seems to be prevalent in many
of Antonio's lines. Since gender identity and its fluidity
are explored throughout this play, the love of Antonio
for Sebastian — not very different from Orsino's growing love for Viola in her male disguise — provides one
more variation on the theme of attraction and gender.

Antonio is unsettled by Sebastian's abrupt desire to
leave. Sebastian explains that his bad luck of late may
rub off on Antonio, which would be poor payment for the
love and kindness that he has shown Sebastian.

Sebastian's language tends to be rhetorical, slightly
stilted, and perhaps insincere. These qualities may hint
at Sebastian's own insecurities. Like many young men,
his attempt to sound worldly may belie his inexperience
and naiveté. Antonio's simple responses, however,
come from the heart and have an emotional immediacy:
He is afraid of losing Sebastian. Sebastian's responses
are almost too polite and seem disingenuous, as if he
were attempting to politely distance himself from one to

whom he owes a large favor. We must also wonder why Sebastian initially dissembled his identity to Antonio. What reason did Sebastian have for saying his name was Roderigo earlier? Name-changing seems to be a habit to which many characters in this play are addicted. Perhaps in this case, it was a feeble attempt at distinguishing himself from his father, who was also named Sebastian. Or more likely, Shakespeare has created a minor echo of the identity/disguise theme.

We learn that Antonio saved Sebastian from drowning. And Sebastian believes that his twin sister Viola died in the shipwreck, moments before he himself was saved. Sebastian praises his sister's beauty and fair mind. He is brought close to tears. Antonio, sympathizing with Sebastian's grief, tells him that he is sorry for his friend's bad fortune. One may also read into Antonio's responses a wounded sarcasm ("If you will not murder me for my love..."), which suggests that Antonio feels as if Sebastian's behavior threatens to accomplish just that — murder his love.

Antonio asks whether he can accompany Sebastian as his servant, but Sebastian refuses. He would prefer to travel alone to Orsino's court. Although Antonio has many enemies there, he decides to secretly follow his friend and risk personal danger.

Act II, Scene 2

Malvolio "returns" the ring to Viola. She realizes this is a sign that Olivia has fallen in love with her male disguise. She wonders how this strange love triangle will turn out in the end.

ACT II, SCENE 2
A street.

[Enter VIOLA, MALVOLIO following.]

Malvolio Were not you even now with the Countess
    Olivia?

Viola Even now, sir; on a moderate pace I have
    since arrived but hither.

Malvolio She returns this ring to you, sir. You   5
    might have saved me my pains, to have taken it away
    yourself. She adds, moreover, that you should put
    your lord into a desperate assurance she will none of
    him; and one thing more, that you be never so hardy
    to come again in his affairs, unless it be to report   10
    your lord's taking of this. Receive it so.

Viola She took the ring of me; I'll none of it.

Malvolio Come, sir, you peevishly threw it to her;
    and her will is, it should be so returned. If it be
    worth stooping for, there it lies in your eye; if not,   15
    be it his that finds it.
    [Exit.]

Viola I left no ring with her. What means this lady?
    Fortune forbid my outside have not charm'd her!
    She made good view of me; indeed, so much
    That sure methought her eyes had lost her tongue,
    For she did speak in starts distractedly.   20
    She loves me, sure; the cunning of her passion
    Invites me in this churlish messenger.
    None of my lord's ring! why, he sent her none.
    I am the man. If it be so, as 'tis,
    Poor lady, she were better love a dream.   25
    Disguise, I see, thou art a wickedness,

NOTES

5.   *returns this ring:* Olivia's ruse to give Cesario a tangible reason for returning. Note the high-handed manner in which Malvolio addresses the messenger.

8.   *desperate assurance:* a certainty that offers no hope.

14.   *so returned:* that is, peevishly (so Malvolio throws the ring down upon the floor, although some actors put the ring on the end of the staff of office and wave it at the messenger).

24.   *I am the man:* Cesario realizes that Olivia has, indeed, fallen for himself rather than for his master.

26.   *wickedness:* Cesario speaks with feeling about the wickedness that arises from women's being deceived (since Eve) by disguise.

Wherein the pregnant enemy does much.

How easy is it for the proper-false

In women's waxen hearts to set their forms!

Alas, our frailty is the cause, not we!   30

For such as we are made of, such we be.

How will this fadge? my master loves her dearly;

And I, poor monster, fond as much on him;

And she, mistaken, seems to dote on me

What will become of this? As I am man,   35

My state is desperate for my master's love;

As I am woman, — now alas the day!

What thriftless sighs shall poor Olivia breathe!

O Time, thou must untangle this, not I!

It is too hard a knot for me to untie!   40

[Exit.]

27.	*pregnant:* quick, resourceful.
28.	*proper-false:* men who are handsome and deceitful.
30.	*frailty:* The distinction between frailty and the woman who is frail is a subtle one.
32.	*fadge:* fall into place.
38.	*thriftless sighs:* extravagant and unprofitable sighs.

COMMENTARY

This scene continues the action that began in Act I, Scene 5. Malvolio has been sent by Olivia to return a ring to Cesario, and he officiously executes his mission. Could there be any task he would enjoy more thoroughly than sending one of Olivia's suitors packing? (Remember that Malvolio is secretly in love with Olivia!) Unfortunately for him, he is delivering a message that has quite the opposite intention — to ensure that Cesario returns to Olivia.

Malvolio attempts to hand over the ring to Cesario, all the while holding it with contempt. The steward adds scornfully that both of them would have saved time and effort by Cesario keeping the ring in the first place. He adds that Cesario should tell the Duke that Olivia has no interest in him and that he should send no more messengers, unless Cesario would like to come again, to report how the Duke takes this news.

Cesario refuses to take the ring, saying, "She took the ring from me; I'll none of it." We know, of course, that this is not true. Cesario never gave her a ring. Cesario has quickly improvised a lie in order to protect Olivia's honor. Cesario gains nothing from saying this for herself, and it is rather one more example of her resourcefulness and her generosity of spirit.

Malvolio, who has no time to waste with peevish messengers, tosses the ring to the ground and insists that if it is worth anything Cesario should pick it up, and then he exits. Malvolio's superciliousness and snooty pride are worth noting, as we shall see later in the story when he is forced to view his social position from an altogether more humble perspective. Shakespeare, a master of contrast, uses bold strokes here, showing us a very churlish Malvolio, which will set off his later change in station and behavior in a more dramatic light.

Cesario is puzzled by the ring, and by Malvolio's speech. It dawns on her that her boy disguise has charmed the eyes of Olivia. She realizes that Olivia is in love with her, and Malvolio's message was both a sign of her passion and an invitation for Cesario to return. Cesario pities Olivia, whose love for Cesario is hopeless.

Her soliloquy leaps from one superior insight to the next. She is quick to see the damage that her disguise has caused and relates it to the ease with which women are tricked by outward appearance. "Our frailty is the cause, not we," Viola says of women, "for such as we are made of, such we be." Later she will say, "I am not that I am." Does this effectively negate her own frailty? If this frailty is based on accepted or learned gender role behavior for women, then by playing Cesario, she does — by playing a man she does not incorporate frailty into the role. One might wonder whether Viola's experience playing a man will have any lasting effect on her conception of being a woman. Perhaps, upon her return to womanhood she might choose to reconstruct her feminine role without those components she deems frail. In addition, Viola is given a rare glimpse of what it is to be a woman — and a woman in love — from a new perspective, that of an outsider, a man, in her scenes with Olivia.

Viola then examines her own predicament. While she is disguised as a man she can never attain her love (Orsino), and when she does reveal herself a woman, Olivia's love will be hopeless. Viola wonders how events will turn out, leaving it up to Time to untangle this knotty mess the lovers are in.

Act II, Scene 3

Late at night at Olivia's manor house, Sir Toby, Sir Andrew, and Feste celebrate with drink and song. Maria warns them to quiet down, but it is too late. Malvolio enters and reprimands them, threatening to throw them out of the house. After he leaves, the others plot their revenge on him.

ACT II, SCENE 3
Olivia's house.

[Enter SIR TOBY and SIR ANDREW.]

Sir Toby Approach, Sir Andrew. Not to be a-bed
after midnight is to be up betimes; and "diluculo
surgere," thou know'st, —

Sir Andrew Nay, by my troth, I know not; but I
know, to be up late is to be up late.

Sir Toby A false conclusion. I hate it as an unfilled   5
can. To be up after midnight and to go to bed then,
is early; so that to go to bed after midnight is to go
to bed betimes. Does not our life consist of the four
elements?

Sir Andrew Faith, so they say; but I think it rather   10
consists of eating and drinking.

Sir Toby Thou'rt a scholar; let us therefore eat
and drink. Marian, I say! a stoup of wine!

[Enter Clown.]

Sir Andrew Here comes the fool, i' faith.

Clown How now, my hearts! did you never see the   15
picture of "We three"?

Sir Toby Welcome, ass. Now let's have a catch.

Sir Andrew By my troth, the fool has an excellent
breast. I had rather than forty shillings I had such a
leg, and so sweet a breath to sing, as the fool has.   20
In sooth, thou wast in very gracious fooling last
night, when thou spokest of Pigrogromitus, of the
Vapians passing the equinoctial of Queubus. 'Twas
very good, i' faith. I sent thee sixpence for thy leman.
Hadst it?

NOTES

2-3.   *diluculo surgere:* to rise early ... (saluberrimum est)
        is the most healthy.

8-9.   *four elements:* earth, air, fire, and water. The Eliza-
        bethans believed that humanity was made up of var-
        ious combinations of these four elements. The
        theory of humors was based upon this theory.

12.   *scholar:* ironic, for Sir Andrew cannot remember the
        lessons that are echoed and parodied by Sir Toby in
        this scene.

13.   *Marian:* affectionate variation on Maria.

        stoup: cup, flagon, or tankard.

16.   *We three:* picture of two donkeys; the viewer made
        up the third! Sir Toby knows this joke, for he calls
        the Clown the third ("ass").

17.   *catch:* musical round.

22.   *Pigrogromitus... :* a fantastic story made up and told
        by Feste; (pigro = lazy, vap = vapid, Queubus = cubus
        [cube] or queue [tail]).

24.   *leman:* sweetheart.

Clown I did impeticos thy gratillity: for Malvolio's   25
nose is no whipstock; my lady has a white hand,
and the Myrmidons are no bottle-ale houses.

Sir Andrew Excellent! why, this is the best fooling,
when all is done. Now, a song.

Sir Toby Come on; there is sixpence for you — let's   30
have a song.

Sir Andrew There's a testril of me too. If one knight
give a —

Clown Would you have a love song, or a song of
good life?

Sir Toby A love song, a love song.

Sir Andrew Ay, ay. I care not for good life.   35

Clown *[Sings.]*
O mistress mine, where are you roaming?
O, stay and hear; your true love's coming,
That can sing both high and low.
Trip no further, pretty sweeting;
Journeys end in lovers meeting,   40
Every wise man's son doth know.

Sir Andrew Excellent good, i' faith.

Sir Toby Good, good.

Clown *[Sings.]*
What is love? 'tis not hereafter;
Present mirth hath present laughter;   45
What's to come is still unsure.
In delay there lies no plenty;
Then come kiss me, sweet and twenty,
Youth's a stuff will not endure.

Sir Andrew A mellifluous voice, as I am true knight.   50

Sir Toby A contagious breath.

Sir Andrew Very sweet and contagious, i' faith.

Sir Toby To hear by the nose, it is dulcet in con-
tagion. But shall we make the welkin dance indeed?
shall we rouse the night-owl in a catch that will draw   55
three souls out of one weaver? shall we do that?

26. *impeticos thy gratillity:* I pocketed your tip myself, for Malvolio pokes his nose into my business, and my girl friend (who is a lady) and I go to the high-class Myrmidons taverns and not to mere lowdown pubs. Feste runs all this together, making paraphrase difficult.

27. *Myrmidons:* a chain of high-class taverns in London, named after the warlike-race of Thessaly, whom Achilles led to the siege of Troy.

32. *testril:* fanciful form of *tester* = sixpence.

50. *mellifluous:* sweetly and smoothly flowing.

51. *contagious:* means either an attractive song or bad breath.

53. *To hear by the nose...:* If one could hear with one's nose this song would be sweetness in the midst of a strong foul smell.

54. *welkin:* sky (used humorously here).

56. *weaver:* Weavers were said to be fond of psalms singing.

Sir Andrew An you love me, let's do't. I am dog at
a catch.

Clown By'r lady, sir, and some dogs will catch well.

Sir Andrew Most certain. Let our catch be, "Thou
knave."

Clown "Hold thy peace, thou knave," knight? I   60
shall be constrained in't to call thee knave, knight.

Sir Andrew 'Tis not the first time I have constrained one to call me knave. Begin, fool. It begins "Hold thy peace."

Clown I shall never begin if I hold my peace.

Sir Andrew Good, i' faith. Come, begin.   65
[Catch sung.]
[Enter MARIA.]

Maria What a caterwauling do you keep here! If
my lady have not called up her steward Malvolio and
bid him turn you out of doors, never trust me.

Sir Toby My lady's a Cataian, we are politicians,
Malvolio's a Peg-a-Ramsey, and "Three merry men   70
be we." Am not I consanguineous? am I not of her
blood? Tillyvally. Lady! *[Sings.]* "There dwelt a
man in Babylon, lady, lady!"

Clown Beshrew me, the knight's in admirable fooling.

Sir Andrew Ay, he does well enough if he be dis-   75
posed, and so do I too. He does it with a better grace,
but I do it more natural.

Sir Toby *[Sings.]* "Oh, the twelfth day of
December," —

Maria For the love o' God, peace!

[Enter MALVOLIO.]

Malvolio My masters, are you mad? or what are   80
you? Have you no wit, manners, nor honesty, but to
gabble like tinkers at this time of night? Do ye make
an ale-house of my lady's house, that ye squeak out
your coziers' catches without any mitigation or

57.   *dog at:* clever at.

66.   *caterwauling:* making a wailing noise like a cat.
From Middle English cat + wawen, to wail (an onomatopoetic word, whose sound echoes its meaning).

69.   *Cataian:* native of Cathay (China); a scoundrel,
rogue, or sharper.

70.   *Peg-a-Ramsey:* the name of a song applied to
Malvolio as a term of reproach by Sir Toby. The bal-
lad, now lost, contains some refrains in which a
henpecked husband longs for his bachelor days with
the words: "Give me my yellow hose again, give me
my yellow hose." This may have suggested the idea
of yellow stockings for gulling Malvolio to
Shakespeare.

71.   *consanguineous:* related by blood.

82.   *tinkers:* Tinkers wandered about mending utensils
and were thought to drink a lot and make noise.

84.   *coziers':* cobblers'.

mitigation: softening of the sound.

remorse of voice? Is there no respect of place, per-   85
sons, nor time in you?

Sir Toby We did keep time, sir, in our catches.
Sneck up!

Malvolio Sir Toby, I must be round with you. My
lady bade me tell you, that, thought she harbours
you as her kinsman, she's nothing allied to your dis-
orders. If you can separate yourself and your mis-   90
demeanors, you are welcome to the house; if not,
an it would please you to take leave of her, she is
very willing to bid you farewell.

Sir Toby "Farewell, dear heart, since I must needs
be gone."

Maria Nay, good Sir Toby.   95

Clown "His eyes do show his days are almost done."

Malvolio Is't even so?

Sir Toby "But I will never die."

Clown Sir Toby, there you lie.

Malvolio This is much credit to you.

Sir Toby "Shall I bid him go?"   100

Clown "What an if you do?"

Sir Toby "Shall I bid him go, and spare not?"

Clown "Oh, no, no, no, no, you dare not!"

Sir Toby Out o' tune, sir! ye lie. Art any more than
a steward? Dost thou think, because thou art vir-   105
tuous, there shall be no more cakes and ale?

Clown Yes, by St. Anne, and ginger shall be hot i'
the mouth too.

Sir Toby Thou'rt i' the right. Go, sir rub your chain
with crumbs. A stoup of wine, Maria!   110

Malvolio Mistress Mary, if you prized my lady's
favour at anything more than contempt, you would
not give means for this uncivil rule. She shall
know of it, by this hand.
[Exit.]

---

86. *time... in our catches:* short musical compositions for three or more voices, which sing the same melody, the second singer beginning the first line as the first goes on to the second line, and so on.

87. *Sneck up!:* Go hang (onomatopoetic sound of a man's neck breaking).

100. *Shall I bid him go?:* Toby and Feste alter the words of the ancient song to fit their present situation.

105–106. *Dost thou think, because thou art virtuous, there shall be no more cakes and ale?:* This is the classic challenge to puritans of every time and place.

109. *Go, sir rub your chain with crumbs:* go polish your steward's chain, which he wore around his neck like a mayoral chain).

Maria Go shake your ears.   115

Sir Andrew 'Twere as good a deed as to drink when
a man's a-hungry, to challenge him the field, and then
to break promise with him and make a fool of him.

Sir Toby Do't, knight. I'll write thee a challenge; or
I'll deliver thy indignation to him by word of mouth.   120

Maria Sweet Sir Toby, be patient for to-night. Since
the youth of the count's was to-day with my lady,
she is much out of quiet. For Monsieur Malvolio,
let me alone with him; if I do not gull him into a
nayword, and make him a common recreation, do   125
not think I have wit enough to lie straight in my
bed. I know I can do it.

Sir Toby Possess us, possess us; tell us something
of him.

Maria Marry, sir, sometimes he is a kind of puritan.

Sir Andrew Oh, if I thought that, I'd beat him like
a dog.

Sir Toby What, for being a puritan? thy exquisite   130
reason, dear knight.

Sir Andrew I have no exquisite reason for't, but I
have reason good enough.

Maria The devil a puritan that he is, or anything
constantly, but a time-pleaser; an affectioned ass,   135
that cons state without book and utters it by great
swarths: the best persuaded of himself, so crammed,
as he thinks, with excellencies, that it is his grounds
of faith that all that look on him love him; and on
that vice in him will my revenge find notable cause   140
to work.

Sir Toby What wilt thou do?

Maria I will drop in his way some obscure epistles
of love, wherein, by the colour of his beard, the shape
of his leg, the manner of his gait, the expressure of
his eye, forehead, and complexion, he shall find him-   145
self most feelingly personated. I can write very like
my lady your niece; on a forgotten matter we can
hardly make distinction of our hands.

---

124.   *gull him:* deceive and trick him.

125.   *nayword:* byword; his name will be synonymous
with laughing-stock.

128.   *puritan:* member of a group in the Church of England
during the sixteenth and seventeenth centuries who
wanted simpler forms of worship and stricter morals
(many puritans settled in New England). Hence, any
person who is very strict in morals and religion (from
Latin *puritas,* purity).

130.   *exquisite:* exact or precise.

135.   *affectioned:* affected, one who puts on airs.

136.   *cons state:* learns passages on etiquette and politics by great chunks, and quotes them at length;
a bore.

142.   *obscure epistles:* letters that make sense but not
clear or complete sense.

146.   *feelingly personated:* sympathetically impersonated
or imitated.

Sir Toby Excellent! I smell a device.

Sir Andrew I have't in my nose too.   150

Sir Toby He shall think, by the letters that thou wilt drop, that they come from my niece, and that she's in love with him.

Maria My purpose is, indeed, a horse of that colour.

Sir Andrew And your horse now would make him   155
an ass.

Maria Ass, I doubt not.

Sir Andrew Oh, 'twill be admirable!

Maria Sport royal, I warrant you. I know my physic will work with him. I will plant you two, and let the   160
fool make a third, where he shall find the letter. Observe his construction of it. For this night, to bed, and dream on the event. Farewell.
[Exit.]

Sir Toby Good night, Penthesilea.

Sir Andrew Before me, she's a good wench.

Sir Toby She's a beagle, true-bred, and one that   165
adores me. What o' that?

Sir Andrew I was adored once too.

Sir Toby Let's to bed, knight. Thou hadst need send for more money.

Sir Andrew If I cannot recover your niece, I am a   170
foul way out.

Sir Toby Send for money, knight. If thou hast her not i' the end, call me cut.

Sir Andrew If I do not, never trust me, take it how you will.

Sir Toby Come, come, I'll go burn some sack; 'tis too late to go to bed now. Come, knight; come,   175
knight.
[Exeunt.]

---

149. *device:* trick.

159. *physic:* medicine (to cure his pride).

161. *construction:* interpretation.

163. *Penthesilea:* Queen of the Amazons, a race of female warriors. A reference to Maria's diminutive stature with, perhaps an appreciative recognition of her spirited behavior.

170. *foul way out:* deep in financial trouble.

172. *cut:* cart-horse, gelded.

174. *burn some sack:* heat some wine with sugar and spices; stay up all night drinking.

COMMENTARY

The scene is Olivia's house, after midnight. Sir Toby and Sir Andrew are drunk and celebrating. They talk a lot of drunken nonsense and parody scholarly discourse, arguing about whether going to bed after midnight is to go to bed late (that night) or early (the next day).

When Feste the fool joins them, a full-out party has broken out, complete with singing and dancing. In most productions, Feste has a musical instrument — a lute — with which he accompanies his songs. We note that this is not the first of their late-night sessions together, as Andrew refers to Feste's fooling of the previous night.

Andrew asks for a song from Feste, and Toby seconds the motion. This play has more songs than any other of Shakespeare's plays. Feste's songs were written with the actor Robert Armin in mind, as he was known to have an excellent singing voice. The many songs and catches contribute to setting the festive mood of the play. The music creates a world that is distinctly different from everyday reality; it is a time of madness, revelry, and love, but even in the carnival world of twelfth night (and the Feast of Epiphany it is modeled on), one cannot escape from the melancholy this music is steeped in. This festive atmosphere is but a brief respite from the daily world of hardship and hard work.

The fool, Feste, provides most of the musical interludes of a Twelfth Night production.
Clive Barda/PAL

It was common practice for the fool to earn his living from singing and fooling. Toby and Andrew offer to pay Feste for a love song. Feste's song touches on themes from the play. Though Feste may be referring to his mistress, Olivia, the song's message is pertinent to all the young lovers in the play. In the first stanza, he sings "journeys end with lovers meeting," and the same can be said for comedies. In the second stanza, the song suggests pleasure should not be postponed, because youth does not last forever. The song might be speaking to any one of the lovers in this play. Seize the day — *carpe diem* — and accept the pleasures of life before it's too late.

Sir Toby suggests that they sing a catch (a song to be sung in rounds by a group), and Andrew suggests the catch, "Thou Knave." And the group sings a rousing, voluble round of "Hold thy peace, Thou Knave." We can assume that it is as unpleasantly grating as it is loud, and soon enough, their caterwauling has caught the attention of Maria.

Maria's warnings fall on deaf ears. Toby cannot take Maria seriously in the role of disciplinarian; they have had too much fun together. Besides, as Toby reminds her ("Am I not consanguineous?"), he and Olivia are family. And to prove that he isn't worried, he launches another catch, "There dwelt a man in babylon..." Followed by a third, "Oh, the twelfth day of December," when Malvolio enters.

Malvolio is a natural at playing the disciplinarian; his job as steward is to keep order around the house. What little power that is at his command, he will use (and probably abuse). He scolds the revelers for turning the household into an ale house, that is, a place for boisterous drunks. He asks whether they have no respect for time, as in the time of night. And Toby slyly answers that they have kept time in their catches. Malvolio warns Toby that if he can't separate his rude behavior from his person, Olivia will be forced to ask Toby to separate himself from her household. Toby bursts into song, mocking the seriousness of Malvolio. Feste joins in with Toby, and the two use their music and fooling to undermine the authority of the steward.

Feste is equally adept at provoking Sir Toby, mocking his false bravado (for example, Toby's claim to live forever is immediately rebuked by the Fool) and instigating a confrontation between the drunken knight and the steward. Toby rises to the challenge, dismissing Malvolio with a withering remark, "go rub your chain with crumbs." And with complete contempt for everything Malvolio has said, Toby orders more wine from Maria.

Because no one else in the room takes Malvolio's presence and power seriously, he turns on Maria. Malvolio admonishes Maria that she is not serving Olivia's interest, and before he exits, promises that he will be sure to let Olivia know it.

The conflict in this house is between two distinct ways of life. First, there is Malvolio, the rational, all-business social climber who lives an early-to-bed, early-to-rise existence. Then there is Toby and his cohorts, who enjoy the pleasures of life; they drink and sing and laugh, stay up late and sleep late. In part, this conflict is

Malvolio (with candle) tries to calm the revelers, Sir Andrew, Feste, and Sir Toby.

a manifestation of the tension between the beginnings of the modern economy — a force that was creating massive social changes in Shakespeare's England — and the time-honored English hospitality that had existed for thousands of years. Malvolio embodies the modern emphasis on economy, whereas Toby and his friends represent the old way of life. Malvolio cannot participate in the festivities or revel in excessive eating and drinking because he cannot help but think of it as a terrible waste of Olivia's resources — and absurd behavior from an economic perspective. Of course, Malvolio's dourness, cold rationalism, and thrift seem just as foolish from Toby's perspective. Life itself is what matters; it is to be experienced, celebrated, and savored.

Malvolio is a killjoy, and the audience, at this point, dislikes him nearly as much as the revelers in the play do. Maria shouts after him to shake his ears, and Andrew suggests challenging him to a duel. Toby says that he will write and deliver the challenge to Malvolio himself. But Maria has a better idea. Maria has a plan to embarrass Malvolio and make his name forever after synonymous with "laughingstock."

Maria suggests that Malvolio is a kind of puritan. And in this, Maria doesn't mean that he is actually a member of the Puritan church, but someone who is self-righteous and severe. Malvolio cannot laugh, he does not like to sing, he will not drink, but it is not because it is against his religion. He is so consumed with imagining his rewards to come — not in heaven, but on earth — to be promoted in social class above these drunken revelers is high on his list. His revenge against them is highest. His desire for advancement and, as we will see, his desire for Olivia are so strong that most of his energies are devoted to restraining himself. Because he cannot share his fantasies with anyone, his capacity for self-repression is astounding. Maria, however, has a good idea what goes on in Malvolio's secret thoughts. Why shouldn't she? She has spent more time in close proximity to Malvolio than any other character, with the possible exception of Olivia. And if familiarity breeds contempt, she knows Malvolio far too well to be friendly.

Maria's plan is to exploit Malvolio's self-importance and pride. Malvolio believes that everyone who sees him loves him, and Maria's revenge will play upon that flaw in him. She will counterfeit, or forge, a love letter from Olivia to him, and leave it where he's sure to find it. And though nameless, the letter will be addressed to someone with Malvolio's qualities. Because Maria's handwriting is indistinguishable from Olivia's, Malvolio can't help but fall for the ploy.

Twelfth Night, in contrast to many of Shakespeare's other plays, lacks a significant action at its center — if it can be said to have a center at all. Instead, the play is made up of sub-plots, love complications, and quite a few songs. The frivolous nature of the counterfeit-letter subplot, however silly its inception, has by the end of this story taken on a life and gravity of its own. It feeds Malvolio's appetite for self love, enabling him to believe Olivia sees him in the same light as he sees himself — worthy of being a Count! And by story's end, this subplot gives Malvolio a taste of self-knowledge — and humility, as well.

Toby and Andrew commend Maria, and her plan. Maria suggests that they meet tomorrow and put the plan into action before she exits. Because it's now too late for bed, at least for these revelers, Toby and Andrew heat some wine and decide to drink until daylight.

Act II, Scene 4

Orsino asks for music to relieve his lovesick pangs. He discusses the difference between the male and female capacity to love with Viola. Viola expresses her love for Orsino with a thinly veiled story about herself as though it were a story about her sister. Orsino, though interested in her "sister's" fate, sends Viola again to Olivia.

ACT II, SCENE 4
The Duke's palace.

[Enter DUKE, VIOLA, CURIO, and Others.]

Duke Give me some music. Now, good-morrow, friends.
Now, good Cesario, but that piece of song,
That old and antique song we heard last night.
Methought it did relieve my passion much,
More than light airs and recollected terms   5
Of these most brisk and giddy-paced times.
Come, but one verse.

Curio He is not here, so please your lordship, that
should sing it.

Duke Who was it?   10

Curio Feste, the jester, my lord; a fool that the lady
Olivia's father took much delight in. He is about the
house.

Duke Seek him out, and play the tune the while.
[Exit CURIO. Music plays.]
Come hither, boy. If ever thou shalt love,
In the sweet pangs of it remember me;   15
For such as I am all true lovers are,
Unstaid and skittish in all motions else,
Save in the constant image of the creature
That is beloved. How dost thou like this tune?

Viola It gives a very echo to the seat   20
Where Love is throned.

Duke   Thou dost speak masterly.
My life upon't, young though thou art, thine eye
Hath stay'd upon some favour that it loves.
Hath it not, boy?

NOTES

1. *music:* the signature-tune of Orsino.

3. *old and antique song:* The Duke's musical taste seems to have been very conservative.

5. *airs:* tunes, melodies.

   recollected terms: studied and artificial expressions.

17. *Unstaid and skittish:* unstable and excitable motions, probably emotions.

21. *Love:* here personified; If Orsino suffers (from unrequited passion), Viola also suffers from unrevealed love.

   masterly: like a master (note the masculine reference when we all know that Cesario is actually female).

23. *favour:* girl (favored one).

Viola   A little, by your favour.

Duke What kind of woman is't?   25

Viola   Of your complexion.

Duke She is not worth thee, then. What years, i' faith?

Viola About your years, my lord.

Duke Too old, by heaven. Let still the woman take
An elder than herself; so wears she to him,
So sways she level in her husband's heart.   30
For, boy, however we do praise ourselves,
Our fancies are more giddy and unfirm,
More longing, wavering, sooner lost and worn,
Than women's are.

Viola   I think it well, my lord.

Duke Then let thy love be younger than thyself   35
Or thy affection cannot hold the bent;
For women are as roses, whose fair flower
Being once display'd, doth fall that very hour.

Viola And so they are. Alas, that they are so;
To die, even when they to perfection grow!   40

[Re-enter CURIO and Clown.]

Duke O fellow, come, the song we had last night.
Mark it, Cesario, it is old and plain;
The spinsters and the knitters in the sun,
And the free maids that weave their thread with bones
Do use to chant it. It is silly sooth,   45
And dallies with the innocence of love,
Like the old age.

Clown Are you ready, sir?

Duke Ay; prithee, sing. *[Music. Song.]*

Clown Come away, come away, death,   50
And in sad cypress let me be laid;
Fly away, fly away, breath;
I am slain by a fair cruel maid.
My shroud of white, stuck all with yew,
O prepare it!   55
My part of death, no one so true
Did share it.

24. *favour:* permission (note the play on the word. Orsino is actually her favored one).

26. *What years:* What age is she?

29. *so wears she to him:* She adapts herself to him.

30. *So sways she level:* so she keeps a steady affection for him.

45. *silly sooth:* simple truth.

46. *dallies:* toys with.

49. *prithee:* I entreat you.

52. *sad cypress:* a coffin of dark cypress wood.

Not a flower, not a flower sweet,
On my black coffin let there be strown;
Not a friend, not a friend greet   60
My poor corpse, where my bones shall be thrown.
A thousand thousand sighs to save,
Lay me, oh, where
Sad true lover never find my grave,
To weep there!   65

Duke There's for thy pains.

Clown No pains, sir; I take pleasure in singing, sir.

Duke I'll pay thy pleasure then.

Clown Truly, sir, and pleasure will be paid, one
time or another.   70

Duke Give me now leave to leave thee.

Clown Now, the melancholy god protect thee; and
the tailor make thy doublet of changeable taffeta,
for thy mind is a very opal. I would have men of
such constancy put to sea, that their business might   75
be everything and their intent everywhere; for that's
it that always makes a good voyage of nothing.
Farewell.
[Exit.]

Duke Let all the rest give place.

[CURIO and Attendants retire.]
Once more, Cesario,
Get thee to yond same sovereign cruelty.
Tell her, my love, more noble than the world,   80
Prizes not quantity of dirty lands;
The parts that fortune hath bestow'd upon her,
Tell her, I hold as giddily as fortune;
But 'tis that miracle and queen of gems,
That nature pranks her in, attracts my soul.   85

Viola But if she cannot love you, sir?

Duke I cannot be so answer'd.

Viola   Sooth, but you must.
Say that some lady, as perhaps there is,
Hath for your love as great a pang of heart

73. *changeable taffeta:* shot silk which changes color as the light changes.

74. *opal:* a gem with changeable colors according to the light.

78. *give place:* leave us alone.

79. *sovereign cruelty:* this cruel woman who rules my life; or this queen of cruelty.

81. *prizes not quantity...:* does not value her real estate.

85. *pranks:* decorates.

86. *Sooth:* truth or truly.

As you have for Olivia. You cannot love her;   90
You tell her so; must she not then be answer'd?

Duke There is no woman's sides
Can bide the beating of so strong a passion
As love doth give my heart; no woman's heart
So big, to bold so much. They lack retention.   95
Alas, their love may be called appetite, —
No motion of the liver, but the palate, —
That suffer surfeit, cloyment and revolt;
But mine is all as hungry as the sea,
And can digest as much. Make no compare   100
Between that love a woman can bear me
And that I owe Olivia.

Viola   Ay, but I know —

Duke What dost thou know?

Viola Too well what love women to men may owe.
In faith, they are as true of heart as we.   105
My father had a daughter loved a man,
As it might be, perhaps, were I a woman.
I should your lordship.

Duke   And what's her history?

Viola A blank, my lord. She never told her love,
But let concealment, like a worm i' the bud,   110
Feed on her damask cheek. She pined in thought,
And with a green and yellow melancholy
She sat like patience on a monument,
Smiling at brief. Was not this love indeed?
We men may say more, swear more; but indeed   115
Our shows are more than will; for still we prove
Much in our vows, but little in our love.

Duke But died thy sister of her love, my boy?

Viola I am all the daughters of my father's house,
And all the brothers too; and yet I know not.   120
Sir, shall I to this lady?

Duke   Ay, that's the theme.
To her in haste; give her this jewel; say,
My love can give no place, bide no denay.
[Exeunt.]

97.   *motion of the liver:* The liver was regarded as the seat of the passions.

        palate: taste-buds in the mouth.

98.   *suffer surfeit:* experience an excess. (note the alliteration of the sibilant-s).

        cloyment: weary by too much of anything sweet and pleasant.

110.   *worm i' the bud:* a cankerworm eating through a rose bud.

111.   *damask:* silky smooth as a Damascus rose.

        pined in thought: brooded over it.

113.   *She sat like patience on a monument:* a perfect simile to express calm endurance and waiting.

121.   *shall I:* (go again) to this lady (Olivia).

        theme: main intent.

123.   *denay:* noun (substantive); old form of denial.

COMMENTARY

At Orsino's palace, the musicians play for the pleasure of Orsino. The Duke asks to hear a song that he heard the night before, as it relieved him of his passion, but the singer (Feste) is not present. While Curio goes off in search of Feste, the Duke and Cesario discuss love.

Orsino, inveterate egotist that he is, imagines himself the model of all true lovers, because he can keep nothing in mind except his loved one. Yet, Orsino's talk of love is not centered on Olivia; it is his own image as a suffering lover that he fixates on. Orsino is in love with the idea of love, but his narcissism prevents him from truly experiencing it. He is incapable of giving himself to another or making a true sacrifice; he is only capable of "performing" love as a one-man show of romanticized suffering.

Cesario, however, is no narcissist; in fact, she willingly abnegates her own identity (Viola) so as to serve her love. Her understanding of love is learned through acts of sacrifice and service; she comes to know her lover by tending to his needs. She even woos Olivia for Orsino, when she would rather woo Orsino for herself.

Shakespeare also differentiates their conception of love in the style of verse that he gives the two characters. Orsino's verse is magniloquent and rhetorical, the verse of public formal utterance. Viola speaks in verse that is intimate and honest.

Orsino finds Cesario's talk of love masterly and assumes that Cesario must be in love, so he asks who Cesario loves. Viola describes her lover, Orsino, elliptically. The Duke advises Cesario to love a woman younger than himself. Despite his many arguments to the opposite, Orsino now claims that a man's love is more giddy and unfirm than a woman's is.

Viola closes the conversation on a melancholy note; after Orsino's comparison of a woman and a rose, implying his interest in a woman dies the moment he has deflowered her (or at least seen the full display of her beauty and womanhood). Viola accepts and mourns the fate of being such a rose: To die, even when they to perfection grow! The line's pathos stems from Viola's recognition that male love — and her beloved Orsino's, in particular — is indeed short-lived and giddy. This information comes as a surprise to Viola, as Orsino would never dare to be so honest on these topics if he knew he were speaking to a woman.

Although Orsino has said that the song is "silly sooth, and dallies with the innocence of love," it expresses a tragic attitude towards life. The theme of the song is the sadness that leads to the death of a young man whose love for a fair cruel maid was unrequited. The song expresses Orsino's mood. His calling it silly, rather than grave, calls attention to his own experience of being an unrequited lover, which he evidently does not take all that seriously.

Orsino attempts to pay Feste for his pains, but Feste would rather be paid for his pleasure. In return for his payment, Feste praises the Duke. At least it seems like praise, but in fact, he is gently mocking Orsino's changeable moods and lack of constancy. And Feste has him nailed, for all his talk of constancy, Orsino never seems to know what he wants. His appetite rules him, but it is not a healthy appetite. He is hungry for music one minute, the next he has had too much music and is sick of it. The same goes for Orsino's pleasure in Feste's fooling. Even Orsino's love for Olivia lacks constancy; he describes it as "giddy" and

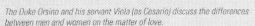

The Duke Orsino and his servant Viola (as Cesario) discuss the differences between men and women on the matter of love.

"light" in one moment, and "hungry as the sea" the next. This is not the first time in this play, or many other of Shakespeare's plays, that the Fool uses his foolery to provide a mirror for the other characters — a mirror designed to jar the viewer into self-knowledge.

After Feste exits, the Duke tells Cesario to go to Olivia again. Cesario asks what happens "if she cannot love you, sir?" but Orsino will not accept that as a possibility. Then Cesario puts the case to him in a different light: Say that some lady loves you as much as you love Olivia, you cannot love her, you tell her so. Mustn't she accept your answer?

Orsino denies that a woman could love with as great a pang of heart as he can. And in contradistinction to his last speech on male love (which he himself characterized as "giddy," "unfirm," and so on), Orsino reverses the terms, declaring women's love all appetite that may suffer surfiet and revolt, while his own love is hungry as the sea and can digest as much. This egotistical nonsense hurts Viola to hear it. She knows the love that women can bear for men. Women are as true in heart, if not truer. Viola tells Orsino a story that is a thinly veiled account of her love for the Duke. The story expresses the quiet sacrifice that she bears for her love; she keeps it hidden and allows it to feed on her youth.

Viola, in her disguise as Cesario, is able to talk to her lover in a way that she could not do as a woman; she takes advantage of this situation and schools Orsino on the realities of love. She counters the Duke's puffed-up rhetoric and narcissism with her own sad story, and in the end, the Duke is moved, but not yet changed, as he sends Cesario to Olivia, saying, "Ay, that's the theme," as if he were playing at courtship.

For all his histrionics and hyperbolic love poetry, Orsino conceives of love as something akin to a game or charade. Orsino's love is insubstantial, something to keep his boredom at bay — although he would never admit it. Yet, in this same scene, the gravity of love and the failure to love or be loved is impressed on us insistently. Love can hardly be spoken of without finding it in close proximity to death. Feste's song is about a young man who dies of unrequited love, as is the story of Viola's fictive twin pining away like Patience on a monument. Love consumes an individual in the same manner that death consumes life — both are processes that ineluctably move toward their conclusions totally beyond an individual's control. While Viola can envision her love as a sacrifice of her life, for Orsino, it is only his interest in a woman that inevitably dies — women, like roses, die once they are revealed/experienced.

Act II, Scene 5

Maria dupes Malvolio with a forged letter. Sir Toby, Fabian, and Andrew watch from behind a box tree. Malvolio promises to obey every item in the letter, word for word. Maria and the rest anticipate Malvolio's ensuing humiliation.

ACT II, SCENE 5
Olivia's garden.

[Enter SIR TOBY, SIR ANDREW, and FABIAN.]

Sir Toby Come thy ways, Signior Fabian.

Fabian Nay, I'll come; if I lose a scruple of this
sport, let me be boiled to death with melancholy.

Sir Toby Wouldst thou not be glad to have the nig-
gardly rascally sheep-biter come by some notable   5
shame?

Fabian I would exult, man. You know, he brought
me out o' favour with my lady about a bear-baiting
here.

Sir Toby To anger him we'll have the bear again;
and we will fool him black and blue. Shall we not,
Sir Andrew?

Sir Andrew An we do not, it is pity of our lives.   10

Sir Toby Here comes the little villain.

[Enter MARIA.]
How now, my metal of India!

Maria Get ye all three into the box-tree. Malvolio's
coming down this walk. He has been yonder i' the
sun practising behaviour to his own shadow this   15
half-hour. Observe him, for the love of mockery;
for I know this letter will make a contemplative
idiot of him. Close, in the name of jesting! Lie thou
there *[throws down a letter]*; for here comes the
trout that must be caught with tickling.   20
[Exit.]
[Enter MALVOLIO.]

Malvolio 'Tis but fortune; all is fortune. Maria
once told me she did affect me; and I have heard

NOTES

1.   *Signior:* Italian title for a gentleman (used famil-
iarly by Sir Toby).

2.   *scruple:* smallest part or iota.

5.   *sheep-biter:* (Malvolio), dog that worries sheep
on the sly.

7.   *bear-baiting:* form of sport in which dogs worried
a bear chained to a post. As a puritan, Malvolio
had probably reported Fabian for bear-baiting to
Olivia, who also disapproved of this cruel sport.

12.   *metal of India:* gold (priceless wench).

17.   *make a contemplative idiot of him:* fool him into
fantastic imaginings of himself as Olivia's lover
and husband.

20.   *trout that must be caught with tickling:* Malvolio
will be caught (trapped) by having his vanity
tickled.

herself come thus near, that should she fancy, it should be one of my complexion. Besides, she uses me with a more exalted respect than any one else that follows her. What should I think on't?   25

Sir Toby Here's an overweening rogue!

Fabian Oh, peace! Contemplation makes a rare turkey-cock of him. How he jets tinder his advanced plumes!

Sir Andrew 'Slight, I could so beat the rogue!   30

Sir Toby Peace, I say.

Malvolio To be Count Malvolio!

Sir Toby Ah, rogue!

Sir Andrew Pistol him, pistol him.

Sir Toby Peace, peace!   35

Malvolio There is example for't; the lady of the Strachy married the yeoman of the wardrobe.

Sir Andrew Fie on him, Jezebel!

Fabian O, peace! now he's deeply in. Look how imagination blows him.   40

Malvolio Having been three months married to her, sitting in my state, —

Sir Toby Oh, for a stone-bow, to hit him in the eye.

Malvolio Calling my officers about me, in my branched velvet gown; having come from a day-bed, where I have left Olivia sleeping, —   45

Sir Toby Fire and brimstone!

Fabian Oh, peace, peace!

Malvolio And then to have the humour of state; and after a demure travel of regard, telling them I know my place as I would they should do theirs, to ask for my kinsman Toby, —   50

Sir Toby Bolts and shackles!

Fabian Oh, peace, peace, peace! now, now.

Malvolio Seven of my people, with an obedient start,   55

26. *overweening:* arrogant, presumptuous.

28. *jets:* struts.

   advanced plumes: raised feathers (like a turkey-cock's).

30. *'Slight:* by God's light (common Elizabethan oath).

38. *Jezebel:* Ahab's shameless wife (1 Kings, xvi et seq.). Not a very appropriate epithet, but what should one expect from Sir Andrew?

43. *stone-bow:* crossbow for throwing stones.

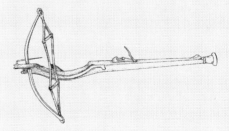

49. *humour of state:* dignified personality of the statesman.

50. *demure travel of regard:* allowing his eye to travel seriously from one to the other in the room.

52. *kinsman:* Sir Toby would have become a relative then. Note: he drops Sir Toby's title, calling him Toby.

make out for him. I frown the while; and perchance
wind up my watch, or play with my — some rich
jewel. Toby approaches; courtesies there to me, —

Sir Toby Shall this fellow live?

Fabian Though our silence be drawn from us with   60
cars, yet peace.

Malvolio I extend my hand to him thus, quenching
my familiar smile with an austere regard of control, —

Sir Toby And does not Toby take you a blow o' the
lips then?

Malvolio Saying, "Cousin Toby, my fortunes having   65
cast me on your niece give me this prerogative of
speech," —

Sir Toby What, what?

Malvolio "You must amend your drunkenness."

Sir Toby Out, scab!

Fabian Nay, patience, or we break the sinews of   70
our plot.

Malvolio "Besides, you waste the treasure of your
time with a foolish knight," —

Sir Andrew That's me, I warrant you.

Malvolio "One Sir Andrew," —

Sir Andrew I knew 'twas I; for many do call me fool.   75

Malvolio What employment have we here? *[Taking up the
letter.]*

Fabian Now is the woodcock near the gin.

Sir Toby Oh, peace! and the spirit of humours intimate reading aloud to him!

Malvolio By my life, this is my lady's hand. These   80
be her very C's, her U's, and her T's; and thus makes
she her great P's. It is, in contempt of question, her
hand.

Sir Andrew Her C's, her U's, and her T's. Why that?

Malvolio *[Reads.]* "To the unknown beloved, this,

57. *my...:* Malvolio was about to say "my chain" indicating his office as steward, but he recalls that
he would not then occupy this lowly place, so
quickly changes to "some rich jewel."

61. *cars:* chariots or carriages (a form of torture in
which the victim was torn apart between two
such vehicles).

77. *gin:* trap (the woodcock was believed to be a
rather unintelligent sort of bird).

78. *spirit of humours:* in this case the spirit of comedies rather than of elements and proportions.

81. *C's...U's...T's:* Some editors believe that this is a
bawdy joke. They argue that "cut" was a word for
the pudendum.

and my good wishes:" — her very phrases! By your   85
leave, wax. Soft! and the impressure her Lucrece,
with which she uses to seal. 'Tis my lady. To whom
should this be?

Fabian This wins him liver and all.

Malvolio *[Reads.]*
Jove knows I love;
But who?   90
Lips, do not move;
No man must know.
"No man must know." What follows? the numbers
altered. "No man must know" — if this should be thee,
Malvolio?   95

Sir Toby Marry, hang thee, brock!

Malvolio *[Reads.]*
I may command where I adore;
But silence, like a Lucrece knife,
With bloodless stroke my heart doth gore.
M, O, A, I, doth sway my life.   100

Fabian A fustian riddle!

Sir Toby Excellent wench, say I.

Malvolio "M, O, A, I, doth sway my life." Nay, but
first, let me see, let me see, let me see.

Fabian What dish o' poison has she dressed him?   105

Sir Toby And with what wing the staniel checks at it!

Malvolio "I may command where I adore." Why she
may command me: I serve her; she is my lady. Why,
this is evident to any formal capacity; there is no
obstruction in this. And the end, — what should that   110
alphabetical position portend? If I could make that
resemble something in me, — Softly! M,O,A,I, —

Sir Toby Oh, ay, make up that; he is now at a cold
scent.

Fabian Sowter will cry upon't for all this, though it
be as rank as a fox.

Malvolio M, — Malvolio; M, — why, that begins my   115
name.

---

86.   *Lucrece:* seal engraved with the head of the Roman matron Lucretia, who committed suicide rather than submit to being dishonored.

93.   *the numbers altered:* the metre changes.

96.   *brock:* badger or skunk.

100. *M,O,A,I,:* One critic suggests that these letters may stand for Mare, Orbis, Aer, and Ignis, i.e., Water, Earth, Air, and Fire, the four elements of which the various humors are composed. Another critic suggests that Shakespeare here threw a glance towards the French essayist, MONTAIGNE. Since Maria composed the letter (in theory), may the letters not have differed from MALVOLIO's name just enough to confuse him?

101. *fustian:* bombastic, ridiculously pompous (when used as an adjective).

106. *staniel:* The hawk is distracted away from the prey by a worthless bird.

114. *Sowter:* dog's name, a bungling hound.

Fabian Did not I say he would work it out? the cur is excellent at faults.

Malvolio M, — but then there is no consonancy in the sequel; that suffers tinder probation. A should follow, but O does.   120

Fabian And O shall end, I hope.

Sir Toby Ay or I'll cudgel him, and make him cry O!

Malvolio And then I comes behind.

Fabian Ay, an you had any eye behind you, you might see more detraction at your heels than fortunes before you.   125

Malvolio M, O, A, I. This simulation is not as the former; and yet, to crush this a little, it would bow to me, for every one of these letters are in my name. Soft! here follows prose.   130
[*Reads.*] "If this fall into thy hand, revolve. In my stars I am above thee; but be not afraid of greatness: some are born great, some achieve greatness, and some have greatness thrust upon 'em. Thy fates open their hands; let thy blood and spirit embrace them;   135
and, to inure thyself to what thou art like to be, cast thy humble slough and appear fresh. Be opposite with a kinsman, surly with servants; let thy tongue tang arguments of state; put thyself into the trick of singularity. She thus advises thee that sighs for thee. Remember who commended thy yellow stockings,   140
and wished to see thee ever cross-gartered. I say, remember. Go to, thou art made, if thou desirest to be so; if not, let me see thee a steward still, the fellow of servants, and not worthy to touch Fortune's fingers. Farewell. She that would alter services with thee,   145
    "THE FORTUNATE-UNHAPPY."
Daylight and champain discovers not more. This is open. I will be proud, I will read politic authors, I will baffle Sir Toby, I will wash off gross acquaintance, I will be point-devise the very man. I do not now fool myself, to let imagination jade me; for   150
every reason excites to this, that my lady loves me.

---

119. *no consonancy in the sequel...:* a pompous punning way of indicating that the consonants are in the wrong order (consonance, sequence).

120. *suffers tinder probation:* does not stand up to the proof (of observation).

125. *Ay... eye* (and the previously mentioned letter I): a play upon these words.

127. *simulation:* method of representing.

128. *to crush this...:* With a little straining it would fit me.

131. *revolve:* here means consider (but Malvolio literally turns around on stage).

137. *slough:* snake skin, garments he wears now.

139. *trick of singularity:* mannerisms that make you stand out from the others.

146. *champain:* flat open country.
discovers: reveals.

147. *open:* The way is clear.
politic: political.

149. *point-devise:* to the point of perfection.

150. *jade:* deceive or fool.

She did commend my yellow stockings of late, she
did praise my leg being cross-gartered; and in this
she manifests herself to my love, and with a kind of
injunction drives me to these habits of her liking. I   155
thank my stars I am happy. I will be strange, stout,
in yellow stockings, and cross-gartered, even with
the swiftness of putting on. Jove and my stars be
praised! Here is yet a postscript.
[Reads.] "Thou canst not choose but know who I   160
am. If thou entertainest my love, let it appear in thy
smiling. Thy smiles become thee well; therefore in
my presence still smile, dear my sweet, I prithee."
Jove, I thank thee. I will smile; I will do everything that thou wilt have me.   165
[Exit.]

Fabian I will not give my part of this sport for a
pension of thousands to be paid from the Sophy.

Sir Toby I could marry this wench for this device.

Sir Andrew So could I too.

Sir Toby And ask no other dowry with her but   170
such another jest.

Sir Andrew Nor I neither.

Fabian Here comes my noble gull-catcher.

[Re-enter MARIA.]

Sir Toby Wilt thou set thy foot o' my neck?

Sir Andrew Or o' mine either?   175

Sir Toby Shall I play my freedom at tray-trip, and
become thy bond-slave?

Sir Andrew I' faith, or I either?

Sir Toby Why, thou hast put him in such a dream,
that when the image of it leaves him he must run   180
mad.

Maria Nay, but say true; does it work upon him?

Sir Toby Like aqua vitae with a midwife.

Maria If you will then see the fruits of the sport,
mark his first approach before my lady. He will

156.   *strange:* distant, stand-offish.

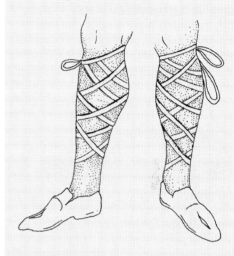

167.   *Sophy:* palace of the Shah of Persia.

173.   *gull-catcher:* Maria (the gull that she has caught
being, of course, Malvolio).

174.   *set thy foot o' my neck:* i.e., act as the victor in a
duel and show that she has him at her mercy.

176.   *tray-trip:* a game played with dice; the object of the
game was to throw three consecutive threes.

182.   *aqua vitae:* literally ardent spirits (high proof alcohol, probably brandy).

midwife: may have been administered to mothers
at childbirth by midwives, or else drunk by midwives
to relieve the tedium of waiting.

come to her in yellow stockings, and 'tis a colour she   185
abhors; and cross-gartered, a fashion she detests; and
he will smile upon her, which will now be so unsuit-
able to her disposition, being addicted to a melancholy as she is, that it cannot but turn him into a notable contempt. If you will see it, follow me.

Sir Toby To the gates of Tartar, thou most excel-   190
lent devil of wit!

Sir Andrew I'll make one too.
[Exeunt.]

189. *notable contempt:* well known object of contempt, notorious.

190. *Tartar:* Tartary, or Tartarus, the infernal regions of classical (Greek) mythology, hell.

Note how Sir Andrew's answers are all feeble reflections of Sir Toby's replies.

COMMENTARY

This scene, the gulling of Malvolio, is one of the most comic of the play. Sir Toby, Sir Andrew, and Fabian (a servant of Olivia's, who also has a long-standing grudge against Malvolio), have met at the appointed time in Olivia's garden, and they can't wait to fool Malvolio black and blue. (Feste, it should be noted, is conspicuously absent.) Maria arrives, and Sir Toby and friends greet the brains of the organization with appropriate enthusiasm. Maria tells them to hide in the box-tree and observe Malvolio, then she drops the counterfeit letter where he will find it and exits.

Fabian, Sir Toby, and Sir Andrew hide in a box-tree to witness the gulling of Malvolio. From a Royal Shakespeare Company production of Twelfth Night.
Clive Barda/PAL

Before Malvolio has even seen the letter, he is dreaming aloud of Olivia and imagining that she loves him. Malvolio is so full of self-love that we are sure the device will work on him. If everyone in the play has an appetite that must be glutted to surfeit before the play's end, with Malvolio, his appetite is his self-love. Malvolio is so hungry for an elevation in status and social class commensurate with his own yet-to-be-recognized greatness, he will feast himself on the counterfeit presentment of his greatness, that is, the preposterous promises of the letter.

As he walks down the path toward the letter, he practices behavior to his own shadow; he pretends to be a Count! He imagines the glorious moment of waking in bed next to the Countess, the velvet gown he would put on, and the haughty behavior that he would practice on the other members of the household. Malvolio imagines aloud an encounter with Sir Toby in which the knight curtsies to Malvolio. Sir Toby, Andrew, and Fabian can hardly contain their anger and disgust. It is worth noting that, although Malvolio's behavior in his fantasies is not so different than in reality, the responses of the other characters to his pride and condescension have changed radically — they recognize his right to behave *as if he were a Count*.

Much of the humor in this scene relies on the amusing commentary of the hidden auditors — Toby, Fabian, and Andrew — as they react to Malvolio's speech and comment on the unfolding action. Malvolio cannot hear their scathing asides, but the audience can; this stage device allows the humor to build while the action they comment on continues without interruption. Shakespeare utilizes this convention to great comic effect in many of his comedies. In *Much Ado About Nothing,* the hidden Dons mock Benedict's conversion from confirmed bachelor to wooer. In *Henry IV,* Prince Hal and Poins overhear Falstaff talking to Doll Tearsheet. And in *Troilus and Cressida,* Shakespeare ups the ante, as Thersites, unseen, mocks Troilus and Ulysses as they observe and comment upon Diomedes and Cressida. In general, the aside is a metatheatric gesture, in which the actors break the imaginary fourth wall between the audience and the action that takes place on stage. The character speaks directly to the audience, giving the nod to the double reality of the play world and the world that is watching the play.

Malvolio is jerked back to reality by the sight of the letter. He recognizes what he thinks is Olivia's handwriting. Malvolio has no trouble imagining himself "the unknown beloved" to whom the letter is addressed and opens the letter.

The letter begins with a riddle, "I may command where I adore." Malvolio gleefully cries out, "Why she may command me: I serve her; she is my lady." But when it comes to the passage, "M.O.A.I. does sway my life," Malvolio falters for a moment. His name may start with the letter M, but the rest of the letters are not in the same order as his name. "And yet, to crush this a little, it would bow to me..." Malvolio twists the text to fit his needs, which may be a subtle joke on the Puritans. The Puritans were thought to have crushed the meaning of the Holy Scriptures into a form that would better serve their own purposes.

Malvolio celebrates the greatness thrust upon him and the letter that he presumes is from Olivia. Nigel Hawthorne is Malvolio in the 1996 film, Twelfth Night. The Everett Collection

The letters MOAI are the first letters of each of the four elements in Latin. M stands for *mare,* or sea; O is *orbis,* or earth; A is *aer,* or air; and I is *ignis,* or fire. Thus Malvolio, by "crushing" the text, would in a sense be shaping the world into his own image, a truly sublime example of a man's hubris preceding his fall. Toby and the others playfully pun on the letters, too. Toby echoes the O.I. with his exclamation, "O, ay...." Fabian puns on the position of the letter O, as in *omega,* the last letter in the Greek alphabet, by saying, "And O shall end, I hope."

The body of the letter exhorts Malvolio to accept the greatness that is thrust upon him; in specific, he should be surly with servants, opposite with kinsman, and put himself into the trick of singularity. He is also advised to wear yellow stockings with cross garters and to smile all the time in Olivia's presence. The letter speaks directly to Malvolio's fantasy self; it perfectly blends concrete references to his present state as a steward and social inferiority to Olivia, as well as to his fantasies of greatness. The verisimilitude of the handwriting in itself could not convince Malvolio to fall for such a trick; he is duped by his own willingness to believe his own fantasies have indeed come true.

Maria has cleverly conceived a device that mimics the steward's own style of speech, which is full of pretentious phrases. And more to the point, this device will turn the sober, methodical steward into his opposite, a sportive fool. He is to wear sportive clothes, instead of his normally sober clothes, and greet the world, or at least Olivia, with smiling. Malvolio is giddy. He thinks all his dreams have come true in an instant, and he swears that he will do everything the letter commends.

Sir Toby and friends howl with laughter and praise the mischievous genius of Maria. Notice that Toby thinks to reward Maria by marrying her, which he feels he could do. This is the second time a possible marriage between Toby and Maria is mentioned (Feste is the first to comment on it in Act I), foreshadowing their marriage in Act V. Here, Maria anticipates the hilarity that will be the result of the first meeting between Olivia and the smiling Malvolio.

But Malvolio's daydreaming aloud makes this scene unbearably funny to watch. The tendency to imagine ourselves in erotic encounters, perhaps aggrandizing ourselves for the sake of fantasy, is universal. To be gulled into believing our fantasies are realities, as is the case with Malvolio, and to suffer the consequences for our egotistical flights of fantasy — the shame and embarrassment — is painful to watch. No doubt, our discomfort stems from the knowledge that it may just as well happen to us in the future – or has already happened in the past! Shakespeare is a masterful observer of the human condition, and it is a testament to his greatness that he is so often able to draw universal truths from the most individual and seemingly idiosyncratic experiences.

Notes

Notes

TWELFTH NIGHT
ACT III

Olivia *I prithee, tell me what thou think'st of me.*

Viola *That you do think you are not what you are.*

Olivia *If I think so, I think the same of you.*

Viola *Then think you right; I am not what I am.*

Olivia *I would you were as I would have you be!*

Viola *Would it be better, madam, than I am?*
I wish it might, for now I am your fool.

Act III, Scene 1

Viola encounters Feste on her way to see Olivia; she enjoys the Fool's witty wordplay. Soon after she runs into Sir Toby and Sir Andrew, Olivia arrives and talks to Viola in private, declaring her love for Viola.

ACT III, SCENE 1
Olivia's garden.

[Enter VIOLA, and Clown with a tabor.]

Viola Save thee, friend, and thy music. Dost thou live by thy tabor?

Clown No, sir, I live by the church.

Viola Art thou a churchman?

Clown No such matter, sir. I do live by the church; for I do live at my house, and my house doth stand by the church.

Viola So thou mayst say, the king lies by a beggar, if a beggar dwell near him; or, the church stands by thy tabor, if thy tabor stand by the church. 10

Clown You have said, sir. To see this age! A sentence is but a cheveril glove to a good wit. How quickly the wrong side may be turned outward!

Viola Nay, that's certain. They that dally nicely with words may quickly make them wanton. 15

Clown I would, therefore, my sister had had no name, sir.

Viola Why, man?

Clown Why, sir, her name's a word; and to dally with that word might make my sister wanton. But indeed words are very rascals since bonds disgraced them. 20

Viola Thy reason, man?

Clown Troth, sir, I can yield you none without words; and words are grown so false, I am loath to prove reason with them.

NOTES

1. *Save thee:* God save thee.

2. *tabor:* small drum used by professional clowns and jesters.

12. *cheveril glove:* kid leather (easily stretchable).

15. *wanton:* not chaste.

Viola I warrant thou art a merry fellow and carest
for nothing.

Clown Not so, sir, I do care for something; but in
my conscience, sir, I do not care for you. If that be
to care for nothing, sir, I would it would make you
invisible.

Viola Art not thou the Lady Olivia's fool?

Clown No, indeed, sir; the Lady Olivia has no folly.
She will keep no fool, sir, till she be married; and
fools are as like husbands as pilchards are to herrings;
the husband's the bigger. I am indeed not her fool,
but her corrupter of words.

Viola I saw thee late at the Count Orsino's.

Clown Foolery, sir, does walk about the orb like
the sun, it shines everywhere. I would be sorry, sir,
but the fool should be as oft with your master as
with my mistress. I think I saw your wisdom there.

Viola Nay, an thou pass upon me, I'll no more with
thee. Hold, there's expenses for thee.

Clown Now, Jove, in his next commodity of hair
send thee a beard!

Viola By my troth, I'll tell thee, I am almost sick
for one — *[aside.]* though I would not have it grow on
my chin. Is thy lady within?

Clown My lady is within, sir. I will construe to
them whence you come. Who you are and what you
would are out of my welkin, I might say element,
but the word is overworn.
[Exit.]

Viola This fellow is wise enough to play the fool;
And to do that well craves a kind of wit.
He must observe their mood on whom he jests,
The quality of persons, and the time,
And, like the haggard, check at every feather
That comes before his eye. This is a practice
As full of labour as a wise man's art;

25

30

35

40

45

50

55

35. *corrupter of words:* an excellent definition of Feste's kind of fooling.

37. *orb:* poetic word for world.

43. *commodity:* quantity of wares, parcel, supply.

48. *construe:* explain (in the scholastic sense).

50. *welkin:* sky (= element).

56. *haggard:* unschooled hawk.

check: swerve aside after.

feather: bird (apart from the true prey).

For folly that he wisely shows is fit,
But wise men, folly-fall'n, quite taint their wit.   60

[Enter SIR TOBY and SIR ANDREW.]

Sir Toby Save you, gentlemen.

Viola And you, Sir.

Sir Andrew Dieu vous garde, monsieur.

Viola Et vous aussi; votre serviteur.

Sir Andrew I hope, sir, you are; and I am yours.   65

Sir Toby Will you encounter the house? my niece
is desirous you should enter, if your trade be to her.

Viola I am bound to your niece, sir; I mean, she is
the list of my voyage.

Sir Toby Taste your legs, sir; put them to motion.   70

Viola My legs do better understand me, Sir, than I
understand what you mean by bidding me taste my
legs.

Sir Toby I mean, to go, sir, to enter.

Viola I will answer you with gait and entrance. But
we are prevented. *[Enter Olivia and Maria.]* Most   75
excellent accomplished lady, the heavens rain
odours on you!

Sir Andrew That youth's a rare courtier. "Rain
odours," well.

Viola My matter hath no voice, lady, but to your   80
own most pregnant and vouchsafed ear.

Sir Andrew "Odours," "pregnant," and "vouchsafed."
I'll get 'em all three all ready.

Olivia Let the garden door be shut, and leave me to
my hearing. *[Exeunt Sir Toby, Sir Andrew, and
Maria.]* Give me your hand, sir.   85

Viola My duty, madam, and most humble service.

Olivia What is your name?

Viola Cesario is your servant's name, fair princess.

---

59. *folly, etc:* The folly Feste shows reveals his basic intelligence and wisdom.

60. *But wise men, etc.:* but wise men who indulge in folly show themselves to be fundamentally foolish.

63. *Dieu vous garde:* the two knights employ French (the language of dueling) out of mocking regard for Cesario.

66. *encounter:* affected way of saying go into.

69. *list:* limit, boundary, purpose.

70. *Taste:* test.

71–72. *understand... understand:* stand under ... comprehend.

74. *gait:* walking (play on gate, entrance).

75. *prevented:* the others have arrived before us (Latin for come-before), hence forestalled.

81. *pregnant:* ready.
vouchsafed: offered, ready, attentive.

Olivia My servant, sir! 'Twas never merry world
Since lowly feigning was called compliment.
You're servant to the Count Orsino, youth.

Viola And he is yours, and his must needs be yours.
Your servant's servant is your servant, madam.

Olivia For him, I think not on him; for his thoughts,
Would they were blanks, rather than fill'd with me !

Viola Madam, I come to whet your gentle thoughts
On his behalf.

Olivia   Oh, by your leave, I pray you,
I bade you never speak again of him;
But, would you undertake another suit,
I had rather hear you to solicit that
Than music from the spheres.

Viola   Dear lady, —

Olivia Give me leave, beseech you. I did send,
After the last enchantment you did here,
A ring in chase of you; so did I abuse
Myself, my servant, and I fear me, you.
Under your hard construction must I sit,
To force that on you, in a shameful cunning,
Which you knew none of yours. What might you think?
Have you not set mine honour at the stake
And baited it with all the unmuzzled thoughts
That tyrranous heart can think? To one of your receiving
Enough is shown. A cypress, not a bosom,
Hideth my heart. So, let me hear you speak.

Viola I pity you.

Olivia   That's a degree to love.

Viola No, not a grize; for 'tis a vulgar proof,
That very oft we pity enemies.

Olivia Why, then, methinks 'tis time to smile again.
O world, how apt the poor are to be proud!
If one should be a prey, how much the better
To fall before the lion than the wolf!
[Clock strikes.]
The clock upbraids me with the waste of time.
Be not afraid, good youth, I will not have you;

90

95

100

105

110

115

120

90. *lowly feigning:* sham humility.

101. *music from the spheres:* According to Pythagoras, the universe consisted of eight hollow spheres, inside of which the earth and all the other planets are fixed. The spheres produced a note each which combined to produce perfect harmony which is inaudible to the human ear. The earth is at the center of this system.

106. *hard construction:* uncharitable interpretation.

111. *receiving:* sensitive understanding.

112. *cypress:* black gauze used for mourning.

115. *grize:* step, whit.

vulgar proof: common knowledge.

120. *lion... wolf:* nobleman... servant. If Olivia sounds bitter, it is only because she is making a great effort to control her feelings.

And yet, when wit and youth is come to harvest,
Your wife is like to reap a proper man.
There lies your way, due west.   125

Viola   Then westward-ho!
Grace and good disposition attend your ladyship!
You'll nothing, madam, to my lord by me?

Olivia Stay,
I prithee, tell me what thou think'st of me.

Viola That you do think you are not what you are.

Olivia If I think so, I think the same of you.   130

Viola Then think you right; I am not what I am.

Olivia I would you were as I would have you be!

Viola Would it be better, madam, than I am?
I wish it might, for now I am your fool.

Olivia Oh, what a deal of scorn looks beautiful   135
In the contempt and anger of his lip!
A murderous guilt shows not itself more soon
Than love that would seem hid. Love's night is noon.
Cesario, by the roses of the spring,
By maidhood, honour, truth and everything,   140
I love thee so, that, maugre all thy pride,
Nor wit nor reason can my passion hide.
Do not extort thy reasons from this clause,
For that I woo, thou therefore hast no cause;
But rather reason thus with reason fetter,   145
Love sought is good, but given unsought is better.

Viola By innocence I swear, and by my youth,
I have one heart, one bosom and one truth,
And that no woman has; nor never none
Shall mistress be of it, save I alone.   150
And so adieu, good madam. Never more
Will I my master's tears to you deplore.

Olivia Yet come again; for thou perhaps mayest move
That heart, which now abhors, to like his love.
[Exeunt.]

141.   *maugre:* despite (Fr. malgre).

143–144.   *Do not extort...cause:* Do not conclude that because I woo you, you have no reason for wooing me...

145.   *But...fetter:* but restrain your reason with the following reasons...

151.   *adieu:* The final form is used for farewell.

COMMENTARY

Viola encounters Feste on her way to Olivia's house. She asks him if he lives by his tabor, that is, does he earn a living by playing his drum. Feste's response shows her exactly how he earns his living: He plays with words. He says that he lives by the church. Is he a churchman, she asks, thinking (or playing at thinking) that he means *by* in the sense of *in accordance to the laws of*. No, he replies, but his house stands by (as in *next to*) the church. This initial exchange, punning on three different meanings and/or usages of the basic word *by*, illustrates the pleasures of wordplay and of discovering the slipperiness of language, even though, taken too far, such wordplay can have dangerous ramifications and prevent any possibility of communication.

Viola shows herself to be as adept at "fool-talk" as Feste is, and she catches Feste off guard (a rare thing in this play) by taking Feste's wordplay to its "logical" conclusion (8–10). When Feste responds, "A sentence is but a chevril's glove to a good wit. How quickly the wrong side may be turned outward," he is momentarily shaken that Viola has bettered him in follying. His response is not merely spoken out of joy that he has found someone else who can play with words as well as he, but it also shows his irritation at this saucy youth (perhaps with a little jealousy, insofar as Olivia does not need his services as much now that Cesario is around).

In this brief exchange, we see that Cesario has practically usurped Feste's role of fool and has cast him unwittingly, if only for a second, into the role of straight man. The fool attempts to show that words cannot be trusted, and that the relationship between words and things is at times arbitrary, yet Viola responds that the fault is not so much in the words as in "they that dally nicely" with them (meaning Feste). Just as a "wanton," or unchaste, woman cannot be entirely blamed for being wanton (that is, it takes two to tango), neither can a word be blamed for the way people abuse it.

As Feste makes the indeterminacy of words and meaning apparent, Viola shows us that gender identity works by the same principle. It is what it is until someone turns it inside out, as she has done. To the world, she is a boy until her gender is turned inside out, and she becomes a woman again.

Cesario asks Feste whether he is Olivia's fool. No, Olivia will keep no fool until she has a husband, he says.

Feste is Olivia's corrupter of words. A fine distinction perhaps, but there is a difference between the foolery of Sir Andrew or the foolish fawning of Orsino compared to the thoughtful fooling of Feste. As a self-proclaimed "corruptor of words," Feste loves words enough to lose his own cares in them. He is thus able to help others forget their cares and find "present mirth" without having to turn to alcohol as Sir Toby does.

Viola pays Feste for his fooling, and in return, he prays that Jove will send Cesario a beard, noticing his hairless chin. Viola replies that she is almost sick for one, turning the phrase to mean a husband (as a wink to the audience, for we alone know that she means Orsino). Viola is an adept corrupter of words herself and can appreciate the difference between simple foolishness (that is, misunderstanding) and good fooling, that is, revealing the double meaning of a word or phrase purposely.

Viola soliloquizes on the nature of the fool's profession; to do it well demands intelligence and sensitivity to other people's moods and limits. He must wisely show the folly of others in a way that is edifying, or as in Feste's enemies, provide an opportunity for self-knowledge to the person wittily attacked. Shakespeare might sum up the demands of his own profession with similar words.

Sir Toby and Sir Andrew greet Cesario. Andrew attempts again to show off his small knowledge of French again. But he is shocked into dumbness (or at least halting English) when he receives a reply in French. At every turn, Viola shows herself to be full of good qualities and hidden talents. She can corrupt words with Feste, philosophize about love with Orsino, and speak French with Andrew. Is it any wonder that Olivia and Orsino are attracted to her company?

Andrew's confused reaction to Cesario's French is followed in quick succession by Sir Toby's "taste your legs" racing jargon comment, which Cesario does not comprehend. Both instances of lack of understanding demonstrate the failure of language to act as a medium for communication. As Feste says, "words have grown so false, I am loath to prove reason with them." Yet if we compare this exchange with Cesario and Feste's earlier exchange in this scene, in which both participants *do* understand each other's double entendres, we notice again that language is not to be blamed for people's failure to communicate with each other.

Cesario greets Olivia with what seems a parody of a courtly poetical expression — at least to Sir Andrew, who notices the *unsavory* connotations of the words, "rain odours" and "pregnant," and files these phrases (which he misunderstands) away in his memory for later use. Thoroughly impressed by such nonsense, this aside explains much about Andrew's manner of education. No doubt he learned his French as well as his mastery of dance in a similar fashion; he steals the scraps of other people's knowledge and talents. And when he attempts to recycle them, he does so in an inane and foolish fashion. Yet Andrew's interjections do serve (however unintentionally) a function in the play by pointing out that Cesario's language has become increasingly strained when talking to Olivia. It is getting more difficult for Viola to maintain her part as Orsino's emissary to Olivia, and her language betrays this difficulty.

Olivia attempts to woo Viola (as Cesario).

Olivia dismisses her followers so that she may be alone with Cesario. Olivia is a person with authority and status; she is the head of her household. But being new to that authority (it is only since her father's death), her natural tendency is to overplay her new role as authoritarian. We saw a hint of this in her imperious command to "Take the fool away!" in Act I, Scene 5. But just as Feste was able to return Olivia to her kinder, gentler self, in this scene, she allows herself to be vulnerable and submit to the will of Cesario, a servant. Her willingness to be vulnerable makes us like her. She does not hide behind her role as head of the household now that she is in love; she surrenders to love.

Olivia, who cannot love Orsino, has no trouble falling in love with Cesario. Why? Is it Viola's wit and youth that make her attractive to Olivia? Her hard-to-get act? Her indifference? Or is it possible that Olivia feels safer giving her love to someone who she knows will not accept it. This way she can feel generous and capable of loving without ever risking her heart. Only her pride is on the line in this scene. Or perhaps Shakespeare wanted to show how arbitrary love is in its origin, that falling in

love is not even dependent on gender. Olivia falls in love with Viola, a woman. Some critics have argued that it is Cesario's feminine appearance that is responsible for Olivia's attraction to her.

Olivia made her love known to Cesario by sending her ring after him. Now, in this scene, Olivia wants to know whether Cesario can love her in return. Olivia is not interested in hearing about Orsino at all, but one word from Cesario would sound sweeter than celestial music. Viola replies that she can only pity Olivia and denies that her pity is allied to any feeling of love or affection.

Though disappointed in Cesario's refusal, Olivia behaves with dignity, and does not fall to pitying herself. Olivia exhibits considerable strength and resilience. But she cannot quite dismiss Cesario without finding out what he thinks of her.

Now follows an interchange of rapid, give-and-take repartee that plays on the nature of their respective identities. Cesario suggests that Olivia has forgotten she is a noble by courting a servant like himself. And Olivia replies that he does the same by forgetting that he was born a gentleman. Viola's answer, "I am not that I am," plays on the question of both rank and gender. She is not only of noble birth; she is also a woman. And growing frustrated with playing her role, or roles, she ends the game by saying she will no longer play Olivia's fool.

When Cesario tells Olivia, "now I am your fool," we remember Feste's claims earlier in this scene that Olivia will "keep no fool till she be married." Throughout this exchange, Cesario and Olivia are so clearly at cross-purposes. Olivia seems to be learning valuable truths about love and herself from Cesario, but to Cesario this scene is a tedious rerun of their earlier encounters.

The exchange is not so tedious for the audience, however. Even though this scene does nothing to further the plot, Shakespeare's language here includes many examples of his masterful use of double meanings. For example, in Cesario's final speech in this scene, she says, "I have one heart, one bosom, and one truth, / And that no woman has; nor never none / Shall be mistress of it, save I alone." We become aware that the *meaning* of this statement is different to the audience (who knows Cesario is in fact a woman, that is, if we forget that the actor playing her is a boy) than it is to Olivia (who thinks Cesario is a man). If Olivia really listened to Cesario's words ("save I alone"), she would have to conclude that Cesario is a woman, but love in this play is not only blind but also deaf.

Olivia seems, on the contrary, to take some comfort in Cesario's words, which are so clearly (to us) meant *not* to lead Olivia on, because she only hears what she wants to hear. Olivia holds out hope because it seems to her that, in this speech, Cesario is not merely rejecting Olivia, but all women. Olivia has become uncannily similar to Orsino as we met him at the beginning of the play, whose hope that Olivia may yet return his affections is fueled by Olivia's refusal of *every* suitor.

Olivia's response to Cesario's scorn is an all-out declaration of love. She is indifferent to Orsino's love but driven madly in love by Cesario's scorn. Why? It is Olivia's pride that cannot withstand this check. If she is as worthy a catch as she believes she is — and Orsino would have her believe that she is — why isn't Cesario in love with her? The fact that he isn't in love with her is a challenge to her pride and her own sense of value as a marriageable woman.

Cesario makes it clear that he will never love Olivia and never more return. In desperation, Olivia asks that Cesario return again, if only to plead to her Orsino's love. It is difficult to tell whether Olivia's final lines are sincere here. Is Olivia really considering changing her mind about Orsino, or is she saying this as another thinly veiled ruse to get Cesario to visit her again? Shakespeare does not directly answer this question, but judging by the next (and final) time Olivia and Cesario play out this scene (III.4.209–225), the latter possibility is the more likely interpretation.

Act III, Scene 2

Sir Andrew, believing his courtship of Olivia is doomed, prepares to leave. Sir Toby persuades him to stay and encourages him to challenge Cesario to a duel in order to win Olivia's respect. Sir Andrew goes off to write his challenge. Maria enters, alerting the others that Malvolio is on his way to Olivia and will soon be disgraced.

ACT III, SCENE 2
A room in Olivia's house.

[Enter SIR TOBY, SIR ANDREW, and FABIAN.]

Sir Andrew No, faith, I'll not stay a jot longer.

Sir Toby Thy reason, dear venom, give thy reason.

Fabian You must needs yield your reason, Sir Andrew.

Sir Andrew Marry, I saw your niece do more favours to the count's serving-man than ever she bestowed upon me. I saw't i' the orchard.   5

Sir Toby Did she see thee the while, old boy? Tell me that.

Sir Andrew As plain as I see you now.

Fabian This was a great argument of love in her toward you.   10

Sir Andrew Will you make an ass o' me?

Fabian I will prove it legitimate, sir, upon the oaths of judgment and reason.

Sir Toby And they have been grand-jurymen since before Noah was a sailor.

Fabian She did show favour to the youth in your   15
sight only to exasperate you, to awake your dormouse valour, to put fire in your heart, and brimstone in your liver. You should then have accosted her; and with some excellent jests, fire-new from the mint, you should have hanged the youth into dumb-   20
ness. This was looked for at your hand, and this was balked. The double gilt of this opportunity you let time wash off, and you are now sailed into the north of my lady's opinion, where you will hang like an

NOTES

5.   *count's serving-man:* Cesario.

13. *prove it legitimate:* An oath has to fulfill three conditions, truth, judgment, and reason; Fabian deliberately omits the first condition, truth.

14. *grand-jurymen:* members of a grand jury, a body that enquired into a case to decide whether it merited going forward to trial.

17–18.   *dormouse valour:* small amount of bravery; sleeping valour.

23. *balked:* missed.

     double gilt: a doubly golden opportunity.

24. *north, etc:* You are now in disfavor with your lady.

icicle on a Dutchman's beard, unless you do redeem   25
it by some laudable attempt either of valour or
policy.

Sir Andrew An't be any way, it must be with
valour; for policy I hate. I had as lief be a Brownist as a politician.

Sir Toby Why then. build me thy fortunes upon the
basis of valour. Challenge me the count's youth to   30
fight with him; hurt him in eleven places. My niece
shall take note of it; and assure thyself, there is no
love-broker in the world can more prevail in man's
commendation with woman than report of valour.

Fabian There is no way but this, Sir Andrew.   35

Sir Andrew Will either of you bear me a challenge
to him?

Sir Toby Go, write it in a martial hand; be curst
and brief; it is no matter how witty, so it be eloquent
and full of invention. Taunt him with the licence of
ink. If thou thou'st him some thrice, it shall not be   40
amiss; and as many lies as will lie in thy sheet of
paper, although the sheet were big enough for the
bed of Ware in England, set 'em down. Go, about
it. Let there be gall enough in thy ink; though thou
write with a goose-pen, no matter. About it.   45

Sir Andrew Where shall I find you?

Sir Toby We'll call thee at the cubiculo. Go.

[Exit SIR ANDREW.]

Fabian This is a dear manakin to you, Sir Toby.

Sir Toby I have been dear to him, lad, some two
thousand strong, or so.

Fabian We shall have a rare letter from him; but   50
you'll not deliver't?

Sir Toby Never trust me, then; and by all means
stir on the youth to an answer. I think oxen and
wainropes cannot hale them together. For Andrew,
if he were opened, and you find so much blood in his   55
liver as will clog the foot of a flea, I'll eat the rest
of the anatomy.

---

27. *policy:* scheming and intrigue.

29. *as lief be:* as soon be or rather be Brownist, adherent of a sect, the Independents, founded in Elizabeth I's reign by Robert Brown, an English Puritan.

33. *love- broker:* go-between in love.

38. *martial:* warlike.

40. *if thou thou'st him:* Thou was a mark of contempt unless the person concerned was a close friend or relative.

43. *bed of Ware:* At Ware, in Hertfordshire, there was an oak bedstead big enough to hold twelve adult persons at once.

44. *gall:* bitterness or malice; also an ingredient of ink.

45. *goose-pen:* the normal quill pen, also held by a "goose" (Sir Andrew) noted for foolishness and cowardice.

46. *cubiculo:* room, chamber.

47. *manakin:* puppet.

48. *dear:* expensive.

54. *wainropes:* wagon-ropes.

Fabian And his opposite, the youth, bears in his vis-
age no great presage of cruelty.

[Enter MARIA.]

Sir Toby Look, where the youngest wren of nine
comes.

Maria If you desire the spleen, and will laugh   60
yourselves into stitches, follow me. Yond gull Malvolio is turned heathen, a very renegado; for there is
no Christian, that means to be saved by believing
rightly, can ever believe such impossible passages
of grossness. He's in yellow stockings.   65

Sir Toby And cross-gartered?

Maria Most villainously, like a pedant that keeps a
school i' the church. I have dogged him, like his
murderer. He does obey every point of the letter
that I dropped to betray him. He does smile his face   70
into more lines than is in the new map with the
augmentation of the Indies; you have not seen such
a thing as 'tis. I can hardly forbear hurling things
at him. I know my lady will strike him. If she do,
he'll smile and take't for a great favour.   75

Sir Toby Come, bring us, bring us where he is.
[Exeunt.]

58. *presage:* foretelling.

59. *youngest wren of nine:* an affectionate allusion to
Maria's diminutive stature, based upon the belief
that the last hatched of the brood would be the
smallest (the wren was also called Our Lady's Hen).

60. *spleen:* "stitches" (from laughter).

61. *gull:* "bird" (he has been gulled, or deceived).

62. *renegado:* traitor to his faith.

67. *pedant:* schoolmaster.

72. *augmentation of the Indies:* the first map of the
world (Wright's Mercator projection of 1600) contained more detail of the Indies than previous maps;
augmentation means addition to.

COMMENTARY

At Olivia's house, Sir Andrew prepares to leave. He
is fed up by the pathetic progress of his courtship
of Olivia. Olivia gives more attention to Cesario — a servant! — than she has ever bestowed on Andrew himself. Sir Toby and Fabian take great pains to convince
Andrew to stay, as their pleasures are still dependent
on Andrew's money. They convince him that Olivia
favors Cesario in his sight to make Andrew jealous. And
the fact that she takes pains to do this proves that Olivia
really cares for Andrew. She hopes to create a situation
in which Andrew might prove his valor to her.

Andrew is easily gulled into believing this story. Why
not — Andrew believes anything that gratifies his need
for respect from others, no matter how preposterous.

*Fabian, Sir Andrew, and Sir Toby plot Sir Andrew's latest move to win Olivia's heart.
From a 1997 Royal Shakespeare Company production of Twelfth Night.
Clive Barda/PAL*

Fabian, seeing that Andrew has bought the story, takes it a step further. He suggests that Andrew should challenge Cesario and beat him into dumbness. Sir Toby suggests a duel, and Andrew agrees.

The challenging letter is to be written in a warlike hand to provoke Cesario. Sir Toby's condescending attitude toward Andrew is palpable. Once again, Sir Toby baits Andrew into manifesting the worst of his nature. The cowardly knight will write a bold challenge, which of course he will be too afraid to carry through to its conclusion.

Andrew goes off to write the challenge. Toby and Fabian mock the foolish knight. Fabian says that Andrew is Sir Toby's puppet and will do whatever Sir Toby devises for him. Toby, for his part, jokes about the vast sums of money (some 2,000 sovereigns) that he has cost Andrew so far. They enjoy themselves, anticipating the fun they will have promoting a duel between Andrew and Cesario.

Sir Toby has grown tired of Andrew. The dull knight grates on his nerves, and now even his money is not quite enough payment to endure his company. Toby has raised the price: Andrew must be his bank *and* his gull. Toby may be a fun-loving drunk, but he is not the loveable harmless rogue that we first imagined; he can be quite nasty.

If we compare Toby's behavior in this scene to Maria's behavior in Act II, Scene 3, we notice some interesting similarities. While Maria proposes the gulling of Malvolio to prevent drunken Sir Toby from taking a more rash action against Malvolio in the earlier scene, Toby proposes the duel to prevent Andrew from taking a more rash action later in the play. Yet while Maria is preventing Toby from taking a more rash action in his own interest out of affection for him, Toby is certainly not attempting to cool Andrew down out of any concern for Sir Andrew. Maria's plot is more good natured than Toby's, and she undertakes it to teach Malvolio a lesson as well as to impress Toby. Toby's plot is designed in part to lead to the death of either Sir Andrew or Cesario.

Though both of these gullings lead to some of the play's most effective comic scenes, the gulling of Malvolio is both more comic and less cruel than the gulling of Sir Andrew. The comedy we find in the duel between Sir Andrew and Cesario has more to do with the way Toby's plot *backfires* on him, while Maria's plot, by contrast, works just as she planned it.

Maria arrives and their enthusiasm shifts from one gulling (Andrew) to another (Malvolio). Maria has dogged the steward, "like his murderer," following Malvolio and observing every nuance of the pompous steward's gulling. Malvolio is dressed in the cross garters and is smiling like an idiot, obeying every point of the letter like a pedant following a text line by line.

Act III, Scene 3

Antonio reveals the reason he is in danger: He has committed an offense against Orsino while at sea. He offers his purse to Sebastian, and the two part ways: Antonio to find them room and board, Sebastian to see the sights of the town.

ACT III, SCENE 3
A street.

[Enter SEBASTIAN and ANTONIO.]

Sebastian I would not by my will have troubled I you;
But, since you make your pleasure of your pains,
I will no further chide you.

Antonio I could not stay behind you. My desire,
More sharp than filed steel, did spur me forth;   5
And not all love to see you, though so much
As might have drawn one to a longer voyage,
But jealousy what might befall your travel,
Being skilless in these parts, which to a stranger,
Unguided and unfriended, often prove   10
Rough and unhospitable. My willing love,
The rather by these arguments of fear,
Set forth in your pursuit.

Sebastian   My kind Antonio,
I can no other answer make but thanks,
And thanks, and ever thanks. Often good turns   15
Are shuffled off with such uncurrent pay;
But, were my worth as is my conscience firm,
You should find better dealing. What's to do?
Shall we go see the reliques of this town?

Antonio To-morrow, sir. Best first go see your lodging.   20

Sebastian I am not weary, and 'tis long to night.
I pray you, let us satisfy our eyes
With the memorials and the things of fame
That do renown this city.

Antonio   Would you'ld pardon me;
I do not without danger walk these streets.   25
Once, in a sea-fight, 'gainst the count his galleys
I did some service; of such note indeed,
That were I ta'en here it would scarce be answer'd.

NOTES

1.   *by my will:* willingly.

8.   *jealousy...travel:* fear of what might befall Sebastian as a stranger in these parts.

16. *shuffled off with such uncurrent pay:* brushed off with careless and ungrateful words (if any), or insincere reward.

22. *memorials:* public monuments, major buildings, statues etc.

25. *not without danger:* understatement for "It is very dangerous for me to..." (the figure of speech is called LITOTES).

28. *ta'en:* taken, captured it would scarce be answered, it (the charge) could scarcely be denied.

Sebastian Belike you slew great number of his people.

Antonio The offence is not of such a bloody nature;   30
   Albeit the quality of the time and quarrel
   Might well have given us bloody argument.
   It might have since been answer'd in repaying
   What we took from them, which, for traffic's sake,
   Most of our city did. Only myself stood out;   35
   For which, if I be lapsed in his place,
   I shall pay dear.

Sebastian   Do not then walk to open.

Antonio It doth not fit me. Hold, sir, here's my purse.
   In the south suburbs, at the Elephant,
   Is best to lodge. I will bespeak our diet,   40
   Whiles you beguile the time and feed your knowledge
   With viewing of the town. There shall you have me.

Sebastian Why I your purse?

Antonio Haply your eye shall light upon some toy
   You have desire to purchase; and your store,   45
   I think is not for idle markets, sir.

Sebastian I'll be your purse-bearer and leave you
   For an hour.

Antonio   To the Elephant.

Sebastian I do remember.
   [Exeunt.]

34.   *traffic's sake:* for the sake of trade and commerce.

36.   *lapsed:* arrested.

39.   *the Elephant:* the Oliphant Tavern (original of the Elephant and Castle) near the Globe Theater.

40.   *bespeak our diet:* order our meals.

43.   *Why I your purse?:* Why do you give me your purse?

44.   *toy:* trifle that catches your fancy.

COMMENTARY

Sebastian and Antonio walk the streets of the city near the Duke's palace. Sebastian is new to the town and eager to walk around and sightsee, but Antonio is liable to be arrested on sight if he is recognized. He has risked this danger for two reasons; first, his desire (love?) for Sebastian; and second, his fear that any harm might befall Sebastian, being a stranger in the town.

Sebastian thanks Antonio and promises that if his financial situation were better, he would pay Antonio with more than words of thanks. Note the interesting fact that while Viola survived the shipwreck with her money intact, Sebastian has apparently lost all his money in the shipwreck. The fact that Sebastian is beholden to Antonio for rescuing him physically, as well as for providing for him economically, places him in a more vulnerable situation than Viola. Clearly Sebastian would prefer to clear himself of *both* debts through economic means, while Antonio holds out hope that Sebastian will return Antonio's *affections,* rather than merely his money. Both of these options would be "more than words of thanks," but clearly Antonio and Sebastian do not have a reciprocal relationship.

Then Sebastian suggests that they go to town and see the sights. Antonio suggests that they secure their lodging first. If the homoerotic subtext is played openly

CliffsComplete *Twelfth Night*   Act III, Scene 3   **113**

in production, Antonio's suggestion to head to their lodgings is usually played as a sexual advance. Sebastian's reply, that he is not tired and would rather satisfy his eyes on the things of renown in town, would be a gentle way of sidestepping the offer.

Antonio asks to be excused. He cannot walk the streets without danger of arrest, and he describes the nature of his trouble with the Duke. He was engaged in a sea battle against the Duke's ships, and although others from his city have cleared things up with the Duke, Antonio has not.

Antonio hands Sebastian his purse and suggests that they meet later at a tavern called The Elephant. Antonio will take care of the details of their lodging and eating arrangements, leaving Sebastian to walk the town and buy anything that his heart desires with Antonio's purse. Sebastian agrees, and they go their separate ways.

Act III, Scene 4

Malvolio, smiling like a fool and wearing brilliant yellow stockings, appears before Olivia and Maria. Olivia imagines that he has gone mad and leaves him in the care of Sir Toby while she goes off to see Cesario. Sir Toby delivers Andrew's challenge to Cesario, and the two reluctant duelists prepare to fight. Antonio, mistaking Cesario for Sebastian, comes to Cesario's defense. Orsino's officers arrest Antonio and cart him off. Cesario is left to ponder Antonio's strange words, which lead her to believe her brother may be alive.

ACT III, SCENE 4
Olivia's garden.

[Enter OLIVIA and MARIA.]

Olivia I have sent after him; he says he'll come.
How shall I feast him? what bestow of him?
For youth is bought more oft than begg'd or borrow'd.
I speak too loud.
Where is Malvolio? he is sad and civil,
And suits well for a servant with my fortunes: 5
Where is Malvolio?

Maria He's coming, madam; but in very strange
manner. He is, sure, possessed, madam.

Olivia Why, what's the matter? does he rave?

Maria No, madam, he does nothing but smile.   10
Your ladyship were best to have some guard about
you, if he come; for, sure, the man is tainted in's
wits.

Olivia Go call him hither. *[Exit Maria.]* I am as mad as he,
If sad and merry madness equal be.

[Re-enter MARIA, with MALVOLIO.]
How now, Malvolio!

Malvolio Sweet lady, ho, ho.   15

Olivia Smilest thou?
I sent for thee upon a sad occasion.

Malvolio Sad, lady! I could be sad. This does
make some obstruction in the blood, this cross-garter-
ing; but what of that? if it please the eye of one, it   20

2.   *bestow of him:* what to bestow on or give him.

4.   *sad and civil:* grave and polite.

5.   *suits well:* fits my own mood.

8.   *possessed:* out of his mind (which has been taken over by the devil).

11. *guard:* to protect her (reference to the ancient belief that all madmen are violent and refractory).

12. *tainted in's wits:* of a diseased mind.

17. *sad:* serious occasion.

is with me as the very true sonnet is, "Please one, and please all."

Olivia Why, how dost thou, man? what is the matter with thee?

Malvolio Not black in my mind, though yellow in my legs. It did come to his hands, and commands shall be executed. I think we do know the sweet Roman hand.

Olivia God comfort thee! Why dost thou smile so and kiss thy hand so oft?

Maria How do you, Malvolio?

Malvolio At your request! yes, nightingales answer daws.

Maria Why appear you with this ridiculous boldness before my lady?

Malvolio "Be not afraid of greatness." 'Twas well writ.

Olivia What meanest thou by that, Malvolio?

Malvolio "Some are born great," —

Olivia Ha!

Malvolio "Some achieve greatness," —

Olivia What sayest thou?

Malvolio "And some have greatness thrust upon them."

Olivia Heaven restore thee!

Malvolio "Remember who commended thy yellow stockings," —

Olivia Thy yellow stockings!

Malvolio "And wished to see thee cross-gartered."

Olivia Cross-gartered!

Malvolio "Go to, thou art made, if thou desirest to be so;" —

Olivia Am I made?

Malvolio "If not, let me see thee a servant still."

23. Olivia is scared. Can this be her sober-suited steward?

27. *Roman hand:* the Italian style of handwriting which was becoming fashionable during the sixteenth century; it resembled printer's italic.

31. *nightingales...daws:* Song birds don't answer to the ugly sound of crows.

48. *made:* a play on "thy fortune's made," maid, and mad.

Olivia Why, this is very midsummer madness. 50

[Enter Servant.]

Servant Madam, the young gentleman of the Count Orsino's is returned. I could hardly entreat him back. He attends your ladyship's pleasure.

Olivia I'll come to him. *[Exit Servant.]* Good Maria, let this fellow be looked to. Where's my cousin 55 Toby? Let some of my people have a special care of him. I would not have him miscarry for the half of my dowry.
[Exeunt OLIVIA and MARIA.]

Malvolio Oho! do you come near me now? no worse man than Sir Toby to look to me! This concurs directly with the letter: she sends him on purpose, 60 that I may appear stubborn to him; for she incites me to that in the letter. "Cast thy humble slough," says she; "be opposite with a kinsman, surly with servants; let thy tongue tang with arguments of state; put thyself into the trick of singularity;" and con- 65 sequently sets down the manner how: as, a sad face, a reverend carriage, a slow tongue, in the habit of some sir of note, and so forth. I have limed her; but it is Jove's doing, and Jove make me thankful! And when she went away now, "Let this fellow be looked 70 to." "Fellow!" not Malvolio, nor after my degree, but "fellow." Why, everything adheres together, that no dram of a scruple, no scruple of a scruple, no obstacle, no incredulous or unsafe circumstance — What can be said? Nothing that can be can come 75 between me and the full prospect of my hopes. Well, Jove, not I, is the doer of this, and he is to be thanked.

[Re-enter MARIA, with SIR TOBY and FABIAN.]

Sir Toby Which way is he, in the name of sanctity? If all the devils of hell be drawn in little, and Legion himself possessed him, yet I'll speak to him. 80

Fabian Here he is, here he is. How is't with you, sir? how is't with you, man?

68. *limed:* trapped as with birdlime (a sticky substance that was spread on tree branches to catch birds).

73. *dram:* small amount.

  scruple: third of a dram or small quantity.

74. *incredulous:* incredible.

78. *in the name of sanctity:* Sir Toby invokes the name of holiness, as he is (pretends to be) dealing with a devil.

79. *Legion:* allusion to the man possessed of many devils in the country of the Gadarenes; refer to Mark, v, 9 and Luke, viii, 30.

Malvolio Go off; I discard you. Let me enjoy my
    private. Go off.

Maria Lo, how hollow the fiend speaks within him!   85
    did not I tell you? Sir Toby, my lady prays you to
    have a care of him.

Malvolio Aha! does she so?

Sir Toby Go to, go to; peace, peace; we must deal
    gently with him. Let me alone. How do you,   90
    Malvolio? how is't with you? What, man! defy the
    devil. Consider, he's an enemy to mankind.

Malvolio Do you know what you say?

Maria La you, an you speak ill of the devil, how he
    takes it at heart! Pray God, he be not bewitched!   95
    My lady would not lose him for more than I'll say.

Malvolio How now, mistress!

Maria O Lord!

Sir Toby Prithee, hold thy peace; this is not the way.
    Do you not see you move him? let me alone with   100
    him.

Fabian No way but gentleness; gently, gently. The
    fiend is rough, and will not be roughly used.

Sir Toby Why, how now, my bawcock! how dost
    thou, chuck?   105

Malvolio Sir!

Sir Toby Ay, Biddy, come with me. What, man!
    'tis not for gravity to play at cherry-pit with Satan.
    Hang him, foul collier!

Maria Get him to say his prayers, good Sir Toby,   110
    get him to pray.

Malvolio My prayers, minx!

Maria No, I warrant you, he will not hear of
    godliness.

Malvolio Go, hang yourselves all! you are idle
    shallow things; I am not of your element. You shall   115
    know more hereafter.
    [*Exit.*]

84.   *private:* privacy.

104.   *bawcock:* fine fellow (from the French, beau coq —
        fine bird).

107.   *Biddy:* common name for a hen (very insulting to
        Malvolio).

109.   *foul collier:* coal-miner (black, like the devil).

Sir Toby Is't possible?

Fabian If this were played upon a stage now, I could condemn it as an improbable fiction.

Sir Toby His very genius hath taken the infection of the device, man. 120

Maria Nay, pursue him now, lest the device take air and taint.

Fabian Why, we shall make him mad indeed.

Maria The house will be the quieter. 125

Sir Toby Come, we'll have him in a dark room and bound. My niece is already in the belief that he's mad. We may carry it thus, for our pleasure and his penance, till our very pastime, tired out of breath, prompt us to have mercy on him, at which time we 130 will bring the device to the bar and crown thee for a finder of madmen. But see, but see!

[Enter SIR ANDREW.]

Fabian More matter for a May morning.

Sir Andrew Here's the challenge, read it. I warrant there's vinegar and pepper in't. 135

Fabian Is't so saucy?

Sir Andrew Ay, is't, I warrant him. Do but read.

Sir Toby Give me. *[Reads.]* "Youth, whatsoever thou art, thou art but a scurvy fellow."

Fabian Good, and valiant. 140

Sir Toby *[Reads.]* "Wonder not, nor admire not in thy mind, why I do call thee so, for I will show thee no reason for't."

Fabian A good note; that keeps you from the blow of the law. 145

Sir Toby *[Reads.]* "Thou comest to the lady Olivia, and in my sight she uses thee kindly; but thou liest in thy throat. That is not the matter I challenge thee for."

Fabian Very brief, and to exceeding good sense — less.

122–123. *take air and taint:* become known and spoil.

131. *bring the device to the bar:* bring the trick out into the open, to be judged (a flavor of the law is in these words).

136. *saucy:* spicy; insolent, rude; refers to vinegar and pepper previously mentioned.

144–145. *keeps you from the blow of the law:* is not actionable in the law courts.

149. *sense-less:* the last word is spoken as an aside to the audience; it is not for Andrew's ears.

Sir Toby *[Reads.]* "I will waylay thee going home,   150
where if it be thy chance to kill me" —

Fabian Good.

Sir Toby *[Reads.]* "Thou killest me like a rogue
and a villain."

Fabian Still you keep o' the windy side of the law;
good.

Sir Toby *[Reads.]* "Fare thee well; and God have
mercy upon one of our souls! He may have mercy   155
upon mine; but my hope is better, and so look to
thyself. Thy friend, as thou usest him, and thy sworn
enemy, Andrew Aguecheek." If this letter move
him not, his legs cannot. I'll give it him.

Maria You may have very fit occasion for't; he is   160
now in some commerce with my lady, and will by
and by depart.

Sir Toby Go, Sir Andrew; scout me for him at the
corner of the orchard like a bum-baily. So soon as
ever thou seest him, draw; and, as thou drawest,   165
swear horrible; for it comes to pass oft that a terrible
oath, with a swaggering accent sharply twanged off,
gives manhood more approbation than ever proof
itself would have earned him. Away!

Sir Andrew Nay, let me alone for swearing.   170
[Exit.]

Sir Toby Now will not I deliver his letter: for the behaviour of the young gentleman gives him out to be
of good capacity and breeding; his employment
between his lord and my niece confirms no less.
Therefore this letter, being so excellently ignorant,   175
will breed no terror in the youth. He will find it
comes from a clodpole. But, sir, I will deliver his
challenge by word of mouth; set upon Aguecheek
a notable report of valour; and drive the gentleman,
as I know his youth will aptly receive it, into a most   180
hideous opinion of his rage, skill, fury and impetu-
osity. This will so fright them both that they will
kill one another by the look, like cockatrices.

153.   *windy side of the law:* windward (protected) side.

163.   *commerce:* business; conversation about something.

164.   *bum-baily:* sheriff's officer of inferior rank who lay
in wait to arrest debtors.

165.   *drawest:* draw thy sword.

177.   *clodpole:* blockhead.

183.   *cockatrices:* mythological creatures, half serpent,
half cockerel, famed for killing at a glance.

[Re-enter OLIVIA, with VIOLA.]

Fabian Here he comes with your niece; give them
    way till he take leave, and presently after him.   185

Sir Toby I will meditate the while upon some horrid
    message for a challenge.
    [Exeunt SIR TOBY, FABIAN, and MARIA.]

Olivia I have said too much unto a heart of stone
    And laid mine honour too unchary out.
    There's something in me that reproves my fault;   190
    But such a headstrong potent fault it is,
    That it but mocks reproof.

Viola With the same 'haviour that your passion bears
    Goes on my master's grief.

Olivia Here, wear this jewel for me, 'tis my picture.   195
    Refuse it not; it hath no tongue to vex you;
    And I beseech you come again to-morrow.
    What shall you ask of me that I'll deny,
    That honour saved may upon asking give?

Viola Nothing but this, your true love for my master.   200

Olivia How with mine honour may I give him that
    Which I have given to you?

Viola   I will acquit you.

Olivia Well, come again to-morrow. Fare thee well.
    [Exit.]

[Re-enter SIR TOBY and FABIAN.]

Sir Toby Gentlemen, God save thee.

Viola And you, sir.   205

Sir Toby That defence thou hast, betake thee to't. Of
    what nature the wrongs are thou hast done him, I
    know not; but thy intercepter, full of despite, bloody
    as the hunter, attends thee at the orchard-end. Dis-
    mount thy tuck, be yare in the preparation, for thy   210
    assailant is quick, skilful, and deadly.

Viola You mistake, sir; I am sure no man hath any
    quarrel to me. My remembrance is very free and
    clear from any image of offence done to any man.

185. *presently:* immediately.

189. *too unchary out:* thriftlessly squandered my good name.

193. *'haviour:* behavior, conduct.

195. *jewel:* diamond brooch containing a miniature portrait of Olivia (Viola probably wants to refuse this gift, but does not do so for fear of offending the countess even further).

208. *thy intercepter:* the one who wants to cut you off and prevent your escape.

210. *Dismount thy tuck:* take thy rapier out of its scabbard or sheath.

be yare in thy preparation: be ready (hence, nimble, brisk) in getting ready for this duel.

211. *thy assailant:* Sir Andrew Aguecheek quick, skilful, and deadly, — but only in Sir Toby's imagination!

Sir Toby You'll find it otherwise, I assure you. 215
Therefore, if you hold your life at any price, betake
you to your guard; for your opposite hath in him
what youth, strength, skill, and wrath can furnish
man withal.

Viola I pray you, sir, what is he?

Sir Toby He is knight, dubbed with unhatched 220
rapier and on carpet consideration; but he is a
devil in private brawl. Souls and bodies hath he
divorced three; and his incensement at this moment is so implacable, that satisfaction can be none
but by pangs of death and sepulchre. Hob, nob, is 225
his word; give't or take't.

Viola I will return again into the house and desire
some conduct of the lady. I am no fighter. I have
heard of some kind of men that put quarrels purposely on others, to taste their valour. Belike this is
a man of that quirk.

Sir Toby Sir, no; his indignation derives itself 230
out of a very competent injury. Therefore, get you
on and give him his desire. Back you shall not to
the house, unless you undertake that with me which
with as much safety you might answer him. Therefore, on, or strip your sword stark naked; for 235
meddle you must, that's certain, or forswear to wear
iron about you.

Viola This is as uncivil as strange. I beseech you,
do me this courteous office, as to know of the
knight what my offence to him is. It is something
of my negligence, nothing of my purpose. 240

Sir Toby I will do so. Signior Fabian, stay you
by this gentleman till my return.
[Exit.]

Viola Pray you, sir, do you know of this matter?

Fabian I know the knight is incensed against you,
even to a mortal arbitrement; but nothing of the 245
circumstance more.

Viola I beseech you, what manner of man is he?

220–221. *dubbed with unhatched rapier:* knighted with his own sword that had not been hacked in battle.

221. *carpet consideration:* while kneeling, not on the field of battle, but on a carpet.

223. *incensement:* anger.

224. *Hob, nob:* hit or miss.

231. *competent injury:* legitimate and substantial wrong.

236. *wear iron:* wear a sword.

245. *mortal arbitrement:* settle a dispute by duelling to the death of one contestant.

Fabian Nothing of that wonderful promise, to read
him by his form, as you are like to find him in the
proof of his valour. He is, indeed, sir, the most skil-   250
ful, bloody, and fatal opposite that you could possibly have found in any part of Illyria. Will you
walk towards him? I will make your peace with
him if I can.

Viola I shall be much bound to you for't. I am one
that had rather go with sir priest than sir knight. I   255
care not who knows so much of my mettle.
[Exeunt.]

[Re-enter SIR TOBY, with SIR ANDREW.]

Sir Toby Why, man, he's a very devil; I have not
seen such a firago. I had a pass with him, rapier,
scabbard and all, and he gives me the stuck in with
such a mortal motion, that it is inevitable; and on
the answer, he pays you as surely as your feet hit   260
the ground they step on. They say he has been
fencer to the Sophy.

Sir Andrew I'll not meddle with him.

Sir Toby Ay, but he will not now be pacified.
Fabian can scarce hold him yonder.   265

Sir Andrew Plague on't, an' I thought he had been
valiant and so cunning in fence, I'ld not have
challenged him. Let him let the matter slip, and I'll
give him my horse, gray Capilet.

Sir Toby I'll make the motion. Stand here, make a   270
good show on't; this shall end without the perdition
of souls. *[Aside.]* Marry, I'll ride your horse as well
as I ride you.
[Re-enter FABIAN and VIOLA.]
[To Fabian.] I have his horse to take up the quarrel; I have persuaded him the youth's a devil.

Fabian He is as horribly conceited of him; and   275
pants and looks pale, as if a bear were at his heels.

Sir Toby *[To Viola.]* There's no remedy, sir; he
will fight with you for oath's sake. Marry, he hath
better bethought him of his quarrel, and he finds

257. *firago:* virago (heroic maiden) For a similar play
on words refer to Humbert Wolfe's definition of a
chaste female cabinet-minister as a *virago
intacta.*

262. *fencer to the Sophy:* taught fencing to the Shah
of Persia.

264. *but he will not now be pacified:* it is clear that Sir
Toby is the instigator of this duel since neither of
the antagonists wishes to meddle with the other.

267. *in fence:* in the art of fencing.

269. *gray Capilet:* the name of the horse with which
Sir Andrew wished to bribe Viola not to fight.

270. *I'll make the motion:* to act as though doing something; nowadays means to do something so casu-
ally that one does not do it at all.

272. *perdition:* loss.

that now scarce to be worth talking of; therefore   280
draw, for the supportance of his vow. He protests
he will not hurt you.

Viola [Aside.] Pray God defend me! A little thing
would make me tell them how much I lack of a
man.

Fabian Give ground, if you see him furious.

Sir Toby Come, Sir Andrew, there's no remedy;   285
the gentleman will, for his honour's sake, have one
bout with you; he cannot by the duello avoid it. But
he has promised me, as he is a gentleman and a soldier, he will not hurt you. Come on; to't.

Sir Andrew Pray God, he keep his oath!

Viola I do assure you, 'tis against my will.   290
[They draw.]

[Enter ANTONIO.]

Antonio Put up your sword. If this young gentleman
Have done offence, I take the fault on me.
If you offend him, I for him defy you.

Sir Toby You, sir! why, what are you?

Antonio One, sir, that for his love dares yet do more   295
Than you have heard him brag to you he will.

Sir Toby Nay, if you be an undertaker, I am for you.
[They draw.]

[Enter Officers.]

Fabian O good Sir Toby, hold! here come the officers.

Sir Toby [To Antonio.] I'll be with you anon.   300

Viola Pray, sir, put your sword up, if you please.

Sir Andrew Marry, will I, sir; and for that I promised you, I'll be as good as my word. He will bear
you easily and reins well.

First Officer This is the man; do thy office.   305

Second Officer Antonio, I arrest thee at the suit
of Count Orsino.

Antonio You do mistake me, sir.

281.   *supportance of his vow:* in order not to break his oath.

282.   *A little thing:* A small rip of the doublet by the opponent's sword would soon reveal the fact that Viola is a woman.

287.   *the duello:* the strict rules of duelling.

298.   *undertaker:* one who is ready to join a fight. A second duel begins, between Sir Toby Belch and Antonio, but this, too, is stopped, by the intervention of Orsino's officers who have come to arrest Antonio (who has been recognized).

304–305.   *He will bear you easily and reins well:* Sir Andrew here gives Sir Toby the horse, gray Capilet.

306.   *office:* duty.

307.   *suit:* on behalf of.

First Officer No, sir, no jot; I know your favour well,
Though now you have no sea-cap on your head.　　　310
Take him away; he knows I know him well.

Antonio I must obey. *[To Viola.]* This comes with seeking
　　you:
But there's no remedy; I shall answer it.
What will you do, now my necessity
Makes me to ask you for my purse? It grieves me　　　315
Much more for what I cannot do for you
Than what befalls myself. You stand amazed;
But be of comfort.

Second Officer Come, sir, away.

Antonio I must entreat of you some of that money.　　　320

Viola What money, sir?
For the fair kindness you have show'd me here,
And, part, being prompted by your present trouble,
Out of my lean and low ability
I'll lend you something. My having is not much;　　　325
I'll make division of my present with you.
Hold, there's half my coffer.

Antonio　　　　　　　　　Will you deny me now?
Is't possible that my deserts to you
Can lack persuasion? Do not tempt my misery,
Lest that it make me so unsound a man　　　330
As to upbraid you with those kindnesses
That I have done for you.

Viola　　　　　　　　　I know of none;
Nor know I you by voice or any feature.
I hate ingratitude more in a man
Than lying vainness, babbling drunkenness,　　　335
Or any taint of vice whose strong corruption
Inhabits our frail blood.

Antonio　　　　　　　O heavens themselves!

Second Officer Come, sir, I pray you, go.

Antonio Let me speak a little. This youth that you see here
I snatch'd one half out of the jaws of death,　　　340
Relieved him with such sanctity of love,
And to his image, which methought did promise
Most venerable worth, did I devotion.

326. *present:* current holdings.

327. *coffer:* chest, treasury, bank.

341. *sanctity of love:* the friendship that is holy.

First Officer What's that to us? The time goes by; away!

Antonio But oh, how vile an idol proves this god!　345
　Thou hast, Sebastian, done good feature shame.
　In nature there's no blemish but the mind;
　None can be called deform'd but the unkind;
　Virtue is beauty, but the beauteous-evil
　Are empty trunks o'erflourish'd by the devil.　350

First Officer The man grows mad; away with him!
　Come, come, sir.

Antonio Lead me on.
　[Exit with Officers.]

Viola Methinks his words do from such passion fly,
　That he believes himself. So do not I.
　Prove true, imagination, O prove true,　355
　That I, dear brother, be now ta'en for you!

Sir Toby Come hither, knight; come hither,
　Fabian; we'll whisper o'er a couplet or two of most
　sage saws.

Viola He named Sebastian. I my brother know
　Yet living in my glass; even such and so　360
　In favour was my brother, and he went
　Still in this fashion, colour, ornament,
　For him I imitate. Oh, if it prove,
　Tempests are kind and salt waves fresh in love.
　[Exit.]

Sir Toby A very dishonest paltry boy, and more a　365
　coward than a hare. His dishonesty appears in
　leaving his friend here in necessity and denying
　him; and for his cowardship, ask Fabian.

Fabian A coward, a most devout coward, religious
　in it.

Sir Andrew 'Slid, I'll after him again and beat him.　370

Sir Toby Do; cuff him soundly, but never draw thy
　sword.

Sir Andrew An I do not, —
　[Exit.]

---

345. *this god:* Sebastian is god-like to the simple-hearted Antonio.

358. *saws:* maxims, aphorisms.

360. *glass:* mirror; her own face is like a mirror image of her brother.

364. *Tempests are kind:* storms produce good results as well as tragic ones.

370. *'Slid:* God's eyelid (a common oath). Sir Andrew's courage is high in the absence of the opponent.

Fabian Come, let's see the event.

Sir Toby I dare lay any money 'twill be nothing yet.
[Exeunt.]

COMMENTARY

Olivia and Maria are in the garden. Olivia waits nervously for Cesario, who has promised to come. How should she treat him when he arrives? Would it seem like she is trying to buy his affections if she gives him a gift? (Note that Olivia's question about the relationship of love and money echoes a theme introduced in the preceding scene, when Antonio offers his purse to Sebastian. For both Antonio and Olivia, love is what moves them to *give* to their beloved — in contrast to Orsino. But Olivia, a more fleshed out and sympathetic character than Antonio, also analyzes the nature of giving, not only for herself but also for the audience. The profound question that Olivia asks has puzzled great philosophers throughout the ages: *How can one truly give if one expects, or even hopes, for something in return?*) Olivia has called for Malvolio as his sober nature is a source of comfort to her in moments like these.

Maria wastes no time in setting up Malvolio's downfall. She tells Olivia that Malvolio has been acting strange lately and is probably possessed. The most evident symptom of his madness is his constant smiling. When Olivia sees the heretofore sober Malvolio smiling, why wouldn't she believe he is mad, especially considering that she has called for Malvolio precisely because of his sober humor? Although clearly Olivia, as head of a household that includes both Malvolio and Sir Toby, has previously sided against Malvolio as "sick of self-love," she values Malvolio at least as much as she does Feste and Sir Toby. The "war" between these characters represents an internal war for Olivia as well.

Malvolio enters, smiling, of course. His appearance is radically altered. His somber mourning clothes have been replaced with sportive yellow stockings, which he calls to Olivia's attention. His sad and civil manner has been replaced by inane smiling. He blows kisses to Olivia, and what is more maddening to Olivia, he offers her a knowing look while alluding to the various lines of the letter that he believes she has written to him.

From Olivia's point of view, Malvolio does seem mad. He is acting completely out of character. She is both bewildered by and concerned for him. Maria has done her job well.

While Malvolio repeats word for word his instructions from the letter — of course, he has memorized every word by heart — Maria must restrain herself from laughing. She is still, however, capable of setting up Malvolio further, asking why he appears "with this ridiculous boldness before my lady?" It's as if she is prompting him for his speech on greatness. Why not? Maria knows what the letter says, and she knows Malvolio. Although some critics have argued that Maria's actions here are deplorable, at this point in the play it is hard *not* to laugh with her. If things were truly harmonious in Olivia's household in the first place, *before* the gulling of Malvolio, these critics would be justified. But even though Maria has temporarily caused great disharmony in Olivia's household, Maria's ends (to make the house "quieter," III.4.140) certainly justify her means. By exposing Malvolio's "secret" desires, Maria is acting quite like the author of this play — for what she does to Malvolio is no more cruel than the madness to which the events of *Twelfth Night* bring Olivia, for example.

A servant announces Cesario's arrival. Before Olivia goes to see Cesario, she tells Maria to have her people look after Malvolio. Clearly, she has great fondness for her steward and truly cares about him. She says she would gladly give half of the dowry she would receive in marriage to ensure that no harm comes to Malvolio.

Olivia leaves, and Malvolio reels with ecstacy. When the fool plays with words, he shows how untrustworthy they are and how easily meanings miscarry. In comparison to the fool's practiced wit, we find Malvolio infected with folly. He cannot help but twist every word and situation inside out to bring further proof of his ensuing pleasure. Olivia's mention of her dowry suggests to Malvolio that she is thinking of marrying him. Olivia calling him "fellow" is misconstrued as further evidence that she now thinks of him as a member of her own social status. Even Olivia's sending Toby to see him contributes to his belief that she loves him and wants to marry him, as it fits the tenor of her letter. This is madness indeed: Malvolio's reason is infected, and his own subjective interpretations of events are out of joint with the reality of the situation.

Fabian and Sir Toby try to subdue the duped Malvolio. From a 1997 Royal Shakespeare Company production of Twelfth Night. *Clive Barda/PAL*

Toby and Fabian come in, looking as though they are prepared to pacify a raving lunatic. The custom at this time was to treat the insane worse than criminals. The insane were often restrained by force, manacled, and thrown into prisons.

Malvolio attempts to dismiss them, but Toby and his cohorts have him surrounded. Toby, with mock concern, suggests that the others leave him alone with the madman. He will try to talk sense into Malvolio. Maria says that she suspects that he has been possessed by the devil. Fabian encourages the others to act gently while they attempt to restrain him, but Malvolio is outraged by their rude treatment and storms off stage.

Fabian concludes that if this scene were played upon the stage no one would believe it. Of course, it *is* being played on a stage, and audiences for 400 years have "believed" it. The fact that Shakespeare includes Fabian's skeptical utterance in the play is one of the more potent devices Shakespeare utilizes to create, paradoxically, the illusion that what we're seeing is real.

By having a character in the play speak as a skeptical realist, Shakespeare usurps the role of the skeptic. Maria is in favor of pursuing Malvolio immediately, before something interferes with the device.

Maria had the idea to gull Malvolio in the first place, and at every moment, Maria works to ensure that the device is seen through to the end, with the maximum potential for harming Malvolio. Fabian worries that they will make him mad for real, and Maria responds, with the subtle smile of a sadist, that the house will be the quieter once Malvolio has been driven mad forever. (The plausibility also exists that Maria means that once Malvolio is gone, Toby will have no one to rebel against, and these strident clashes will end.) Toby senses what Maria is hinting at, and suggests that they lock up Malvolio in a dark room, as was customary for lunatics in those days. The others agree.

Sir Andrew enters, and the second comic subplot is put in motion. Andrew has written what he believes to be a fiery challenge to Cesario — full of vinegar and pepper. Toby reads the letter aloud, and what to Andrew seems fiery seems to Toby, Fabian, and the audience a cowardly and ridiculous challenge. Fabian mocks the tenor of the note in his many asides.

Sir Toby promises Andrew that he will deliver the challenge. Meantime, he suggests Andrew wait at the orchard's edge prepared to confront Cesario. Sir Toby advises him to swear horribly and brandish his sword, and Andrew exits, ready to swear.

Toby will deliver the challenge himself by word of mouth. Andrew's note is too ignorant to breed fear in Cesario. Toby will distort Andrew's skill and rage in a manner so terrifying that Cesario will be as afraid to fight Andrew, as Andrew will be to fight him.

For one last time, Olivia and Cesario appear alone together. Once again they play out their scene, in which Olivia woos Cesario, and Cesario tries to reject Olivia politely, while halfheartedly speaking on behalf of Orsino. This time, Olivia does most of the talking. Although Olivia would do anything to win Cesario's love, a part of her condemns her passions for leading her to behave so unwisely. Her passion, however, is stronger than her awareness of doing herself wrong. She cannot stop herself from begging Cesario to return again, though she knows it is hopeless. If Orsino's philosophy is correct (and in some ways it is), until Olivia's appetite surfeits, sickens, and dies, she will have no control over herself.

Sir Toby and Fabian approach Viola as she leaves Olivia. Sir Toby tells her to defend herself, and quickly, for her assailant is bloody-minded and waits for her at the orchard-end. Viola is sure that some mistake has been made; she has done no one wrong.

Toby assures her that there is no mistake. Sir Andrew is a devil in private brawl, he's killed three men, and he is so incensed that only Cesario's death will satisfy him. Cesario's first impulse is to return to Olivia's house to beg protection, but Sir Toby tells Cesario that she must face the knight or face Toby himself — there is no retreating when honor is at stake.

Cesario demands to know what her offense has been, and Toby agrees to ask the knight, leaving Fabian to prevent her from running away. Fabian talks up the bloodthirsty rage and fierce quality of Sir Andrew, while Toby has a go at Sir Andrew.

Sir Toby plays the same game with Andrew, describing Cesario's deadly skills with the rapier. Andrew says that he will not confront him. It's too late, says Toby, the man will not be pacified. Andrew offers to give Cesario his gray horse if he will agree to let the matter slip. Hoping to keep the horse for himself, Toby says he will try to negotiate a peace. In some ways, this scene recalls, in way of contrast, a scene in *A Midsummer Night's Dream.* Puck, attempting to undo the confusion and increasingly physical violence he has unleashed as two Athenian men, Demetrius and Lysander, prepare to duel to prove their love for Helena, conjures a fog under cover of which he pretends that he is both Lysander (to Demetrius) and Demetrius (to Lysander). By consistently goading the two rivals to fight, yet preventing them from coming in contact with each other, Puck is able to tire them out and thus prevent the fight. In *Twelfth Night,* by contrast, we know that Toby is not really interested in negotiating a peace. We see Sir Toby as a kind of *anti-Puck,* stirring up a fight between two characters who do not want to fight.

Sir Toby's plan works up to a point. Yet the fact that neither Sir Andrew nor Cesario can, in their hearts, play the role Sir Toby has concocted for them, for his own amusement (and financial gain), helps direct some of the humor in this scene *against* Sir Toby. If Maria's gulling of Malvolio was good foolery (certainly Feste was glad to play a part in it, while he is conspicuously absent from Toby's duel-plot), Toby's plot becomes dangerous, not only to others but also to himself, as we shall see. Not only does Toby not realize that Cesario (either because of temperament or because of gender) would prove less inclined to fight (if not, strictly speaking, a coward) than he thought, but it is becoming clearer that Toby's drunken sensibility, like that of a modern-day junkie, is leading him to pathological actions to support his habit. It would be a mistake to call Toby evil, however, for in many ways the play indulges his vices and his particular form of excess, as much as it indulges Orsino's and Olivia's. Through this indulgence, however, Toby (and the others) may come to see the truth about hmself and how others perceive his actions. He, too, (as Cesario says of Olivia earlier in this act) is not who he thinks he is.

After another round of gulling, the opposites are prepared to fight. Toby has skillfully manipulated a confrontation between the two — a man who dissembles manhood with false words and a woman who dissembles manhood with a false appearance. Significantly, Andrew and Cesario are equally matched in this contest; one is no more or less of a man than the other. To be false in words or false in appearance is one and the same thing in this play.

With Fabian pushing on Cesario, and Toby pushing on Andrew, the two meet face to face, draw their swords, and panic. Just as the two would-be duelers touch sword tips, Antonio arrives. In yet another example of identity confusion, Antonio mistakes Cesario for Sebastian and offers to fight in his place. This amusing parody of a duel is now upstaged by the real thing, as Sir Toby and Antonio draw swords and fight.

The "willing combatants," Cesario and Sir Andrew are egged on to a duel. From a 1997 Royal Shakespeare Company production of Twelfth Night. *Clive Barda/PAL*

Officers of the Duke arrive and inform Antonio that he has been recognized and is under arrest. Antonio turns to Cesario (remember that he has mistaken him for Sebastian) and tells him that this result is what comes from looking for his friend. Then he asks for the return of his purse.

Cesario, of course, denies the knowledge of any purse. The officers tell Antonio that he must come away, and Antonio is desperate; he must have his purse back to purchase a proper defense. He cannot understand how his friend could be so ungrateful. As the officers drag him away, he recounts how he saved this youth's life in a shipwreck and how this same youth now has betrayed him. The officers are not interested and drag him off stage.

Viola partly guesses that Antonio must have saved her brother Sebastian. At least she hopes that this might explain the confusion. Viola prays that her imagination on this point proves true. She exits with the hope that her brother may still be alive.

Toby is momentarily flustered by the intrusion of real violence but waits only a moment before he returns his attention to the would-be duelers. He and Fabian adopt a new strategy. They call Andrew's attention to Cesario's lack of courage and dishonesty. Sir Andrew immediately recovers his false bravado; he will go after Cesario and cuff him soundly. Exit all in search of Cesario.

Notes

Notes

Notes

TWELFTH NIGHT
ACT IV

Clown *Alas, sir, how fell you beside your five wits?*

Malvolio *Fool, there was never man so notoriously abused. I am as well in my wits, fool, as thou art.*

Clown *But as well? then you are mad indeed, if you be not better in your wits than a fool.*

Act IV, Scene 1

Feste mistakes Sebastian for Cesario. Sir Toby and Andrew also mistake Sebastian for Cesario and attack him. Feste runs off to alert Olivia of the melee. Olivia parts the fray, sends Sir Toby off, and declares her love to Sebastian, who is more than delighted to accept her love.

ACT IV, SCENE 1
The street before Olivia's house.

[Enter SEBASTIAN and Clown.]

Clown Will you make me believe that I am not
sent for you?

Sebastian Go to, go to, thou art a foolish fellow.
Let me be clear of thee.

Clown Well held out, i' faith! No, I do not know   5
you; nor I am not sent to you by my lady, to bid you
come speak with her; nor your name is not Master
Cesario; nor this is not my nose neither. Nothing
that is so is so.

Sebastian I prithee, vent thy folly somewhere else;   10
Thou know'st not me.

Clown Vent my folly! he has heard that word of
some great man, and now applies it to a fool. Vent
my folly! I am afraid this great lubber, the world,
will prove a cockney. I prithee now, ungrid thy
strangeness and tell me what I shall vent to my lady.   15
Shall I vent to her that thou art coming?

Sebastian I prithee, foolish Greek, depart from rne.
There's money for thee; if you tarry longer,
I shall give worse payment.

Clown By my troth, thou hast an open hand.   20
These wise men that give fools money get themselves
a good report — after fourteen years' purchase.
[Enter SIR ANDREW, SIR TOBY and FABIAN.]

Sir Andrew Now, sir, have I met you again? there's
for you. *[Striking Sebastian.]*

Sebastian Why, there's for thee, and there, and there.
Are all the people mad?   25
[Beating Sir Andrew.]

NOTES

3. *go to:* an expression of impatience.

5–9. *I...so:* These lines are said sarcastically by Feste.

10. *vent:* utter (spoken scornfully).

13. *lubber:* oaf.

14. *cockney:* those who spoke the dialect and fancy speech of citizens of London.

19. *worse payment:* blows, probably.

Sir Toby Hold, sir, or I'll throw your dagger o'er
the house.

Clown This will I tell my lady straight; I would not
be in some of your coats for two pence.
[Exit.]

Sir Toby Come on, sir; hold.

Sir Andrew Nay, let him alone. I'll go another way   30
to work with him: I'll have an action of battery
against him, if there be any law in Illyria; though
I struck him first, yet it's no matter for that.

Sebastian Let go thy hand.

Sir Toby Come, sir, I will not let you go. Come,   35
my young soldier, put up your iron. You are well
fleshed; come on.

Sebastian I will be free from thee. What wouldst
thou now? If thou darest tempt me further, draw thy
sword.

Sir Toby What, what? Nay, then I must have an
ounce or two of this malapert blood from you.   40

[Enter OLIVIA.]

Olivia Hold, Toby; on thy life I charge thee, hold!

Sir Toby Madam!

Olivia Will it be ever thus? Ungracious wretch,
Fit for the mountains and the barbarous caves,
Where manners ne'er were preach'd! out of my sight!   45
Be not offended, dear Cesario.
Rudesby, be gone!
[Exeunt SIR TOBY, SIR ANDREW and FABIAN.]
          I prithee, gentle friend,
Let thy fair wisdom, not thy passion, sway
In this uncivil and unjust extent
Against thy peace. Go with me to my house,   50
And hear thou there how many fruitless pranks
This ruffian hath botch'd up, that thou thereby
Mayst smile at this. Thou shalt not choose but go.
Do not deny. Beshrew his soul for me,
He started one poor heart of mine in thee.   55

31. *action of battery:* lawsuit for assault (yet Sir Andrew began it!).

40. *malapert:* impertinent.

48. *rudesby:* ruffian.

51. *fruitless pranks:* unprofitable practical jokes.

52. *botch'd up:* started; clumsily put together.

54. *Beshrew:* confound, curse.

55. *started:* startled.

Sebastian What relish is in this? how runs the stream?
  Or I am mad, or else this is a dream.
  Let fancy still my sense in Lethe steep;   57.   *Lethe:* the classical river of unmindfulness.
  If it be thus to dream, still let me sleep!

Olivia Nay, come, I prithee; would thou'dst be ruled by me!

Sebastian Madam, I will.   60

Olivia   Oh, say so, and so be!
  [Exeunt.]

COMMENTARY

In the street before Olivia's house, Feste has been sent by Olivia to find Cesario. When he meets Sebastian, he naturally mistakes him for Cesario (the two are twins), and of course, Sebastian does not know what the Fool is talking about. Sebastian believes the Fool is playing a joke on him, and Feste believes Cesario is playing a joke on him. They talk at cross-purposes, until Sebastian tires of the Fool and pays him to leave.

One significant difference that we notice between Sebastian and Cesario is Sebastian's readiness to resort to violence, or threats of violence. Cesario would never threaten the fool. Shakespeare differentiates the twins in their manner of diction, as well as by certain traits that are related to traditional gender role behaviors. Viola is more mature in her thinking and more giving; Sebastian is quicker to resort to violence. Olivia and Orsino may be blind to such differences, but Shakespeare's insight into the subtleties of character individuation is unfailing.

Sir Andrew also has the misfortune of mistaking Sebastian for Cesario. Filled with venom left over from the preceding scene, he strikes Sebastian and unexpectedly receives a sound beating in return. Sir Toby physically takes hold of Sebastian and pulls him off of Andrew. Feste goes off to find Olivia and let her know what her mad uncle and his friend have done to her young man.

Toby and Sebastian draw swords. They are prevented from fighting by the cry of Olivia, who demands that they stop immediately. She tells Toby to leave her sight, and then takes Sebastian aside believing, as everyone else has, that he is Cesario.

Sebastian, who has been mocked by a fool, punched by a stranger, and challenged to a duel by a second stranger, believes he has stumbled into a town in which everyone has gone mad. But now, as the beautiful Olivia ministers to his bruises, he is unsure whether he is mad or in a dream — all that he is sure of is that he should like to keep dreaming. The mad world of Illyria upon which Sebastian has stumbled is much like the "improbable fiction" of which Fabian spoke in the previous act, yet Sebastian accepts the madness (as we in the audience are clearly meant to) and is rewarded for this attitude.

In this act, we finally see the truth of Olivia's claim, "Love sought is good, but given unsought is better." Of course unbeknownst to Olivia, that statement applies to her as much as it does to Sebastian. Neither Sebastian nor Olivia were searching for each other, and one would be tempted to draw the conclusion that Shakespeare is saying that true love may come about more because of accidents such as these than it does through direct declarations of desire and protracted wooing in words. Olivia, delighted by Cesario's newfound receptivity to her love, proposes marriage, and Sebastian accepts at once. The two dash off in search of priest.

Act IV, Scene 2

To please Maria and Sir Toby, Feste disguises himself as Sir Topas the curate and visits the imprisoned Malvolio. Feste returns to Malvolio a second time, without a disguise, and promises to bring writing materials so that Malvolio can send a letter to Olivia.

ACT IV, SCENE 2
A room in Olivia's house.

[Enter MARIA and Clown.]

Maria Nay, I prithee, put on this gown and this beard; make him believe thou art Sir Topas the curate. Do it quickly; I'll call Sir Toby the whilst. *[Exit.]*

Clown Well, I'll put it on, and I will dissemble myself in't; and I would I were the first that ever dissembled in such a gown. I am not tall enough to become the function well, nor lean enough to be thought a good student; but to be said an honest man and a good housekeeper goes as fairly as to say a careful man and a great scholar. The competitors enter.

[Enter SIR TOBY and MARIA.]

Sir Toby Jove bless thee, Master Parson.

Clown Bonos dies, Sir Toby; for, as the old hermit of Prague, that never saw pen and ink, very wittily said to a niece of King Gorboduc, "That that is, is"; so I, being Master Parson, am Master Parson; for, what is "that" but "that," and "is" but "is"?

Sir Toby To him, Sir Topas.

Clown What ho, I say! peace in this prison!

Sir Toby The knave counterfeits well; a good knave.

Malvolio *[Within.]* Who calls there?

Clown Sir Topas the curate, who comes to visit Malvolio the lunatic.

Malvolio Sir Topas, Sir Topas, good Sir Topas, go to my lady.

NOTES

1. *Nay, etc.:* Feste may have been unwilling to put on this disguise.

2. *Sir:* usual title for Elizabethan clergymen.

    Topas: the jewel, topaz, was popularly believed to cure madness.

3. *curate:* one who has the cure or care of souls; a parish priest.

4. *dissemble:* deceive.

    There is some satire of the ecclesiastical type in these lines, but it is not bitter or personal.

10. *competitors:* colleagues (Sir Toby and Maria).

13. *Bonos dies:* Latin for good day

    hermit of Prague and *niece of King Gorboduc:* figments of Feste's vivid imagination.

Clown Out, hyperbolical fiend! how vexest thou
this man! talkest thou nothing but of ladies?　　　25

Sir Toby Well said, Master Parson.

Malvolio Sir Topas, never was man thus wronged.
Good Sir Topas, do not think I am mad; they have
laid me here in hideous darkness.　　　30

Clown Fie, thou dishonest Satan! I call thee by the
most modest terms; for I am one of those gentle
ones that will use the devil himself with courtesy.
Sayest thou that house is dark?

Malvolio As hell, Sir Topas.　　　35

Clown Why, it hath bay windows transparent as
barricadoes, and the clearstories towards the south
north are as lustrous as ebony; and yet complainest
thou of obstruction?

Malvolio I am not mad, Sir Topas; I say to you,　　　40
this house is dark.

Clown Madman, thou errest. I say, there is no
darkness but ignorance, in which thou are more
puzzled than the Egyptians in their fog.

Malvolio I say, this house is as dark as ignorance,　　　45
though ignorance were as dark as hell; and I say,
there was never man thus abused. I am no more
mad than you are. Make the trial of it in any constant question.

Clown What is the opinion of Pythagoras concerning wild fowl?　　　50

Malvolio That the soul of our grandam might haply
inhabit a bird.

Clown What thinkest thou of his opinion?

Malvolio I think nobly of the soul, and no way ap-
prove his opinion.　　　55

Clown Fare thee well. Remain thou still in darkness. Thou shalt hold the opinion of Pythagoras ere
I will allow of thy wits; and fear to kill a woodcock,
lest thou dispossess the soul of thy grandam. Fare
thee well.

25. *hyperbolical fiend:* diabolical is not good enough for Feste; he suggests an exaggerated devil.

37. *barricadoes:* barricades (which are not transparent).

clearstories: clerestories, that is, small windows above the arches in a church or high up in the hall of a great house.

39. *obstruction:* of the light (the place is dark); the word as used here reminds us of Malvolio's triumphant entrance earlier before Olivia when he complained of the crossqartering obstructing his veins.

44. *Egyptians... fog:* see Exodus 10: 22–23.

48. *constant question:* properly ordered interrogation.

49. *Pythagoras:* Greek philosopher and mathematician who taught that after death human souls passed into animals the type of which corresponded to the quality of the life lived before death.

54. As a Puritan, Malvolio could not agree with Pythagoras's pre-Christian teachings about life after death.

Malvolio Sir Topas, Sir Topas!　　　　　　　　　　60

Sir Toby My most exquisite Sir Topas!

Clown Nay, I am for all waters.

Maria Thou mightst have done this without thy
beard and gown: he sees thee not.

Sir Toby To him in thine own voice, and bring me　　65
word how thou findest him. I would we were well
rid of this knavery. If he may be conveniently delivered, I would he were, for I am now so far in
offence with my niece that I cannot pursue with any
safety this sport to the upshot. Come by and by to　　70
my chamber.
[*Exeunt SIR TOBY and MARIA.*]

Clown [*Singing.*] Hey, Robin, jolly Robin,
Tell me how thy lady does.

Malvolio Fool!

Clown "My lady is unkind, perdy."

Malvolio Fool!　　　　　　　　　　　　　　　75

Clown "Alas, why is she so?"

Malvolio Fool, I say!

Clown "She loves another" — Who calls, ha?

Malvolio Good fool, as ever thou wilt deserve well
at my hand, help me to a candle, and pen, ink, and　　80
paper. As I am a gentleman, I will live to be thankful to thee for't.

Clown Master Malvolio?

Malvolio Ay, good fool.

Clown Alas, sir, how fell you beside your five wits?

Malvolio Fool, there was never man so notoriously　　85
abused. I am as well in my wits, fool, as thou art.

Clown But as well? then you are mad indeed, if
you be no better in your wits than a fool.

Malvolio They have here propertied me; keep me
in darkness, send ministers to me, asses, and do all　　90
they can to face me out of my wits.

64. *he sees thee not*: because the place is dark (perhaps this was why Feste was reluctant to put on
the beard and gown in the first place).

66. *well rid*: Sir Toby wishes they were out of this
affair. He senses trouble with Olivia over this
"joke."

70. *upshot*: logical conclusion.

73. *Jolly Robin...*: lyrics from a song attributed to
Thomas Wyatt.

84. *fell you... five wits*: lost your reason.

89. *propertied me*: made a tool of.

Clown Advise you what you say; the minister is
  here. Malvolio, Malvolio, thy wits the heavens restore! endeavour thyself to sleep, and leave thy vain
  bibble babble.

Malvolio Sir Topas!   95

Clown Maintain no words with him, good fellow.
  Who, I, sir? not I, sir. God be wi' you, good Sir
  Topas. Marry, amen. I will, sir, I will.

Malvolio Fool, fool, fool, I say!

Clown Alas, sir, be patient. What say you, sir? I   100
  am shent for speaking to you.

Malvolio Good fool, help me to some light and
  some paper. I tell thee, I am as well in my wits as
  any man in Illyria.

Clown Well-a-day that you were, sir!   105

Malvolio By this hand, I am. Good fool, some ink,
  paper, and light; and convey what I will set down to
  my lady. It shall advantage thee more than ever the
  bearing of letter did.

Clown I will help you to't. But tell me true, are   110
  you not mad indeed? or do you but counterfeit?

Malvolio Believe me, I am not; I tell thee true.

Clown Nay, I'll ne'er believe a madman till I see
  his brains. I will fetch you light and paper and ink.

Malvolio Fool, I'll requite it in the highest degree.   115
  I prithee, be gone.

Clown *[Singing.]* I am gone, sir.
  And anon, sir,
  I'll be with you again,
  In a trice,   120
  Like to the old Vice,
  Your need to sustain;
  Who, with dagger of lath,
  In his rage and his wrath,
  Cries, aha! to the devil: 125

94.   *vain bibble babble:* see I Timothy 6:20; 2 Timothy 2:16.

101.   *shent:* rebuked, reproved, blamed.

107.   *convey:* carry to my lady.
108.   *advantage thee:* profit or reward thee.

115.   *requite:* repay, reimburse.

121.   *old Vice:* comic character in the mediaeval morality plays.

Like a mad lad,
Pare thy nails, dad;
Adieu, goodman devil.
[Exit.]

128. *goodman:* title for a person of social rank, but not of noble birth.

COMMENTARY

Malvolio has been locked up in a dark room in the cellar of Olivia's house by Sir Toby and his cohorts. Maria seems to have come up with a new way to torture Malvolio. She waits outside Malvolio's cell as Feste disguises himself as Sir Topas the curate.

Putting on the curate's gown, Feste jests that he will dissemble himself (pretend to be a curate), and that he wishes he were the first that ever dissembled himself in such a gown (pretended to be virtuous). This harks back to Feste's quip to Olivia in Act I, Scene 5: "...cucullus non facit monachum," that is, the cowl does not make the monk, as well as to his equivocal comments to Cesario about living by the church. Feste uses his wit to criticize hypocrisy, false appearances, and any force that sets itself in opposition to experiencing the pleasures of life. His targets include the church, Olivia's protracted mourning, Orsino's self-proclaimed constancy, and Malvolio's moral rectitude and social climbing.

Feste sums up the question of being and identity in this play by saying, "That that is, is; so I, being Master Parson, am Master Parson...." Or to put it another way, we are the roles we play, while we play them. Malvolio, the somber puritanical steward locked in a room for madmen, is a madman; Viola, while she plays Cesario, is the handsome young gentleman desired by Olivia; and so on, until the role no longer suits the occasion.

Disguised as Sir Topas, Feste calls into the prison and announces that he has come to visit Malvolio the lunatic. Malvolio is relieved to hear the parson's voice, for he fondly imagines that his deliverance from prison is near. And as it is deliverance from darkness that Malvolio craves, Feste, in the guise of Sir Topas, offers Malvolio enlightenment. Feste parodies the language of the church, suggesting that Malvolio's darkness is ignorance.

In an attempt to prove his sanity to the parson, Malvolio asks to have his reason put to the test. Feste asks him what the opinion of Pythagoras was concerning wild fowl, and Malvolio correctly answers that he believed in the transmigration of human souls into animals. He adds that he himself does not believe this, for he thinks nobly of the soul.

Shakespeare may mean to convey that pagan elements had crept into Christian religion. The Twelfth Night celebration of the Epiphany in Shakespeare's day had taken on elements of the Roman Saturnalia. This play, which some claim was first performed on Twelfth Night, is much more concerned with the festive holiday spirit of the Saturnalia than the Christian ceremony of the Epiphany. Although Shakespeare had to be careful that his plays did not appear too pagan, if he had hopes that the plays would be performed, it is also clear that the morality of this play is at least as pagan as it is Christian.

Certainly, the institutionalized Elizabethan church did not teach the path of excess of *Twelfth Night,* which has more in common with Dionysian revels than it does with a church service. Shakespeare understood that human nature in civilized Elizabethan society had become somewhat too repressed, and even though Shakespeare himself, at times, takes great pleasure in that world, his harshest criticisms are for moralists who judge others for indulging in what Christians call "sins." One is hard pressed to come up with any example in Shakespeare in which the judger is not judged at least as harshly as those he judges. In this sense, Shakespeare's morality is both pagan and Christ-like, but it is more like what Jesus taught ("judge not, lest ye be judged") than it is like the morality of many professed Christians.

Feste leaves Malvolio in his darkness to join Toby and Maria. Maria notes that Feste might have acted the part of the parson without his disguise, as Malvolio could not see him in the dark. Toby suggests that Feste should return to Malvolio in his regular voice to find out how he is doing.

Toby has grown weary of this business. He is worried that Olivia will never forgive him (66–71). He has just abused Sebastian, remember, and now he is abusing her steward, about whom we know she cares a great deal. Toby is beginning to see that things have gone too far, and things that are enjoyable in moderation can be harmful if taken to extremes.

Feste re-enters as himself, singing. Malvolio calls out to him for help, asking for ink and paper and a candle so that he can write a note to Olivia. Feste asks how Malvolio went mad, and Malvolio answers, "I am as well in my wits, fool, as thou art." Feste's questioning of Malvolio's wits hearkens back to their first confrontation

when Malvolio implied that the fool's wits were infirm. Now, however, Malvolio can no longer afford to act superior to the fool. Perhaps the gulling has served a positive function, if it has taught Malvolio humility.

Malvolio complains of his treatment — he claims to have been notoriously abused — and Feste tells him to watch his words, for the minister is here. Feste then assumes his ecclesiastical voice again and gives Malvolio another pearl of specious wisdom. By changing from one voice to another in rapid succession, Feste gives Malvolio the impression that he has two visitors instead of one.

Finally, having had his fun, and perhaps beginning to feel slightly guilty for torturing the pathetic steward, Feste promises to bring Malvolio some ink and paper. Feste leaves singing. Feste's participation in Malvolio's gulling is benign for the most part, as it comes late (he takes no part in the initial planning) and leads to his eventual release.

Act IV, Scene 3

Sebastian is puzzled and amazed by his strange good fortune; he cannot decide whether it is a dream, everyone is mad, or he is truly lucky. Olivia begs him to marry her quickly to allay her worries and he readily agrees.

ACT IV, SCENE 3
Olivia's garden.

[Enter SEBASTIAN.]

Sebastian This is the air; that is the glorious sun;
This pearl she gave me, I do feel't and see't;
And though 'tis wonder that enwraps me thus,
Yet 'tis not madness. Where's Antonio, then?
I could not find him at the Elephant;   5
Yet there he was; and there I found this credit,
That he did range the town to seek me out.
His counsel now might do me golden service;
For though my soul disputes well with my sense,
That this may be some error, but no madness,   10
Yet doth this accident and flood of fortune
So far exceed all instance, all discourse,
That I am ready to distrust mine eyes,
And wrangle with my reason, that peruades me
To any other trust but that I am mad,   15
Or else the lady's mad; yet, if 'twere so,
She could not sway her house, command her followers,
Take and give back affairs and their dispatch
With such a smooth, discreet, and stable bearing
As I perceive she does. There's something in't   20
That is deceivable. But here the lady comes.

[Enter OLIVIA and Priest.]

Olivia Blame not this haste of mine. If you mean well,
Now go with me and with this holy man
Into the chantry by. There, before him,
And underneath that consecrated roof,   25
Plight me the full assurance of your faith,
That my most jealous and too doubtful soul
May live at peace. He shall conceal it
Whiles you are willing it shall come to note,

NOTES

2. *This pearl:* evidence of Olivia's love.

6. *credit:* general view or belief; report.

8. *counsel:* advice, guidance.

18–20. *Take...she does.:* undertake business matters with skill and reason.

21. *deceivable:* mistaken.

24. *chantry:* private chapel.

26. *Plight me:* pledge me.

27. *jealous:* anxious, worried.

29. *to note:* to public notice.

What time we will our celebration keep   30
According to my birth. What do you say?

Sebastian I'll follow this good man, and go with you;
And, having sworn truth, ever will be true.

Olivia Then lead the way, good father; and heavens so shine,
That they may fairly note this act of mine!   35
[*Exeunt.*]

31.   *my birth:* Olivia is a countess in her own right now, and deserves a full public wedding ceremony when the time comes.

COMMENTARY

In Olivia's garden, Sebastian revels in his good fortune. He can't help wondering whether the events of the day aren't too wonderful to be real. No, it's not a dream; the pearl she gave him is real; he can attest to that. In need of advice, he thinks of Antonio, who might help reason out this mad situation, but Sebastian has not been able to find him.

Notice that while Sebastian is interested in finding Antonio, it is not because he misses him; rather Antonio's advice would do Sebastian golden service, that is, it would help him to pierce the mystery of his situation and decide whether he should marry Olivia. Here is another distinguishing characteristic that differentiates Viola from her brother. Where Viola is constantly giving of herself for others, Sebastian seems a bit opportunistic. He readily accepts pearls and kindness from Olivia. With Antonio, the man who saved his life and took care of him for three months, Sebastian is interested in seeing him only when Antonio can provide him a "golden service". He is either insensitive to Antonio's feelings for him or very naïve.

Sebastian reasons that Olivia must be sane. She could not hold authority in her house if she were mad. And he has seen the servants obey her commands, so she does hold authority. Sebastian sums up the mad world of this play when he says, "there's something in't that is deceivable." He simply cannot believe that love can be this easy. We know that he is right; it is likely that Olivia would not have fallen for Sebastian so easily had she not thought he was Cesario. But the fact that Olivia chooses to stick by Sebastian, even when she finds out that he is not who she first fell for, reveals that part of Sebastian's function is to provide a stark contrast with other love plots. The other plots in this play are, by contrast, so much ado about nothing. The other characters (Orsino, Olivia, and Viola) have made the notion of love so difficult that, by this point in the play, Sebastian brings a certain refreshing quality in the ease with which he finds love.

Olivia arrives with a priest. She apologizes for rushing the marriage, but she has a jealous mind and too many doubts to find any peace until they have their full rites in the church. Apparently, she either suspects that the person she thinks is Cesario will change his mind, or fears that Cesario's sudden acceptance, after such protracted wooing and rejection, may be a dream. The marriage will be kept a secret; they will have a public ceremony later, in keeping with her rank. Sebastian agrees, and they go off arm and arm to the chantry. For Olivia, there is also something "deceivable" in it, but she, like Sebastian, is willing to suspend disbelief.

Notes

Notes

Notes

CLIFFSCOMPLETE

TWELFTH NIGHT
ACT V

Duke *One face, one voice, one habit, and two persons,*
A natural perspective, that is, and is not!

. . . .

Antonio *How have you made division of yourself?*
An apple, cleft in two, is not more twin
Than these two creatures. Which is Sebastian?

Act V, **Scene 1**	**Orsino asks Feste to send Olivia to him. Officers bring Antonio before Orsino. Antonio recounts the ingratitude of Viola. Olivia arrives and informs Orsino that Viola is her husband. Viola denies this, and Olivia sends for a priest to prove its truth. Sir Andrew and Sir Toby enter bleeding and blame Viola for their wounds. Sebastian enters, and all the mistakes of identity are correctly explained. Orsino asks Viola to marry him; they will share a wedding ceremony with Sebastian and Olivia. Malvolio's letter is delivered, and he is freed. He learns that he has been deceived by Maria and Toby and swears to get his revenge.**

ACT V, SCENE 1
The street before Olivia's house.

[Enter Clown and FABIAN.]

Fabian Now, as thou lovest me, let me see his letter.

Clown Good master Fabian, grant me another request.

Fabian Anything.

Clown Do not desire to see this letter.

Fabian This is, to give a dog, and in recompense   5
desire my dog again.

[Enter Duke, VIOLA, CURIO, and Lords.]

Duke Belong you to the Lady Olivia, friends?

Clown Ay, sir, we are some of her trappings.

Duke I know thee well. How dost thou, my good
fellow?

Clown Truly, sir, the better for my foes and the   10
worse for my friends.

Duke Just the contrary, the better for thy friends.

Clown No, sir, the worse.

Duke How can that be?

Clown Marry, sir, they praise me and make an ass   15
of me; now my foes tell me plainly I am an ass: so
that by my foes, sir, I profit in the knowledge of

NOTES

1. *his:* Malvolio's.

8. *trappings:* belongings (relate to "Belong you...?" in the previous line).

myself, and by my friends I am abused: so that, conclusions to be as kisses, if your four negatives make
your two affirmatives, why then, the worse for my   20
friends and the better for my foes.

Duke Why, this is excellent.

Clown By my troth, sir, no, though it please you
to be one of my friends.

Duke Thou shalt not be the worse for me. There's   25
gold.

Clown But that it would be double-dealing, sir, I
would you could make it another.

Duke Oh, you give me ill counsel.

Clown Put your grace in your pocket, sir, for this
once, and let your flesh and blood obey it.

Duke Well, I will be so much a sinner, to be a dou-   30
ble-dealer; there's another.

Clown Primo, secundo, tertio, is a good play; and
the old saying is, the third pays for all. The triplex,
sir, is a good tripping measure; or the bells of Saint
Bennet, sir, may put you in mind; one, two, three.   35

Duke You can fool no more money out of me at
this throw. If you will let your lady know I am here to
speak with her, and bring her along with you, it
may awake my bounty further.

Clown Marry, sir, lullaby to your bounty till I come   40
again. I go, sir, but I would not have you to think
that my desire of having is the sin of covetousness;
but, as you say, sir, let your bounty take a nap, I
will awake it anon.
[Exit.]

Viola Here comes the man, sir, that did rescue me.

[Enter ANTONIO and Officers.]

Duke That face of his I do remember well;   45
Yet, when I saw it last it was besmear'd
As black as Vulcan in the smoke of war.
A bawbling vessel was he captain of,
For shallow draught and bulk unprizable,

19–20. *four negatives make your two affirmatives:* Feste knows his logic well. He means kissing.

23. *troth:* truth.

28. *grace:* the title of a Duke, and the source of all charity.

32. *Primo, etc.:* first, second, third; refers to a counting game played with dice.

33. *triplex:* triple time in music for dancing.

34. *Saint Bennet:* probably one of the St. Bennet (Benedict) churches in the city of London.

39. *bounty:* generosity.

40. *lullaby to your bounty:* may your generosity sleep sweetly until I come again to reawaken it.

44. *the man:* Antonio.

47. *Vulcan:* Roman god of fire and metal-work.

48. *bawbling:* small.

49. *unprizable:* worthless.

With which such scathful grapple did he make   50
With the most noble bottom of our fleet,
That very envy and the tongue of loss
Cried fame and honour on him. What's the matter?

First Officer Orsino, this is that Antonio
That took the Phoenix and her fraught from Candy;   55
And this is he that did the Tiger board,
When your young nephew Titus lost his leg.
Here in the streets, desperate of shame and state,
In private brabble did we apprehend him.

Viola He did me kindness, sir, drew on my side;   60
But in conclusion put strange speech upon me,
I know not what 'twas but distraction.

Duke Notable pirate! thou salt-water thief!
What foolish boldness brought thee to their mercies,
Whom thou, in terms so bloody and so dear,   65
Hast made thine enemies?

Antonio   Orsino, noble sir,
Be pleased that I shake off these names you give me.
Antonio never yet was thief or pirate,
Though I confess, on base and ground enough,
Orsino's enemy. A witchcraft drew me hither.   70
That most ingrateful boy there by your side,
From the rude sea's enraged and foamy mouth
Did I redeem; a wreck past hope he was.
His life I gave him and did thereto add
My love, without retention or restraint,   75
All his in dedication; for his sake
Did I expose myself, pure for his love,
Into the danger of this adverse town;
Drew to defend him when he was beset:
Where being apprehended, his false cunning,   80
Not meaning to partake with me in danger,
Taught him to face me out of his acquaintance,
And grew a twenty years removed thing
While one could wink; denied me mine own purse,
Which I had recommended to his use   85
Not half an hour before.

Viola   How can this be?

---

50. *scathful grapple:* damaging attack.

51. *bottom of our fleet:* ship of our fleet.

52. *That, etc.:* that even those who had suffered loss envied him his success and honored him for his famous achievement.

55. *fraught:* freight, cargo.

  Candy: ancient capital of Crete.

59. *brabble:* brawl.

  apprehend: seize or arrest.

60. *drew:* drew his sword.

61. *strange speech:* unintelligible words.

62. *distraction:* madness.

71. *ingrateful:* ungrateful (Antonio thinks the boy is Sebastian, whereas we know it is Viola in disguise still).

72. *rude:* rough.

  mouth: personification of the sea.

75. *retention:* withholding or holding back.

82. *face me out of his acquaintance:* brazenly deny ever having known me.

85. *recommended to his use:* urged upon him.

Duke When came he to this town?

Antonio To-day, my lord; and for three months before,
No interim, not a minute's vacancy,
Both day and night did we keep company.   90

[Enter OLIVIA and Attendants.]

Duke Here comes the countess; now heaven walks on earth.
But for thee, fellow, — fellow, thy words are madness.
Three months this youth hath tended upon me;
But more of that anon. Take him aside.

Olivia What would my lord, but that he may not have,   95
Wherein Olivia may seem serviceable?
Cesario, you do not keep promise with me.

Viola Madam!

Duke Gracious Olivia, —

Olivia What do you say, Cesario? Good my lord,   100

Viola My lord would speak; my duty hushes me.

Olivia If it be aught to the old tune, my lord,
It is as fat and fulsome to mine ear
As howling after music.

Duke   Still so cruel?

Olivia Still so constant, lord.   105

Duke What, to perverseness? you uncivil lady,
To whose ingrate and unauspicious altars
My soul the faithfull'st offerings hath breathed out
That e'er devotion tender'd! What shall I do?

Olivia Even what it please my lord, that shall become him. 110

Duke Why should I not, had I the heart to do it,
Like to the Egyptian thief at point of death,
Kill what I love? — a savage jealousy
That sometimes savours nobly. But hear me this:
Since you to non-regardance cast my faith,   115
And that I partly know the instrument
That screws me from my true place in your favour,
Live you the marble-breasted tyrant still;
But this your minion, whom I know you love,
And whom, by heaven I swear, I tender dearly,   120

89. *No interim:* no interruption.

107. *ingrate:* ungrateful.

unauspicious altars: unhappy places of worship.

112. *Egyptian thief:* reference to Thyamis, a character in a Greek novel, who tried to kill his lover Chariclea to prevent her from falling into the hands of their enemies, but who killed the wrong person; Chariclea escaped. Translated into English in 1569 (Theagenes).

119. *minion:* darling; also servant.

Him will I tear out of that cruel eye,
Where he sits crowned in his master's spite.
Come, boy, with me; my thoughts are ripe in mischief.
I'll sacrifice the lamb that I do love,
To spite a raven's heart within a dove.   125

Viola And I, most jocund, apt, and willingly,
To do you rest, a thousand deaths would die.

126. *jocund:* merrily.

127. *To do you rest:* to give you peace of mind.

Olivia Where goes Cesario?

Viola   After him I love
More than I love these eyes, more than my life,
More, by all mores, than e'er I shall love wife.   130
If I do feign, you witnesses above
Punish my life for tainting of my love!

131. *feign:* pretend.

132. *tainting:* spoiling.

133. *beguiled:* betrayed and tricked.

Olivia Ay me, detested! how am I beguiled!

Viola Who does beguile you? who does do you wrong?

Olivia Hast thou forgot thyself? is it so long?   135
Call forth the holy father.

Duke   Come, away!

Olivia Whither, my lord? Cesario, husband, stay.

Duke Husband!

Olivia   Ay, husband: can he that deny?

Duke Her husband, sirrah!

Viola   No, my lord, not I.

Olivia Alas, it is the baseness of thy fear   140
That makes thee strangle thy propriety.
Fear not, Cesario; take thy fortunes up;
Be that thou know'st thou art, and then thou art
As great as that thou fear'st.
[Enter Priest.]
                                        Oh, welcome, father!
Father, I charge thee, by thy reverence,   145
Here to unfold, though lately we intended
To keep in darkness what occasion now
Reveals before 'tis ripe, what thou dost know
Hath newly pass'd between this youth and me.

Priest A contract of eternal bond of love,   150
Confirm'd by mutual joinder of your hands,

150. *contract:* marriage-agreement.

151. *mutual joinder:* reciprocal joining.

Attested by the holy close of lips,
Strengthen'd by interchangement of your rings;
And all the ceremony of this compact
Seal'd in my function, by my testimony: 155
Since when, my watch hath told me, toward my grave
I have trevell'd but two hours.

Duke O thou dissembling cub! what wilt thou be
When time hath sow'd a grizzle on thy case?
Or will not else thy craft so quickly grow,   160
That thine own trip shall be thine overthrow?
Farewell, and take her; but direct thy feet
Where thou and I henceforth may never meet.

Viola My lord, I do protest —

Olivia   Oh, do not swear!
Hold little faith, though thou hast too much fear.   165

[*Enter SIR ANDREW.*]

Sir Andrew For the love of God, a surgeon! Send
one presently to Sir Toby.

Olivia What's the matter?

Sir Andrew He has broke my head across and has
given Sir Toby a bloody coxcomb too. For the love   170
of God, your help! I had rather than forty pound
I were at home.

Olivia Who has done this, Sir Andrew?

Sir Andrew The count's gentleman, one Cesario.
We took him for a coward, but he's the very devil incardinate.

Duke My gentleman, Cesario?   175

Sir Andrew 'Od's lifelings! Here he is! You broke
my head for nothing; and that that I did, I was set
on to do't by Sir Toby.

Viola Why do you speak to me? I never hurt you:
You drew your sword upon me without cause;   180
But I bespake you fair, and hurt you not.

Sir Andrew If a bloody coxcomb be a hurt, you
have hurt me: I think you set nothing by a bloody
coxcomb. [*Enter SIR TOBY and Clown.*] Here comes

152. *Attested:* witnessed by.

holy close of lips: kissing.

154. *ceremony of this compact:* ritual of the matrimonial agreement. The language of the priest is both legal and theological, since he has performed a civil and a religious ceremony within the last two hours.

158. *dissembling cub:* deceiving youth.

159. *sow'd a grizzle on thy case:* grown a beard on your face.

170. *coxcomb:* ludicrous name for the head.

174. *incardinate:* incarnate (in the flesh).

176. *'Od's lifelings:* God's lifelings (a common Elizabethan oath).

177–178. *set on to do't:* put up to it (by).

Sir Toby halting; you shall hear more: but if he had
not been in drink, he would have tickled you other-   185
gates than he did.

Duke How now, gentleman! how is't with you?

Sir Toby That's all one; has hurt me, and there's
the end on't. Sot. didst see Dick surgeon, sot?

Clown Oh, he's drunk, Sir Toby, an hour agone;   190
his eyes were set at eight i' the morning.

Sir Toby Then he's a rogue, and a passy measures
pavin. I hate a drunken rogue.

Olivia Away with him! Who hath made this havoc
with them?   195

Sir Andrew I'll help you, Sir Toby, because we'll
be dressed together.

Sir Toby Will you help? an ass-head and a coxcomb
and a knave, a thin-faced knave, a gull!

Olivia Get him to bed, and let his hurt be looked to.   200

[Exeunt Clown, FABIAN, SIR TOBY, and SIR ANDREW.]
[Enter SEBASTIAN.]

Sebastian I am sorry, madam, I have hurt your kinsman;
But, had it been the brother of my blood,
I must have done no less with wit and safety.
You throw a strange regard upon me, and by that
I do perceive it hath offended you.   205
Pardon me, sweet one, even for the vows
We made each other but so late ago.

Duke One face, one voice, one habit, and two persons,
A natural perspective, that is, and is not!

Sebastian Antonio, O my dear Antonio!   210
How have the hours rack'd and tortured me
Since I have lost thee!

Antonio Sebastian are you?

Sebastian   Fear'st thou that, Antonio?

Antonio How have you made division of yourself?
An apple, cleft in two, is not more twin   215
Than these two creatures. Which is Sebastian?

184. *halting:* limping.
185. *othergates:* otherwise (than).
189. *sot:* fool.
191. *set:* glazed or glassy with drink.
192. *passy measures pavin:* Italian passermezzo pavana, a slow and stately dance.
194. *havoc:* devastation.
197. *dressed:* have our wounds bandaged.
198. *Will you help, etc:* Sir Toby's scorn for Sir Andrew here falls into downright irritation and contempt.
209. *natural perspective:* an optical device common in Elizabethan times was the glass which showed one image when viewed from the front, and another image when viewed from an angle.
211. *rack'd:* reference to the rack, an instrument of torture.

Olivia Most wonderful!

Sebastian. Do I stand there? I never had a brother;
Nor can there be that deity in my nature,
Of here and everywhere. I had a sister,   220
Whom the blind waves and surges have devour'd.
Of charity, what kin are you to me?
What countryman? what name? what parentage?

Viola Of Messaline. Sebastian was my father;
Such a Sebastian was my brother too,   225
So went he suited to his watery tomb.
If spirits can assume both form and suit,
You come to fright us.

Sebastian   A spirit I am indeed;
But am in that dimension grossly clad
Which from the womb I did participate.   230
Were you a woman, as the rest goes even,
I should my tears let fall upon your cheek,
And say, "Thrice-welcome, drowned Viola!"

Viola My father had a mole upon his brow.

Sebastian And so had mine.   235

Viola And died that day when Viola from her birth
Had number'd thirteen years.

Sebastian Oh, that record is lively in my soul!
He finished indeed his mortal act
That day that made my sister thirteen years.   240

Viola If nothing lets to make us happy both
But this my masculine usurp'd attire,
Do not embrace me till each circumstance
Of place, time, fortune, do cohere and jump
That I am Viola: which to confirm,   245
I'll bring you a captain in this town,
Where lie my maiden weeds; by whose gentle help
I was preserved to serve this noble count.
All the occurrence of my fortune since
Hath been between this lady and this lord.   250

Sebastian *[To Olivia.]* So comes it, lady, you have been
     mistook;
But nature to her bias drew in that.

219–220. *deity in my nature/Of here and everywhere:* reference to the idea (expressed clearly in the English Book of Common Prayer) that it is against the nature of things for anything to be in more than one place at the same time.

226. *suited:* dressed.

234. *mole:* congenital spot on the skin, usually brown; a birth-mark, evidence of identification.

247. *maiden weeds:* girl's clothes.

251. *mistook:* archaic form for mistaken.

253. *But nature to her bias:* nature led you truly in this (else you would have been married to a girl).

You would have been contracted to a maid;
Nor are you therein, by my life, deceived;
You are betroth'd both to a maid and man.   255

Duke Be not amazed; right noble is his blood.
If this be so, as yet the glass seems true,
I shall have share in his most happy wreck.
[To Viola.] Boy, thou hast said to me a thousand times
Thou never shouldst love woman like to me.   260

Viola And all those sayings will I over-swear;
And all those swearings keep as true in soul
As doth that orbed continent the fire
That severs day from night.

Duke   Give me thy hand;
And let me see thee in thy woman's weeds.   265

Viola The captain that did bring me first on shore
Hath my maid's garments. He upon some action
Is now in durance, at Malvolio's suit,
A gentleman, and follower of my lady's.

Olivia He shall enlarge him. Fetch Malvolio hither;   270
And yet, alas, now I remember me,
They say, poor gentleman, he's much distract.
[Re-enter Clown with a letter, and FABIAN.]
A most extracting frenzy of mine own
From my remembrance clearly banish'd his.
How does he, sirrah?   275

Clown Truly, madam, he holds Beelzebub at the
stave's end as well as a man in his case may do: has
here writ a letter to you; I should have given 't to you
to-day morning, but as a madman's epistles are no
gospels, so it skills not much when they are   280
delivered.

Olivia Open't, and read it.

Clown Look then to be well edified when the fool
delivers the madman. *[Reads.]* "By the Lord,
madam," —

Olivia How now! art thou mad?   285

263. *orbed continent the fire:* the stars.

268. *in durance:* waiting trial in prison.
suit: instigation.

276. *Beelzebub:* Satan.

278–279. *epistles... gospels:* letters... good news.

282–283. *fool delivers the madman:* play on words (to further delay Malvolio's now inevitable deliverance from the dark room?). A play on the two meanings as in delivering a speech and delivering somebody from prison.

Clown No, madam, I do but read madness; an
your ladyship will have it as it ought to be, you
must allow Vox.

Olivia Prithee, read i' thy right wits.

Clown So I do, madonna; but to read his right
wits is to read thus: therefore perpend, my princess,   290
and give ear.

Olivia Read it you, sirrah. *[To Fabian.]*

Fabian *[Reads.]* "By the Lord, madam, you wrong
me, and the world shall know it. Though you have
put me into darkness and given your drunken cousin
rule over me, yet have I the benefit of my senses as   295
well as your ladyship. I have your own letter that
induced me to the semblance I put on; with the
which I doubt not but to do myself much right, or
you much shame. Think of me as you please. I leave
my duty a little unthought of, and speak out of my   300
injury."
"THE MADLY-USED MALVOLIO."

Olivia Did he write this?

Clown Ay, madam.

Duke This savours not much of distraction.

Olivia See him deliver'd, Fabian; bring him hither.   305
[Exit FABIAN.]
My lord, so please you, these things further thought on,
To think me as well a sister as a wife,
One day shall crown the alliance on't, so please you,
Here at my house and at my proper cost.

Duke Madam, I am most apt to embrace your offer.   310
[To Viola.] Your master quits you; and for your service
done him,
So much against the mettle of your sex,
So far beneath your soft and tender breeding,
And since you call'd me master for so long,
Here is my hand. You shall from this time be   315
Your master's mistress.

Olivia   A sister! you are she.

[Re-enter FABIAN with MALVOLIO.]

---

288. *Vox:* Latin for voice. The Clown uses a solemn and ridiculous voice to make fun of Malvolio.

290. *perpend:* listen carefully.

297. *induced me:* led me.

semblance: the costume as recommended by the letter.

300. *THE MADLY-USED MALVOLIO:* suggests that though he has been treated as though he were mad, the truth is otherwise.

308. *One day shall crown the alliance on't:* The double marriage shall take place at the same time, at Olivia's house, and at her expense.

316. *master's mistress:* an irresistible play on masculine-feminine words.

Duke Is this the madman?

Olivia   Ay, my lord, the same.
  How now, Malvolio?

Malvolio   Madam, you have done me wrong,
  Notorious wrong.

Olivia   Have I, Malvolio? no.

Malvolio Lady, you have. Pray you, peruse that letter.   320
  You must not now deny it is your hand.
  Write from it, if you can, in hand or phrase;
  Or say 'tis not your seal, not your invention.
  You can say none of this; well, grant it then,
  And tell me, in the modesty of honour,   325
  Why you have given me such clear lights of favour,
  Bade me come smiling and cross-garter'd to you,
  To put on yellow stockings and to frown
  Upon Sir Toby and the lighter people;
  And, acting this in an obedient hope,   330
  Why have you suffer'd me to be imprison'd,
  Kept in a dark house, visited by the priest,
  And made the most notorious geck and gull
  That e'er invention play'd on? tell me why.

Olivia Alas, Malvolio, this is not my writing,   335
  Though, I confess, much like the character;
  But out of question 'tis Maria's hand.
  And now I do bethink me, it was she
  First told me thou wast mad; then camest in smiling,
  And in such forms which here were presupposed   340
  Upon thee in the letter. Prithee, be content.
  This practice hath most shrewdly pass'd upon thee;
  But when we know the grounds and authors of it,
  Thou shalt be both the plaintiff and the judge
  Of thine own cause.   345

Fabian   Good madam, hear me speak.
  And let no quarrel nor no brawl to come
  Taint the condition of this present hour,
  Which I have wonder'd at. In hope it shall not,
  Most freely I confess, myself and Toby
  Set this device against Malvolio here,   350
  Upon some stubborn and uncourteous parts

332.   *geck and gull:* dupe.

We had conceived against him. Maria writ
The letter at Sir Toby's great importance;
In recompense whereof he hath married her.
How with a sportful malice it was follow'd,   355
May rather pluck on laughter than revenge,
If that the injuries be justly weigh'd
That have on both sides pass'd.

Olivia Alas, poor fool, how have they baffled thee!

Clown Why, "some are born great, some achieve   360
greatness, and some have greatness thrown upon
them." I was one, sir, in this interlude, one Sir Topas,
sir; but that's all one. "By the Lord, fool, I am not
mad." But do you remember? "Madam, why
laugh you at such a barren rascal? an you smile not,   365
he's gagged." and thus the whirligig of Time brings
in his revenges.

Malvolio I'll be revenged on the whole pack of you.
[Exit.]

Olivia He hath been most notoriously abused.

Duke Pursue him, and entreat him to a peace.
He hath not told us of the captain yet.   370
When that is known and golden time convents,
A solemn combination shall be made
Of our dear souls. Meantime, sweet sister,
We will not part from hence. Cesario, come;
For so you shall be, while you are a man;   375
But when in other habits you are seen,
Orsino's mistress and his fancy queen.
[Exeunt all, but Clown.]

Clown *[Sings.]*
When that I was and a little tiny boy,
  With hey, ho, the wind and the rain,
A foolish thing was but a toy,   380
  For the rain it raineth every day.

But when I came to man's estate,
  With hey, ho, the wind and the rain,
'Gainst knaves and thieves men shut their gate,
  For the rain it raineth every day.   385

355. *sportful malice:* in this trick there is more matter for laughter than revenge though all Malvolio can see is revenge.

356. *pluck on:* induce.

359. *baffled thee:* shamed thee, brought him to confusion.

366. *whirligig:* continual whirling, spinning top.

371. *convents:* summons, call together.

378. The boy (Stage 1).

382. The grown men (Stage 2).

But when I came, alas! to wive,
  With hey, ho, the wind and the rain,
  By swaggering could I never thrive,
  For the rain it raineth every day.

But when I came unto my beds,   390
  With hey, ho, the wind and the rain,
  With tosspots still had drunken heads,
  For the rain it raineth every day.

A great while ago the world begun,
  With hey, ho, the wind and the rain,   395
  But that's all one, our play is done,
  And we'll strive to please you every day.
[Exit.]

386.   Married state (Stage 3).

390.   Senility (Stage 4).

394.   The end (Stage 5).

COMMENTARY

The last act consists of one long important scene, in which most of the play's plot complications are resolved. In the street before Olivia's house, Fabian meets Feste carrying Malvolio's letter to Olivia. Although Feste is reluctant to let Fabian see the letter, we will see that he is in no rush to deliver it.

The Duke and his attendants arrive. From the heights of his ducal authority and pretension, Orsino has trouble recognizing Feste as anything beyond Olivia's property, but the Fool is quick to jest him into awareness. Feste's doublespeak only appears to be irrational; in fact, it cuts through the nonsense of propriety and civil lies and gets straight to the truth. Why does Feste say that he is better for his foes and worse for his friends? Because friends will lie to him and allow him to make an ass of himself, whereas enemies will tell him when he is an ass, providing him with self-knowledge. Notice that he says this to Orsino, a man surrounded by attendants who protect him from seeing his true self and allow him to continue being an ass — in love, at least.

Feste's "four negatives make your two affirmatives" prophetically suggests that the four lonely lovers will come together to make two affirmatives (vows of marriage), which will conclude with kisses. The Duke, pleased with Feste's verbal acrobatics, pays him with gold. Feste cleverly begs a second gold piece and, receiving it, attempts to wheedle a third from the duke without luck. As Feste leaves, he tells the Duke's generosity to go to sleep until he comes back to awaken it again.

Enter Antonio, in the custody of the Duke's officers. Viola tells Orsino that the prisoner is the same man who rescued her from the duel with Andrew and begs the Duke to show him leniency. Orsino, however, remembers Antonio from their fight at sea. At that time, Antonio's face was smeared as black as the god Vulcan with battle smoke. The Duke claims that Antonio performed so bravely in battle that even his sworn enemies (says Orsino, his sworn enemy) remembered his feats afterwards and spoke of his valor.

The play's final act will include a reunion of brother and sister, Sebastian and Viola. From a 1997 Royal Shakespeare Company production of Twelfth Night. Clive Barda /PAL

The officers recount the incidents of Antonio's arrest, and Orsino addresses him as a thief and a pirate. Antonio admits to being Orsino's enemy, but not a thief. Cesario's ingratitude, however, is his main concern. Again he recounts the story of Sebastian's rescue, his giving his purse to Sebastian, and the rude treatment he received by Cesario (whom he believes is Sebastian), which he ascribes to fear and cowardice.

Attempting to get to the bottom of this confusion, Orsino asks when Antonio came to town. Today, he says, and until today he has spent every moment of the last three months with this ungrateful youth. Olivia and her attendants arrive, preventing the Duke from unraveling the matter any further.

For the first time in the play, Olivia and Orsino are on stage together. Olivia is courtly but not courteous in her greeting of Orsino. There is more than a hint of cold condescension in her attitude toward the Duke; he has pestered her for so long with his messengers, and now, finally, it is over. She has married someone else: Cesario.

But to Olivia's surprise and concern, she finds Cesario, her husband, at Orsino's side. Has he broken his promise already? Cesario is bewildered by this exchange. Is Olivia mad? Although Cesario has never sworn her love or affections in words to Olivia, she has continued to visit her. And as we know, words are not to be trusted in this play; perhaps her visits have led Olivia on. Cesario is worried that Orsino may misunderstand and jump to dangerous conclusions. One thing that we can count on in Shakespeare's plays: Never trust a mediary when it comes to courting; no matter how well intentioned, they usually drive a wedge between the lover and the beloved.

For example, in *A Midsummer Night's Dream,* Oberon's attempt to bring Helena and Demetrius together does not work as he intended. In *Much Ado About Nothing,* Don Pedro offers simple remedies to bring both pairs of lovers together, which also fail to work as planned. In *Twelfth Night,* Shakespeare adds a twist to this theme, by making Viola/Cesario *both* the well-intentioned mediary as well as the person who will lose at love if her proxy wooing is successful. At this moment in the story, Cesario has clearly not been successful in bringing Orsino and Olivia together. In the process, she is losing the trust of the Duke. When she

(Viola/Cesario) pleads for Olivia to listen to the Duke and ignore his messenger (Cesario), things could hardly seem to get worse for her, but they do.

Olivia has no interest in hearing anything from or about the Duke. Cesario is her one and only concern. Orsino's love being narcissistic, turns to wounded pride, and he lashes out in rage. His pride cannot stand the thought of being cast to non-regardance, the worst fate possible to his egotistic self-love. Orsino surmises that Olivia loves Cesario, his messenger. All his love turns to a murderous rage that will only be appeased by a sacrifice. Why not kill the one he loves, but who is it that he really loves? Olivia or Cesario? He threatens Olivia, but ultimately he decides on Cesario as the perfect sacrifice to his wounded pride. He will deprive Olivia of her love object: Cesario. But maybe Cesario has already become his own subconscious love object.

Orsino will sacrifice the lamb he loves, Cesario, to spite the raven-hearted Olivia. In contrast, Viola willingly volunteers to give her life for her lover's (Orsino's) peace. She even asks the gods to punish her for tainting her love if she does not willingly give herself over to this death for love. She will not have self-love taint her love.

Some argue that Viola's passivity here is hard to accept. While the others err on the side of self-indulgence in this play, Viola tends to over-indulge in self-sacrifice. It is not by chance that Viola is only called by her name once in the entire play; for the majority of the play, Viola has usurped herself in the form of Cesario. Yet such usurping of self, however dangerous, is vindicated by the end of this play. Even though at this moment the play is closer than ever to taking a tragic turn, Viola's very passivity (in contrast to Desdemona's similar passivity in *Othello,* in which her willingness to sacrifice herself to Othello's anger leads to her death, as well as to the death of Othello), is, ironically, what allows her to ultimately win the one she loves.

If most of the characters are unwitting victims of their own unhealthy and selfish desires, Feste and Viola are the exception. Feste keeps his distance from the absurdity of love and ambition through his indifference to it, his playful stance outside the mad courtship rituals. Viola is not indifferent to love but rather so respectful of it that she would die before travestying her passion with vain courtly courtship.

Olivia is inconsolable. She can't imagine how Cesario could forget his vows or deny his affection for her. Cesario refuses to be accused of willfully leading her on, as he never beguiled her. Olivia calls for the holy father. The Duke is furious at his perceived betrayal, crying, "Her husband, sirrah!" Viola denies it all. The priest arrives and attests to the fact that the marriage between Olivia and Cesario has recently taken place.

Orsino, convinced by the priest, calls Cesario a "dissembling cub," and although he is wrong in believing

Viola (as Cesario) and Orsino. From the 1996 film, Twelfth Night, *with Imogen Stubbs and Stephen Mackintosh. The Everett Collection*

Cesario is married, he is at least in part right. Cesario has dissembled to Orsino for the length of their time together, being a woman disguised as a boy.

Sir Andrew enters calling for a surgeon for Sir Toby. He reports that Cesario has bloodied both Toby and himself. The plot continues to thicken. How could Cesario be with the Duke and Olivia in one place and Toby and Andrew in another at the same time? Cesario, knowing of only their earlier mock duel, denies having hurt Andrew.

Toby and Feste enter, and indeed, Toby is bloodied and in need of a surgeon. Feste reports that the surgeon has passed out drunk, leading Toby to assert ironically, "I hate a drunken rogue!" If the purpose of a revel is to feast our appetites to excess, then Sir Toby has finally reached that point; he can no longer tolerate drinking in excess. And moments later, when Andrew offers to help, Sir Toby rebuffs him, calling him "a thin faced knave, a gull!" Sir Toby has had enough of gulling Andrew too, it seems.

Sebastian enters, and the denouement of all the identity complications is set to begin. Cesario and Sebastian are both dressed as men and look strikingly similar. The Duke is dumbfounded and imagines he is seeing a natural optical illusion, "one face, one voice, one habit, and two persons..."

Sebastian's feelings for Antonio seem to have grown more intense by virtue of his absence. When they were together, Sebastian could not say enough to persuade Antonio that they would be better apart, and now, having lost Antonio, Sebastian speaks of it as torture. His language is more passionate and less rhetorical than we have previously heard him speak. Though when the cards are on the table, Sebastian will abandon Antonio yet again without another word. Like the character of Antonio in *The Merchant of Venice,* this Antonio is left at the end of the play with the loss of a dear friend (and/or love interest), but he is not entirely excluded from the happy ending. At least his feud with Duke Orsino is now over. This may be small consolation to Antonio, but it is a significant development.

Antonio is nonplussed by this strange circumstance. He manages to say only, "Sebastian, are you?" and remains silent for the rest of the play. Olivia is both amazed and relieved to see her husband has not deserted her.

Sebastian and Viola turn toward each other with hope and bewilderment. Remember that Viola is dressed as a man, and her hair, which has always been long and full, has been cut in a man's style. While this vision explains part of Sebastian's hesitance, the rest is wonderment at seeing his own likeness, a veritable doppelganger, or double. He cannot stop the rush of questions that tumble from his mouth, "What kin are you to me? What countryman? What name? What parentage?" And though all of Viola's answers seem to say that Cesario is indeed his sister, he remains puzzled by her masculine outward form.

Shakespeare stretches out the recognition scene for as long as possible in order to create and sustain dramatic tension. We have waited the whole play for this moment to come; he will take his time. Viola finally confirms that she is indeed Viola, Sebastian's sister, and that she has served the Duke in this male habit since the shipwreck.

Sebastian explains to Olivia that it was due to these unfortunate and strange circumstances that they have come to be married so quickly. Yet it is also lucky as otherwise she would have been married to a maid. Olivia has no immediate response to this turn of events. If her love for Cesario was based on the wit and plucky intelligence of Viola, her personality and not her looks, as we can assume it was, how can she so easily accept this substitution? In personality, Sebastian and Viola do not seem twins at all; their personalities are as different as their manner of speech. Sebastian lacks the playful charm of Viola; he lacks her sense of humor and sense of improvisation. In part, we must accept the match as the convention of dramatic comedies: They end in marriage, period. (Though we can wonder how they will get along as a married couple.)

The Duke, for his part, happily accepts the change and asks Viola if she is able to love him. She swears that she can, and the Duke asks for her hand, both figuratively and literally. So much for his constancy! He has converted his love for Olivia to Viola without a moment's hesitation. Notice that the notion of the Duke being constant is upheld and lauded by himself, by Valentine, and even Olivia. It is only Viola and Feste who have questioned his constancy in this play.

Before the happy ending can be consummated, Orsino asks to see Viola in her woman's clothing. We learn that the captain who has kept her clothes for her has been thrown into durance (that is, restraint by physical force) by Malvolio. A curious fact, when and why this has happened we never learn, though it may just be an excuse to bring Malvolio on stage so that Shakespeare can tie up all the plot lines in one shot.

Olivia sends for Malvolio, as Feste (with the letter he has yet to deliver in all this time) enters with Fabian. Feste's excuse for not having delivered the letter sooner is that as it was written by a madman, and because a madman's letters are not to be trusted, he didn't see the need to hurry. Olivia asks Feste to read it aloud. Feste reads the letter in an affected voice, as if he himself were the madman. Olivia is annoyed by his persistent clowning in the matter, and she asks Fabian to read it aloud.

Malvolio's letter is well reasoned and not at all the letter of a madman. His claim to have the benefit of his senses as well as Olivia does is both true and telling. They are both sane, though they have both behaved madly. Olivia was insensible to Cesario's dissembling and fell in love with a woman; Malvolio, too, was taken in by the dissembling of Maria's note and fell in love with Olivia.

Orsino notes that the letter does not seem mad at all, and Olivia asks that Malvolio be brought to her. While they wait for him, Olivia suggests that Orsino and Viola should marry at her own and Sebastian's public nuptial at her expense. Orsino agrees and joyfully dismisses Cesario from his role as servant to play the new role of a woman and wife to Orsino.

Malvolio re-enters glowering with rage and indignation, saying, "Madam, you have done me wrong, / Notorious wrong." Olivia denies this fact. And Malvolio shows the forged letter to her, asking her to deny the fact she wrote it. He also asks why she would have him imprisoned and humiliated in such a fashion. Olivia looks at the letter and realizes it is Maria's writing. She promises Malvolio that he shall be both plaintiff and judge of his own cause.

Fabian confesses the part that he and Sir Toby played in the affair and explains that it was in response to Malvolio's stubbornness and uncourteous behavior towards them. He covers for the part Maria played in the gulling, ascribing the origin of the idea to Toby. We learn that Toby has married Maria, bringing this minor subplot to its expected conclusion. Remember that Toby had almost promised to marry Maria as a reward for her gulling of Malvolio. (Will this marriage fair any better than the marriage of Sebastian and Olivia?)

Feste takes the opportunity to remind Malvolio of his pride, which preceded, and in Feste's estimate, precipitated his fall. Malvolio's haughty put-downs of the fool in the earlier acts have now been revenged, as "thus the whiligig of Time brings in his revenges." Not clear, however, is whether Malvolio learns anything from his ordeal, or even whether he should. Though he has wronged others in the play, he has been wronged himself. In effect, Malvolio may be more a man sinned against than a man sinning. Malvolio runs off swearing to be revenged on the whole lot of them.

In lines of stately blank verse, Orsino ends the courtly part of the play. They must pursue Malvolio and entreat him to a peace. Malvolio still has Viola's captain in durance, and Orsino will not marry Viola until he has seen her in her woman's weeds (clothes).

Orsino maintains that he will continue to call Viola by her male name, Cesario, until she has her woman's clothing. Shakespeare has added this minor complication in order to avoid ending the comedy with Orsino kissing Viola on stage, especially while disguised as Cesario (a boy actor dressed in boy's clothes).

Feste is left with the last word. His song returns us to the world of wind and rain, in which a boy becomes a man, swaggers, marries, ages, and dies while the rain raineth every day. The fiction of the play dissolves as the fourth wall (the imaginary wall between audience and players) is broken; Feste speaks directly to the audience, informing them that the play is done. Yet, the scope of this epilogue expands to include not just this one play, but a never-ending cycle of performances. And against reality's wind and rain, we can do no more or less than strive to please each other and enjoy our short residence on earth.

An appropriate ending to a play filled with music, Feste closes in song.

Notes

Notes

Notes

CLIFFSCOMPLETE REVIEW

Use this CliffsComplete Review to gauge what you've learned and to build confidence in your understanding of the original text. After you work through the review questions, the problem-solving exercises, and the suggested activities, you're well on your way to understanding and appreciating the works of William Shakespeare.

IDENTIFY THE QUOTATION

Identify the following quotations by answering these questions:

* Who is the speaker of the quote?
* What does it reveal about the speaker's character?
* What does it tell us about other characters within the play?
* Where does it occur within the play?
* Where does it show us about the themes of the play?
* What significant imagery do you see in the quote, and how do these images relate to the overall imagery of the play?

1. If this fall into thy hand, revolve. In my stars I am above thee; but be not afraid of greatness: some are born great, some achieve greatness, and some have greatness thrust upon 'em.

2. Out o' turn, sir! ye lie. Art any more than a steward? Dost thou think, because thou art virtuous, there shall be no more cakes and ale?

3. What will become of this? As I am man, My state is desperate for my master's love; As I am woman, — now alas the day! — What thriftless sighs shall poor Olivia breathe!

O Time, thou must untangle this, not I! It is too hard a knot for me to untie!

4. If music be the food of love, play on; Give me excess of it, that, surfeiting, The appetite may sicken and so die.

5. Oh, what a deal of scorn looks beautiful In the contempt and anger of his lip! A murderous guilt shows not itself more soon Than love that would seem hid. Love's night is noon.

6. After him I love More than I love these eyes, more than my life, More, by all mores, than e'er I shall love wife. If I do feign, you witnesses above Punish my life for tainting my love!

7. ...for as the old hermit of Prague, that never saw pen and ink, very wittily said to a niece of King Gorboduc, "That that is, is"; so I, being Master Parson, am Master Parson; for, what is "that" but "that," and "is" but "is"?

8. That quaffing and drinking will undo you. I heard my lady talk of it yesterday; and of a foolish knight that you brought in one night here to be her wooer.

TRUE/FALSE

1. T F   At the end of the play, we see Orsino marry Viola.

2. T F   Maria decides to play a trick on Malvolio to get him to stop drinking.

3. T F   Feste sings songs to Orsino as well as to Olivia.

4. T F   Nobody in the play, except the audience, knows that Viola is in love with Orsino until the final scene.

5. T F   Olivia says she would consider Malvolio as a possible lover were she not in love with Cesario.

6. T F   Neither Viola (Cesario) nor Sir Andrew want to fight each other, but they are forced into it by Sir Toby.

7. T F   Orsino is melancholy because he is mourning his dead sister.

8. T F   When Antonio asks Sebastian for the money he gave him, Sebastian gets angry and refuses to pay him back.

9. T F   Viola is dressed in her "woman's weeds" for only one scene in the entire play.

MULTIPLE CHOICE

1. The last words in the play are had by _____.
   a. Malvolio
   b. Orsino
   c. Feste
   d. the Sea Captain

2. Which of the following characters is *not* in love with Olivia?
   a. Sir Andrew
   b. Sir Toby
   c. Malvolio
   d. Orsino

3. Which of the following characters does Orsino say he wants to kill?
   a. Feste
   b. Olivia
   c. Cesario
   d. Sebastian

4. The main setting for the play takes place in _____.
   a. Arden
   b. Stratford-on-Avon
   c. Illyria
   d. Verona

5. When Feste visits Malvolio in the dark cell, he disguises himself as _____.
   a. a woman
   b. a preacher
   c. the duke
   d. Sir Toby

6. When Olivia tells Cesario, "But we will draw the curtain, and show you the picture," she then shows Cesario _____.
   a. the mosaic on the ceiling of her antechamber
   b. a picture of herself that her dead father painted for her
   c. her face
   d. a ring

7. Malvolio decides to wear yellow stockings and go cross-gartered because _____.
   a. he wants to be a fool like Feste
   b. Toby and Maria steal all his other clothes
   c. he is beginning to go mad
   d. his reason persuades him that this will win Olivia over

FILL IN THE BLANK

1. Olivia and Viola have both mourned the loss of a _____.

2. Viola has left her _____ in the care of the sea captain.

3. Malvolio reads a letter that he believes is from Olivia, but it was written by _____.

4. Antonio is afraid to be seen in Illyria because of an act he committed against _____.

5. Malvolio believes that he is talking to Sir Topas, but it is really _____.

6. Sir Andrew, Sir Toby, and Feste disturb the house with _____.

7. Sebastian is indebted to Antonio because he saved him from _____.

8. Olivia falls in love with Cesario, but she marries _____.

9. Feste earns his living by singing and _____.

10. Malvolio dresses himself to please Olivia by wearing _____.

DISCUSSION

Use the following questions to generate discussion:

1. Three characters are in love with Olivia: Malvolio, Sir Andrew, and Orsino. How are their feelings and methods of courtship similar? How are they different?

2. Orsino and Viola discuss the difference between the way men love and the way women love. Do you believe there is a difference? Has it changed at all since Shakespeare's time? If so, how?

3. In the course of the play does the Duke's understanding of love change? What if anything does he learn? If Viola schools him in love, how does this occur, when does it occur, and what indications in the text suggest the Duke's ideas of love have matured?

4. Compare and contrast Olivia's first speech in which she reveals her love for Cesario to Orsino's first speech in which he reveals his love for Olivia. How are they similar? How different? In your opinion, does one represent a deeper love than the other?

5. The sober and serious Malvolio is transformed into a sportive yellow-gartered buffoon. What other characters in this play behave in a manner contrary to their true nature? Is there a difference between wearing a disguise and acting "out of character"?

6. Feste says, "Words have grown so false, I am loath to prove reason with them" (III.1.24–25). Give examples of language that fails to communicate a character's intended meaning. Is the speaker aware a miscommunication has occurred? Is the listener?

7. Contrast Maria's scheme to gull Malvolio with Sir Toby's scheme to trick Sir Andrew into fighting Cesario. What initially motivates their scheming? Are they good-natured pranks? Or are they malicious tricks?

8. Do you feel sorry for Malvolio? Or is he partially responsible for his own downfall? Does your assessment of Malvolio change in the course of the play? If so, when?

9. Olivia is in mourning for the loss of her brother at the play's beginning. How does this affect her choice of companions? Do you think that she was once closer in friendship to the more festive characters?

10. Late in the play, Malvolio says, "I am as well in my wits, fool, as thou art"(IV.2.86). Compared to his first exchange with Feste in Act I, there is a perceptible difference in his attitude toward the fool. What is this difference? And what might be responsible for it? Has he changed for the better?

11. There is much wooing by proxy in this play. Name three characters that use mediaries in their courtship. Are they successful? What do you think Shakespeare's attitude towards mediaries is? What about the people who use them?

12. Is constancy a virtue or a vice in this play? Are there any characters that display true constancy in this play? Who are they? And what are they constant to?

13. When Olivia tells Malvolio he is sick of self-love, what does she mean by this? Are there other characters that might be said to suffer from self-love? Give examples from the play to support your claim.

14. With regard to disposition, situation, and relationship to the other characters in this play, Feste and Viola have many similarities. Compare and contrast their attitudes toward love, disguises, and the pleasures of life.

15. Of the three marriages in the play, which is most likely to succeed? Which is the least likely to succeed? For what reasons?

ACTIVITIES

The following activities can springboard you into further discussions and projects:

1. Ask two female students to play Viola and Olivia and a male student to play Orsino. Read Act II, Scene 4, Lines 16–47 and Act III, Scene 1, Lines 98–172. Then recast all the parts with male students, as it would have been performed in Shakespeare's day, and repeat the two scenes. How do these casting changes affect the scenes? How does it change your understanding of Olivia's relationship with Viola? How does it change your understanding of Orsino's?

2. Create a sequel to *Twelfth Night*, coming up with a new story that begins one month after the original play's ending. Was the play's original ending really a happy one? Which marriages have succeeded? Have any failed? Does Malvolio get his revenge? How?

3. Divide students into groups and ask each group to present a brief performance in which the identity of at least one character is hidden from the others. What questions might reveal their identity? Are some facts harder than others to conceal? What items can serve to prove someone's true identity? What elements of identity are based on physical appearance? Social class? Learned behavior? Heredity?

4. Make a list of your favorite characters (those you positively identify with the most) and least favorite characters in the play. Make a list and rank the characters. Explain what is it about this character you admire or don't admire.

5. Take one scene from *Twelfth Night, or What You Will* and update it, word-for-word, in modern slang, and then act the scene out in class. Be sure not to miss any crucial ideas or phrases, even if they seem at first to be mere Elizabethan "babble."

6. *Twelfth Night* is performed often and in a variety of ways. Sometimes it's acted as if it's a comedy with a happy ending; other times it's acted in darker ways. Sometimes lines, and even

entire scenes, are taken out. If possible, attend a local production of the play. Bring this book along and follow the play. After the play is over, conduct an interview with one of the actors, or the director, and ask them why they interpreted the play the way they did.

7. View a film adaptation of *Twelfth Night*. (The Trevor Nunn movie or the BBC version are great places to start.) Set up a panel discussion in class, in which you play movie critic. Discuss whether the version of the play you saw on film lives up to your expectations. What is gained by making Shakespeare's plays into movies? What is lost? Are too many lines cut from the play? Do certain characters seem less admirable than you expected? Are there things in the movie that allowed you to understand things in the play text better? Are there things in the movie that you feel would have Shakespeare "rolling in his grave"?

8. Although *Twelfth Night* was written 400 years ago, and the world it presents is, in many ways, quite different than our own, the play is still very popular, because in many ways the world is still quite similar. Make a list of things that have changed between now and Shakespeare's times (for example, we have no professional fools, and women seem to have more freedom than they did in Shakespeare's time). Are these changes good things? Bad things?

9. When *Twelfth Night* is performed, the theatre company usually hires a musician to write new melodies (and devise new instrumentation) for the songs. The words, for example, to "O mistress mine," can be set quite easily as a modern "blues" form. Other songs have been rendered on stage in a variety of ways. Take one of the songs from the play and devise a novel way to perform it.

10. Feste is a professional fool. We no longer have such professional fools. Or do we? Look through the newspapers, the Web, television, and so on, at famous celebrities and public figures (such as politicians) and consider the ways in which they are similar to, and different from, Feste. Make a list and compare it with your classmates'.

ANSWERS

Identify the quotation

1. From Act II, Malvolio reading the letter that he mistakenly believes Olivia has written to him.

2. From Act II, Sir Toby excoriates Malvolio, putting down his puritanical attitude.

3. From Act II, Viola upon realizing that Olivia has fallen in love with her disguise.

4. From Act I, Orsino expresses his love sickness to his musicians and attendants.

5. From Act III, Olivia comments that even Cesario's scorn seems beautiful to her.

6. From Act V, Viola would give up her life before she would give up her love for Orsino.

7. From Act IV, Feste speaks to the power of mistaken identity as he dons a parson's persona.

8. From Act I, Maria chastises Sir Toby for his drinking habit and his questionable selection of company, Sir Andrew.

True/False

1. False 2. False 3. False 4. True 5. False 6. True
7. False 8. False 9. True

Multiple Choice

1. a 2. b 3. c 4. c 5. b 6. c 7. d.

Fill in the Blank

1. brother and father 2. woman's clothes
3. Maria 4. Orsino 5. Feste 6. singing catches
7. drowning 8. Sebastian 9. fooling 10. yellow
stockings, cross-gartered

CLIFFSCOMPLETE RESOURCE CENTER

The learning doesn't need to stop here. Cliffs-Complete Resource Center shows you the best of the best: great links to information in print, on film, and online. And the following aren't all the great resources available to you; visit **www.cliffsnotes.com** for tips on reading literature, writing papers, giving presentations, locating other resources, and testing your knowledge.

EDITIONS

Different editions of Shakespeare's plays incorporate not only various versions of the dramas but insightful and interesting background information and critical comments as well. Each of the editions listed below will provide unique perspectives while covering the basics.

Bevington, David, ed. *The Complete Works of Shakespeare*. New York: Harper Collins, 1997.

Evans, G. Blakemore, ed. *The Riverside Shakespeare*. Boston: Houghton Mifflin, 1974.

Wells, Stanley and H. J. Oliver. *Four Comedies*. New York: Penguin, 1994.

BOOKS AND ARTICLES

Bamber, Linda. *Comic Women, Tragic Men: A Study of Gender and Genre in Shakespeare*. Stanford, CA: Stanford University Press, 1982.

A seminal book of feminist criticism. Argues that there is a structural relationship between gender and genre in Shakespeare, and that women in Shakespeare's comedies, however free and heroic they may seem, are never confronted with an either/or choice in the way that men in Shakespeare's tragedies are. According to Bamber, women are thus denied insight and catharsis in Shakespeare.

Barber, C.L. *Shakespeare's Festive Comedy*. Princeton: Princeton University Press, 1959.

A classic study of Shakespeare's comedies. Argues that all of Shakespeare's festive comedies, including *Twelfth Night* (to which Barber devotes a lengthy chapter), move from a repressed world, through a world of carnivalesque "release" to end finally with a clarification that profoundly restructures the individual as well as society. Barber believes that the scapegoating of Malvolio is necessary for the festive conclusion to occur.

Barton, Ann, "*As You Like It* and *Twelfth Night*: Shakespeare's Sense of an Ending." *Shakespearean Comedy*. Ed. Malcolm Bradbury and David Palmer. London: Stratford-upon-Avon-Studies, 1972. 160-172.

Barton compares the endings of two of Shakespeare's most celebrated comedies to conclude that *Twelfth Night* is the darker of the two, leaving much unresolved.

Berry, Ralph. *Shakespeare's Comedies: Explorations in Form*. Princeton, NJ: Princeton University Press, 1972.

A skeptical reading of the societies presented in the comedies. Berry often takes C.L. Barber to task for reducing the complexity in the plays, and has much more reading for the figures that are excluded from the "happy ending" (Malvolio, for example).

Boyce, Charles. *Shakespeare A to Z.* New York: Dell, 1990.

A useful introduction. With entries on plays, characters, actors, Shakespeare's contemporaries, and more.

Burckhardt, Sigurd. *Shakespearean Meanings.* Princeton: Princeton University Press, 1968.

An early example of what has since come to be known as "metadramatic criticism." Burckhardt argues that Shakespeare's plays tell us much about how they were written, that each character may be read as an aspect of Shakespeare himself as he wrote to balance the various disparate elements of his psyche. See especially Burckhardt's chapter on "The Poet As Fool and Priest," which helps illuminate aspects of *Twelfth Night* often overlooked in other criticism.

Doyle, John and Ray Lischner. *Shakespeare For Dummies.* Foster City: Wiley Publishing, Inc., 1999.

This guide to Shakespeare's plays and poetry provides summaries and scorecards for keeping track of who's who in a given play, as well as painless introductions to language, imagery, and other often intimidating subjects.

Eagleton, Terry. *William Shakespeare.* Oxford: Basil Blackwell, 1986.

One of the more enjoyable Marxist readings of Shakespeare's plays, Eagleton (unlike other Marxist critics, such as Elliot Krieger) brings a sense of humor to his social analysis of class structure in *Twelfth Night.*

Evans, Bertrand. *Shakespeare's Comedies.* Oxford, Clarendon Press, 1960.

Evans argues that in every comedy, the plot is structured around the notion of "discrepant awareness." The characters who have more knowledge of their surroundings (such as the true identity of Viola) have more power, while the characters who remain ignorant that a trick is being played on them (such as Malvolio in the dark prison) have less. The audience, usually, has the most power, as we alone know certain things (that Sebastian is alive, for example).

French, Marilyn. *Shakespeare's Division of Experience.* New York, Ballantine Books, 1981.

Another early feminist study focusing on gender differences in Shakespeare. Similar to Bamber, but more sympathetic toward the comedies and the power that women wield in them.

Frye, Northrop. "The Argument of Comedy." *English Institute Essays 1948.* Ed. D.A. Robertson. New York: 1949. 59-73.

Frye, Northrop. *A Natural Perspective : The Development of Shakespearean Comedy and Romance.* New York: Columbia University Press, 1965.

Two classic early studies, which argue that Shakespearean comedy deals with issues of mythic importance. Frye is less interested in the psyches of the characters than he is in the functions they serve in creating a fiction that serves a ritualistic function.

Garber, Marjorie. *Coming of Age in Shakespeare.* New York: Methuen, 1981.

Taking Margaret Mead's anthropological study of Samoans as its starting point, Garber focuses on the moments in Shakespeare's plays when the characters go through rites of passages, and the crises that are involved with them.

Girard, Rene. *A Theatre of Envy: William Shakespeare.* New York: Oxford University Press, 1991.

One of the most engaging studies in recent years, Girard criticizes Freudian readings of Shakespeare and suggests that identity and desire in Shakespeare are always due to imitation. Of particular interest for readers of *Twelfth Night* is his theory of love triangles in this and other plays.

Goddard, Harold. *The Meaning of Shakespeare.* Vol 1. and 2. Chicago: University of Chicago Press, 1951.

One of the best written traditional accounts of Shakepeare. Goddard sees Shakespeare's plays as long visionary poems, akin to Blake's and Emerson's essays. Although Goddard believes that the comedies are lesser achievements than the tragedies, his discussion of *Twelfth Night* raises some very interesting questions about the morality of the play.

Greenblatt, Stephen. *Shakespearean Negotiations.* Berkeley, University of California Press, 1988.

A "New Historicist" critic, Greenblatt's chapter on *Twelfth Night* gives interesting insight into early modern ideas of gender identity through a lengthy investigation of medical records of the time. Greenblatt argues that Shakespeare's erotic tension is always based on "friction." Desire, whether heterosexual or homosexual, is rarely, if ever, fulfilled in Shakespeare's plays. The erotic tension and frustration itself is what, paradoxically, satisfied Shakespeare's audiences.

Hartman, Geoffrey. "Shakespeare's Poetical Character in *Twelfth Night." Shakespeare and the Question of Theory.* Ed. Patricia Parker and Geoffrey Hartman. New York: Metheun, 1985. 37-53.

This groundbreaking re-evaluation considers the complexities and importance of fool-talk and witty banter in *Twelfth Night.* According to Hartman, language creates characters in Shakespeare (and not vice versa), and the ability to lose oneself in language is something *Twelfth Night,* in particular, indulges in. Language, however, with its tendency to never end, is opposed to the plot, which requires an ending to the play.

Hawkins, Harriet. *The Devil's Party: Critical Counterinterpretations of Shakesperean Drama.* New York: Clarendon Press, 1985.

Argues that Shakespeare's plays are largely beyond good and evil, that Shakespeare was deeply suspicious of official codes of morality, and believed that repression was more often the cause of evil than the cure for it.

Howard, Jean. "The Difficulties of Closure: An Approach to the Problematic in Shakespearian Comedy," *Comedy from Sheridan to Shakespeare.* Ed. A. R. Braunmulller and J.C. Bulman. Newark, University of Delaware Press, 1986. 113-28.

A postmodern investigation, that also takes Barber's notion of "resolution" at the end of the comedies to task. Yet Howard considers the lack of closure, or a so-called "happy ending," to make the plays even more festive and playful than Barber's reading with its 1950s' values that, according to Howard, deny the various differences that cannot be absorbed by the end of the play (homosexuality, for example).

Kirsch, Arthur. *Shakespeare and the Experience of Love.* Cambridge, Cambridge University Press, 1981.

A Christian-inflected reading of the comedies in light of the New Testament. Kirsch's high-minded reading sometimes takes itself too seriously.

Leggatt, Alexander. *Shakespeare's Comedy of Love.* London: Methuen, 1974.

An analysis that claims every comedy attempts to find a balance between "romantic" and "realistic" notions of love.

MacCary, W.T. *Friends and Lovers: The Phenomenology of Desire in Shakespearean Comedy.* New York: Columbia University Press, 1985.

A Freudian reading, focusing largely on the tension between same-sex friendship and heterosexual love that occurs in the psyche of the leading male character in each of the comedies.

Nevo, Ruth. *Comic Transformations in Shakespeare.* New York: Methuen, 1980.

A reading of Shakespeare's comedies informed by the spirit of Ovid's metamorphosis.

Pequigney, Joseph. "The Two Antonios and Same Sex Love in *Twelfth Night* and *The Merchant of Venice.*" *English Literary Renaissance* 22:2 (Spring 1992) 201-21.

Through close textual analysis, Pequigney makes a convincing case that Antonio, if not necessarily Sebastian, is clearly meant to be portrayed as homosexual. Pequigney also discusses how many other critics have taken great pains to ignore these passages, or go out of their way to deny any homosexuality in Shakespeare.

Rackin, Phyllis. "Androgyny, Mimesis, and the Marriage of the Boy Heroine on the English Renaissance Stage." *PMLA* 102 (1987):29-41.

Rackin investigates five transvestite heroines in Elizabethan English, including three from Shakespeare plays. Rackin argues that by the time of King James, fear of the homosexual implications of cross-dressing, coupled with fear of the subversive machinations of a play dominated by a female character, led to the gradual decline of such heroines in plays of this period. Even in the three Shakespeare plays that Rackin discusses, we see the comic heroine become increasingly passive (from Portia in *The Merchant of Venice* to Viola in *Twelfth Night*).

Williamson, Marilyn. *The Patriarchy of Shakespeare's Comedies.* Detroit, MI.: Wayne State University Press, 1986.

Similar to Erickson's book, but even more pessimistic about the possibilities for women to transcend the patriarchal limitations of Shakespeare's times.

INTERNET

"Mr. William Shakespeare & the Internet"
daphne.palomar.edu/shakespeare/

This site attempts two things: First, to be a complete annotated guide to the scholarly Shakespeare resources available on Internet. Second, to present new Shakespeare material unavailable elsewhere on the Internet, such as A Shakespeare Timeline, which gives the key events of Shakespeare's life and work along with related documentary evidence. There are several supporting pages to the timeline: A Shakespeare genealogy. A chart showing the relevant family relationships and dates. A Shakespeare Timeline Summary Chart, showing the events of Shakespeare's life in outline along with important contemporary events and publications. It also includes: The Shakespeare Canon. Rowe's Some Acount of the Life &c. of Mr. William Shakespear, prefaced to his 1709 edition of the Works. Charles and Mary Lamb's Tales From Shakespeare. The Prefatory materials from the First Folio.

"The Complete Works of William Shakespeare"
tech-two.mit.edu/Shakespeare/

This is the Web's first edition of the Complete Works of William Shakespeare. Including: Shakespeare discussion area, complete works, Bartlett's familiar Shakespearean quotations.

"Shakespeare's Globe"
www.rdg.ac.uk/globe/

This site, sponsored by the University of Reading (UK), is dedicated to providing background information on Shakespearean performance in original conditions. Centered around the construction of a replica of the Globe playhouse in London, it includes pages devoted to the original Globe and other playhouses in Early Modern London, reports and photographic documentaries on reconstruction and performances at the new Globe, and also some practical information.

"Proper Elizabethan Accents"
www.renfaire.com/Language/index.html

This site provides a guide for proper pronunciation of Elizabethan English. Topics include: pronunciation, vocabulary, and grammar.

FILM

Twelfth Night. Directed by Trevor Nunn. Performed by Helena Bonham Carter, Imogen Stubbs, Toby Stephens, Stephen Mackenzie, Nigel Hawthorne, and Ben Kingsley. 1996.

Set in Victorian-era England, this film adaptation successfully captures much of the frivolity and good nature of the Shakespeare text.

CLIFFSCOMPLETE READING GROUP DISCUSSION GUIDE

Use the following questions and topics to enhance your reading group discussions. The discussion can help get you thinking — and hopefully talking — about Shakespeare in a whole new way!

DISCUSSION QUESTIONS

1. The character of Viola is an example of one of Shakespeare's *breeches heroines* — female characters who masquerade as men. Some scholars describe breeches heroines as characters who *use deception as a path toward freedom*. In what ways is this description appropriate for Viola? What else does she use deception for? When is deception justified for anyone?

2. From the first to the last moment of the play, music plays a major role in *Twelfth Night*. In fact, *Twelfth Night* has served as inspiration for original orchestral compositions, and most productions of the play hire a composer to write original music for the poetry provided by Shakespeare. If you were directing a production of *Twelfth Night*, what type of music would you use — traditional Elizabethan instruments and melodies? Light and airy? Dynamic and passionate?

3. In addition to the several songs that Shakespeare includes in *Twelfth Night*, many of the scenes feel like they could benefit from musical underscoring. What type of music could you use for the following:

   * Viola's arrival to Illyria
   * Sir Toby and Sir Andrew's drinking scenes
   * Orsino and Olivia's discovery that Viola is a woman
   * Malvolio's entrance with yellow stockings and cross-garters
   * Malvolio's final threat and exit

4. Modern psychologists suggest that well-adjusted people are often *psychologically androgynous*, meaning one's personality has no connection to either gender. By playing a man, does Viola become less feminine? Does she become more masculine? By the play's end, does she achieve a degree of psychological androgyny?

5. *Twelfth Night* features many stock romantic and comic elements — a shipwreck, high-born lovers, disguises, separated siblings, mistaken identity, a pompous fool, a clever girl, and a generally happy ending, to name just a few. How does Shakespeare make these and other elements unique and interesting within *Twelfth Night*? How do modern romantic comedies (films, plays, books, television shows) compare with *Twelfth Night* in the use of these stock romantic and comic elements?

6. In comedies, often the obstacles that block young lovers from getting together are parents, society, money, or politics. In *Twelfth Night*, however, the major obstacles are deceit and self-deception. How difficult are these obstacles to overcome? Do the obstacles in *Twelfth Night* make the play more realistic than other comedies? Do they make the play less comical?

7. In many ways, Festes the clown seems like the spokesperson for *Twelfth Night.* His songs and lines can be viewed as commentary on the plot and characters in the play. What are the benefits of viewing Festes as the spokesperson of the play? Is there a down side?

8. If you were producing new stage or film version of *Twelfth Night,* how would you cast the role of Festes? Is he old and weary? Young and spry? How well does he sing and dance? How would you costume him? Does he wear a traditional clown mask? How does the casting and costuming of Festes affect the meaning of the entire play?

9. Because *Twelfth Night* is set almost entirely in the fictional land of Illyria, directors and set designers often create elaborate sets and lighting effects. Productions have been set in wintry wonderlands, pastel pastoral fields, and riotous Mardi Gras celebrations, to name just a few. How do you envision Illyria? Occasionally, a production will be set in a realistic location such as a modern Adriatic fishing town. How does a realistic setting affect the meaning of the play? What does it add? What does it take away?

10. From Shakespeare's time until the mid-1800s, actors played Malvolio as an unsympathetic, purely comic creation. After this time, actors began playing the character more sympathetically. In 1884, actor Henry Irving played Malvolio as a wholly tragic figure, arousing pity from the audience while Malvolio is in prison. How is the play different with a comic Malvolio? A sympathetic Malvolio? A tragic Malvolio?

11. Many film and stage productions of *Twelfth Night* begin the play with Act I, Scene 2 (Viola's arrival to Illyria) and work material from Act I, Scene 1 into later scenes in the play. What does this reorganization add to the play? Is it a good artistic choice? What does reorganizing the scenes take away from the play?

Notes

Index

C

E

continued

continued

Q

R

Shakespeare's Comedy of Love, 179
Shakespeare's Division of Experience, 178
Shakespeare's Festive Comedy, 177
Shakespeare's Globe Web site, 180
'Shakespeare's Poetical Character in *Twelfth Night*," 179
Shakespearean comedy
    defined, 19
    distinguished from tragedy, 19
Shakespearean Meanings, 178
Shakespearean Negotiations, 179
sheets, folding to form pages, 16
Sir Andrew Aguecheek
    agreeing to challenge Cesario to a duel, 110
    agreeing to stay another month, 43
    anticipating Malvolio's humiliation, 86
    blaming Viola for his wounds, 151, 165
    calling for a surgeon for Sir Toby, 165
    celebrating with drink and song, 71, 77
    character description, 42
    character portrayal, 43
    comic scene setting techniques, 42–43
    confused by Cesario's French, 104
    duel with Cesario, 24
    failure in role of gentleman, 23
    foolish knight, 38
    goes in search of Cesario, 129
    interjections as a function in the play, 105
    mistaking Sebastian for Cesario, 135, 137
    offering his gray horse to Cesario, 238
    persuaded to stay and win Olivia's heart, 109
    playful pun on the counterfeit letter's riddle, 93
    plotting revenge on Malvolio, 71
    portrayed as a boastful idiot, 43
    praising Maria's genius, 94
    prancing around like a fool, 43
    preparing to duel Cesario, 128
    preparing to leave, 107, 109

    put down by Maria, 43
    reacting to Malvolio's speech, 93
    representing time-honored English hospitality, 78
    stealing scraps of other people's knowledge, 105
    suggesting Sir Toby challenge Malvolio to a duel, 78
    threatened by Sebastian, 20
    watching Maria dupe Malvolio with a forged letter, 86, 92
    writing a challenge to Cesario, 107
Sir Toby Belch
    abusing Sir Andrew Aguecheek's trust, 42
    announcing Cesario, 57
    anticipating Malvolio's humiliation, 86
    blaming Viola for his wounds, 151, 165
    celebrating with drink and song, 71, 77
    character description, 42
    comic scene setting techniques, 42–43
    compared to Falstaff in *Henry IV,* 42
    compared to Feste, 42, 57
    convincing Sir Andrew Aguecheek to stay another month, 43
    delivering Sir Andrew's challenge to Cesario, 114, 128
    describing Cesario's dueling skills to Sir Andrew, 128
    description of love, 20
    directing Sir Andrew, 23
    failing to take Maria seriously, 77–78
    growing tired of Sir Andrew Aguecheek, 110
    in need of a surgeon, 165
    life of the party, 42
    marrying Maria, 166
    mistaking Sebastian for Cesario, 135, 137
    mocking Sir Andrew Aguecheek, 110
    Olivia's uncle, 38
                                            continued

continued

Notes

Notes

Notes

Notes

CliffsNotes™

CLIFFSCOMPLETE

Hamlet
Julius Caesar
King Henry IV, Part I
King Lear
Macbeth
The Merchant of Venice
Othello
Romeo and Juliet
The Tempest
Twelfth Night

Look for Other Series in the CliffsNotes Family

LITERATURE NOTES

Absalom, Absalom!
The Aeneid
Agamemnon
Alice in Wonderland
All the King's Men
All the Pretty Horses
All Quiet on the Western Front
All's Well & Merry Wives
American Poets of the
 20th Century
American Tragedy
Animal Farm
Anna Karenina
Anthem
Antony and Cleopatra
Aristotle's Ethics
As I Lay Dying
The Assistant
As You Like It
Atlas Shrugged
Autobiography of Ben Franklin
Autobiography of Malcolm X
The Awakening
Babbit
Bartleby & Benito Cereno
The Bean Trees
The Bear
The Bell Jar
Beloved
Beowulf
Billy Budd & Typee
Black Boy
Black Like Me

Bleak House
Bless Me, Ultima
The Bluest Eye & Sula
Brave New World
Brothers Karamazov
Call of Wild & White Fang
Candide
The Canterbury Tales
Catch-22
Catcher in the Rye
The Chosen
Cliffs Notes on the Bible
The Color Purple
Comedy of Errors…
Connecticut Yankee
The Contender
The Count of Monte Cristo
Crime and Punishment
The Crucible
Cry, the Beloved Country
Cyrano de Bergerac
Daisy Miller & Turn…Screw
David Copperfield
Death of a Salesman
The Deerslayer
Diary of Anne Frank
Divine Comedy-I. Inferno
Divine Comedy-II. Purgatorio
Divine Comedy-III. Paradiso
Doctor Faustus
Dr. Jekyll and Mr. Hyde
Don Juan
Don Quixote
Dracula
Emerson's Essays
Emily Dickinson Poems
Emma
Ethan Frome
Euripides' Electra & Medea
The Faerie Queene
Fahrenheit 451
Far from Madding Crowd
A Farewell to Arms
Farewell to Manzanar
Fathers and Sons
Faulkner's Short Stories
Faust Pt. I & Pt. II
The Federalist
Flowers for Algernon
For Whom the Bell Tolls
The Fountainhead
Frankenstein
The French Lieutenant's Woman
The Giver
Glass Menagerie & Streetcar
Go Down, Moses

The Good Earth
Grapes of Wrath
Great Expectations
The Great Gatsby
Greek Classics
Gulliver's Travels
Hamlet
The Handmaid's Tale
Hard Times
Heart of Darkness & Secret Sharer
Hemingway's Short Stories
Henry IV Part 1
Henry IV Part 2
Henry V
House Made of Dawn
The House of the Seven Gables
Huckleberry Finn
I Know Why the Caged Bird Sings
Ibsen's Plays I
Ibsen's Plays II
The Idiot
Idylls of the King
The Iliad
Incidents in the Life of a Slave Girl
Inherit the Wind
Invisible Man
Ivanhoe
Jane Eyre
Joseph Andrews
The Joy Luck Club
Jude the Obscure
Julius Caesar
The Jungle
Kafka's Short Stories
Keats & Shelley
The Killer Angels
King Lear
The Kitchen God's Wife
The Last of the Mohicans
Le Morte Darthur
Leaves of Grass
Les Miserables
A Lesson Before Dying
Light in August
The Light in the Forest
Lord Jim
Lord of the Flies
Lord of the Rings
Lost Horizon
Lysistrata & Other Comedies
Macbeth
Madame Bovary
Main Street
The Mayor of Casterbridge
Measure for Measure
The Merchant of Venice

Middlemarch
A Midsummer-Night's Dream
The Mill on the Floss
Moby-Dick
Moll Flanders
Mrs. Dalloway
Much Ado About Nothing
My Ántonia
Mythology
Narr. …Frederick Douglass
Native Son
New Testament
Night
1984
Notes from Underground
The Odyssey
Oedipus Trilogy
Of Human Bondage
Of Mice and Men
The Old Man and the Sea
Old Testament
Oliver Twist
The Once and Future King
One Day in the Life of
 Ivan Denisovich
One Flew Over Cuckoo's Nest
100 Years of Solitude
O'Neill's Plays
Othello
Our Town
The Outsiders
The Ox-Bow Incident
Paradise Lost
A Passage to India
The Pearl
The Pickwick Papers
The Picture of Dorian Gray
Pilgrim's Progress
The Plague
Plato's Euthyphro…
Plato's The Republic
Poe's Short Stories
A Portrait of the Artist…
The Portrait of a Lady
The Power and the Glory
Pride and Prejudice
The Prince
The Prince and the Pauper
A Raisin in the Sun
The Red Badge of Courage
The Red Pony
The Return of the Native
Richard II
Richard III
The Rise of Silas Lapham
Robinson Crusoe